GESTAPO CHIEF

The 1948 Interrogation of
HEINRICH MÜLLER

by Gregory Douglas

VOLUME

From Secret U.S. Intelligence Files

1st Edition

Copyright 1997 by Gregory Douglas

Published by R. James Bender Publishing,
P.O. Box 23456, San Jose, California 95153
Phone: (408) 225-5777
Fax: (408) 225-4739

Printed in the United States of America

ISBN No. 0-912138-68-8

Title page photo:
Heinrich Müller and Regierungsrat Scholz, a personal friend from Bavaria.

Table of Contents

Foreword

The revelations of *Gestapo Chief: The 1948 Interrogation of Heinrich Müller* continue to reverberate on both sides of the Atlantic. The German edition sold out two printings before it was banned by the German government, while the American edition has been predictably ignored by the mainstream media in the United States.

A book as extraordinary as *Gestapo Chief* may demand a high level of verification considering that it flies in the face of orthodox history. In the spirit of independent confirmation, it was surprising and gratifying soon after the appearance of Volume I last year, when I received a telephone call from noted author and intelligence expert, William Corson. He said that he not only accepted the reality of the post-war career of Heinrich Müller, but that he knew the name of the man who interrogated Müller in 1948, a name Gregory Douglas was not privy to at the time. Corson immediately sent me to the first chapter of his book *Widows,* where a profile of James Speyer Kronthal instantly revealed character traits and background that identified him as "Q" in the interrogation. Kronthal was CIA station chief in Bern, Switzerland, in 1948. None of this background was known to Gregory Douglas before his first book was published.

The first volume shook the foundations of conventional history, positing such heretical facts as Roosevelt's pre-knowledge of the Pearl Harbor attack, Adolf Hitler's escape from Berlin at the end of the war, and other iconoclastic satchel charges. But what could possibly be left for a second volume?

Volume II continues the interview, with additional facts that make Volume I seem almost genteel by comparison. The idea that the former chief of the Gestapo could be given a new name and the U.S. Army rank of brigadier general astound many. But the evidence that Müller is primarily responsible for the employment by the United States government of a long list of Nazis, some of whom were wanted for specific war crimes, will cause outrage in extreme liberal sectors even at this late date. Recall the furor over the trial of Klaus Barbie, who was only a lieutenant in the Gestapo.

As the interviews develop in Volume II, it becomes obvious that Müller was President Harry Truman's most important asset in identifying and ousting many of the communists who had found their way into the government during the Roosevelt/Wallace administration.

This continuing story of the post-war eminence of one of the most powerful figures in the Third Reich, and the studied non-reaction of mainstream media and historical writers toward it, may find its best metaphor in one of Edgar Allen Poe's most famous stories wherein Montresor (this book's author) mortars another brick into the cellar wall behind which a languishing Fortunato (the accepted history of WWII) wails with ever-weakening plaint. Volume II of *Gestapo Chief* is significant, and there may yet be one or two bricks to be placed before the wall is finished, and the muffled voice within is heard no more. *In Pace Requiescat!*

Frank D. Thayer, PhD.
New Mexico State University,
Las Cruces

Gregory Douglas has produced a historical *tour de force*. Meticulously researched and authoritatively edited. Anyone, regardless of their intellectual orientation, who dismisses the reality and contents of Müller's files and his relationship with American Intelligence out of hand, does so at their own risk.

William R. Corson

William R. Corson has been involved with the intelligence community for most of his adult life. Corson, who holds a Ph.D. in economics, is a retired Colonel of the USMC and was executive secretary of the joint Department of Defense/Central Intelligence Agency commission on anti-terrorism. He worked with the CIA on the highest levels and in 1977 published a book, "The Armies of Ignorance," the standard work on the history of US intelligence.

Where possible, each revelation has been challenged and examined using all available resources to include: individual, military records, released US communications intercepts and captured documents. To date, the Müller documents have met every challenge.

Robert T. Crowley

Robert T. Crowley attended the US Military Academy at West Point and has served in both the Army Military Intelligence and the Office of Naval Intelligence. Following his tours of duty, Crowley joined the Central Intelligence Agency and rose to a high-level advisory position within it. One of his fields of expertise was the Soviet KGB and he is co-author of the acclaimed work "The New KGB."

Author's Acknowledgments

As these works progress, the author must look further and further afield to locate obscure information and confirmation. FOIA requests now concentrate on Müller's new postwar persona, on those who worked with him after the war, on family members, on real estate holdings and fine art auction catalogs, to mention only a few.

There are, however, specific persons to whom the author is indebted and they are: Mr. Robert Wolfe, formerly of the US National Archives; Karl Müller, grandson of Heinrich Müller, whose assistance has been noteworthy in tracking down postwar connections and personas, and who certainly possesses all of his grandfather's Bavarian charm and intelligence; Dr. William R. Corson; Lt. Col. Robert Crowley; Mr. Paul Elston of the BBC who made very helpful suggestions, that the author was pleased to act upon; Dr. Frank D. Thayer for his overviews; Mr. Willi Korte for his suggestions about stolen art; Christian Wehrschutz of Vienna for his research on Swiss bank accounts and CIA operations in Switzerland; Lt. Col. Ed Milligan USA (Ret.) of Alexandria, VA; Col. James Critchfield, USA (Ret.) of Williamsburg, VA for important material concerning Reinhard Gehlen and his CIA-run organization; Mr. Thomas Belknap, for an in-depth discussion about the "Paperclip" operation, and a number of former associates of Heinrich Müller in the United States, Canada and Germany who have been most helpful, if demanding, of anonymity.

And last, but surely not least, many hours of painstaking work were performed by Brenda Miles and Stan Cook in an effort to catch elusive technical errors. Their labor has resulted in a smoother transition of my ideas and words.

Essays in Mendacity

The first volume of the series on Heinrich Müller, Chief of the Gestapo, was the author's first book on any subject and because of the controversial nature of much of the material, it was necessary to carefully check out each and every fact, publication of which could cause controversy in various predictable circles.

The documents used in the book were subjected to various tests by different agencies and individuals. For example, the CIC papers on Globocnik, his buried treasure and his use by British and US intelligence, were checked and rechecked from every angle. The typewriters were correct to the period. The authors were in place at the times specified, and their handwriting matched known samples in official US archives. A computer check of the writing styles of both contributors to what we now refer to as the Sereny file matched perfectly with known original documents.

The German intelligence transcript of the Roosevelt-Churchill scrambled conversation of November 26, 1941 is an original document and both the composition of the paper and the typewriter used indicate that the document was entirely authentic to the period.

The positive information on the authentication of the Globocnik papers was very clearly covered in a lengthy, illustrated article appearing in the British paper, *The Independent*, on Sunday of July 19, 1992. The author of this article was Gitta Sereny. It was this positive commentary on the originality of the Globocnik documents that persuaded three publishers to accept the manuscript for publication. As an act of courtesy, in retrospect an error of judgment, the author thanked Sereny for giving the impetus to the publication to the first volume taken from the Müller papers.

The book first appeared in print in Germany, put out by the publishing house of Druffel Verlag, and at once began selling very well, achieving bestseller status within six months. The English version, published by Bender Publications, was a slower starter but following favorable book reviews and national advertising, also sold very well. Both publishing companies, as well as the Spanish publisher, have indicated that the book has benefited tremendously from referrals. Pleased readers inform their friends and so the good work prospers. These sales were materially assisted when a private foundation bought up nearly half the first run to distribute to college, and some lower level, libraries.

The great bulk of the correspondence to both the publisher and the author was very favorable and positive. There were, however, some virulent exceptions. As a case in point, Sereny wrote a book review in a tabloid British paper in which she completely reversed the facts that she had published in her 1992 article. Sereny claimed that all the documents in the book had been fakes, and that the book was "a piece of filth." Her comments resulted in lawsuits for defamation against both Sereny and her publisher by the author, and this specific aspect of the matter cannot be discussed any further.

Among other suspect comments, Sereny now claimed to have absolute proof that Globocnik died in British captivity. This so-called absolute proof consists of an out of focus photograph purporting to show the corpse of Globocnik wrapped in a rug, and a sad commentary on the poor quality of modern government technicians. Earlier photographs on the same subject were obvious fakes and the new picture obviously came from the same source.

No doubt Sereny hopes her original and obscure article about the CIC papers published in 1992 is forgotten. Or perhaps, even more likely, Sereny herself does not recall what she once wrote and persuaded reluctant publishers to accept the authenticity of these important and pivotal papers as a reason for publishing. It may be interesting to print excerpts from the original article.

Sereny speaks of having received a copy of the CIC report from an American source, not this author, and of being intrigued with its implications. Securing a £30,000 advance from the London *Sunday Times* on the strength of her belief that the documents were original, Sereny began her investigations which eventually led her to Washington, DC.

> *The first person I turned to was Dr. Robert Wolfe at the National Archives in Washington, a world authority on the Third Reich and its aftermath. When he saw the document, he was horrified: if authentic, it recorded the most outrageous act his country-and Britain- would have committed after the war. True, the language seemed extravagant in places, but many CIC agents were men of foreign extraction whose English was stilted. And the patchiness of the 'sanitizing' could be due to the inexperience or apathy of the clerks who prepared documents for release under the Freedom of Information Act. In view of the then-recent disclosures of the CIC's misdeeds in the case of Klaus Barbie, it seemed only too possible that the document was genuine.*
>
> *And when Dr. Wolfe took it to the director of the Fort Meade Repository, Colonel Walsh, his reaction was that, except for a declassification stamp which was missing (not a unique occur-*

*rence), it looked authentic. Col. Walsh would assign an assistant
to look for either the original, or any other documents that might
substantiate it.*

*Dr. Wolfe had soon found in the National Archives another
report by Special Agent Severin Wallach, concerning the 20 July
plot on Hitler's life; it confirmed that Wallach had indeed been
working in Berlin at the time when the report was written. But
given the urgency Dr. Wolfe had impressed on Fort Meade, their
search appeared frustratingly halfhearted.*

*At the end of April, Wolfe decided that restraint was ineffec-
tive, and wrote an official letter, requesting all information held
on Müller or Globocnik. Col. Walsh was on holiday, but a few
days later Dr. Wolfe had a phone call from an assistant to say
that they had no information at all on Müller-the head of Nazi
Germany's secret police. That was incredible enough, but it was
followed by a letter extending this absence of knowledge to
Globocnik: they claimed to have nothing at all on the man in
charge of the murder of Jews in Poland.*

Sereny then mentions the Annex written by Wallach's superior in the Berlin
CIC, Captain Andrew L. Venters:

*This was an even more disturbing document, allegedly
written by Wallach's superior, Andrew Venters, whose signature
was immediately authenticated from known documents.*

Sereny continues that Wolfe, unable to penetrate the defenses of the
Intelligence Command at Ft. Meade, contacted the OSI or Office of Special
Investigations, a branch of the US Department of Justice which investigated
cases of illegal entry into the United States by individuals who might be wanted
for alleged war crimes. This agency had better investigative powers than Wolfe
and discovered that the Meade facility, in fact, had easily located material on
both Müller and Globocnik. None of this material was made available to
Wolfe, however. Sereny continues:

*The OSI was ready now to undertake an official investiga-
tion, Their remit included access to the Fort Meade archives,
forensic examination by the FBI and pyscho-linguistic analysis
of the documents I had presented to them.*

*The FBI's report was inconclusive: the many-times copied
document did not lend itself to forensic examination but the
typewriters and typefaces were of the correct period. The OSI
now had some information about the putative signatories of the
documents, though they were both dead. Severin Wallach and
Andrew Venters, his operations officer who countersigned the
first report and was the author of the "Annex," had worked as
a team in Berlin at the relevant time. And it was quite normal
for a Special Agent to prepare a report while the Operations*

Officer wrote an "Annex"- an explanation or extension of the report.

In Washington, several former CIC officers had been contacted and, while some were understandably reticent and all were appalled at the prospect of further scandalous disclosures, none seemed to consider that it was impossible. Severin Wallach, Viennese by birth and a lawyer by profession, was described as a brilliant and solitary man, convinced of the Soviet threat. He had run 30 to 60 agents at any one time, and conceived a number of projects which he 'kept very close to his chest.' And Venters, the alleged author of the 'Annex,' was apparently prone to high-flown language.

A former CIC officer whom I visited in Germany, who had worked closely with both men for years, provided an authoritative 'bottom line.' 'It is extraordinary' he said, 'whoever produced this had to have been in-or closely advised by someone from-Region VIII. The format is right, the methodology is correct and, given the personalities of the two people who allegedly wrote this, even the tone and the breadth of the concept fits.'

Even a cursory reading of Sereny's evaluation of the CIC file would give any reader the clear impression that while American experts and officials may have been shocked and dismayed by the contents of the papers, there was no proof of any kind that the documents were fakes. In point of fact, when the author wrote to Robert Wolfe in 1993 following the initial Sereny article, he promptly replied, in a letter on official National Archives stationary that…"based on all the internal evidence, the documents would appear to be authentic."

With the Sereny article and the Wolfe letter in essential agreement as to matters of fact, the Müller book included the CIC documents as authentic and made direct references to both the letter and the article.

On April 21, 1996, Sereny wrote a series of reviews on books she viewed as hostile to her favorite topic: the Holocaust. Sereny claimed that the entire Müller book was a tissue of lies, in general, and that the CIC documents concerning the capture of Globocnik, his faked suicide and the looting of his funds by British officials were deliberate fakes, in specific, known as such to the author. How Sereny could come to such a contorted conclusion is not difficult to assess. In her original article, Sereny herself supplies the obvious answer:

> *That weekend, I discussed the situation with four top OSI officials in Washington. There was complete agreement that a document so potentially damaging to the British and US governments had to be thoroughly examined.*

Had to be more than thoroughly examined. If the examination could prove, as it clearly did not, that the document was a hoax, then the matter was concluded and an appropriate article by Sereny, trumpeting her brilliant success in uncovering this hoax could appear in the London paper justifying their expenditure of £30,000.

Unfortunately, Sereny could not write such an article since all of her discoveries pointed to an opposite conclusion. Nevertheless, if she were able to convince her editor that such were the case, the fact that she was actively cooperating in assisting both the British and US governments in concealing a deadly secret could be forgotten and her fees unreturned.

Sereny states in her diatribe that…

> …he maliciously thanks me for my research into the authenticity of the key documents, without which this book could not have been written.

It is evident that this public connection of Sereny's name to the CIC papers forced her to distance herself as far from this conclusion as possible:

> Many questions raised by the behavior of various parties to the investigation remain unanswered. Why, for instance, were the OSI's efforts so halfhearted, with only one investigator left to pursue the matter, largely in (sic) his own time? Why did Fort Meade lie to Dr. Wolfe about the existence of files on two important Nazis? Why has there been no attempt in Washington to discredit the forged documents officially…?

In the first volume of the Müller series is a copy of Mr. Wolfe's authenticating statement. Sereny had to have read this statement since she reviewed all the material in which it was included. It should be of some interest to note that at no time subsequent to her knowledge of Wolfe's statement, and the publication of her 1996 article, did Sereny or anyone representing her or her paper ever make any attempt to contact Wolfe to ascertain if, in fact, he made such a statement.

It can be seen in the documentation published in the first volume that US official records on Heinrich Müller contained material about his postwar activities which are forbidden to be released on the grounds of National Security. That would account for the lack of comment from either the British or American government—comment which could publicize even more devastating material than the small CIC file. It would also account for Sereny's frantic attempts to distance herself from her earlier published remarks by printing an injudicious outburst of malicious defamation.

In matters of historical accuracy, only the former Soviet Union was more mendacious than official British sources. There were a number of British officers directly connected with Globocnik after his capture. These names were supplied by Sereny in a published article as a result of her own investigations: Brigadier Guy Wheeler of Military Intelligence; Lt. Ted Burkett, also of MI; Major Ken Hedly of the 4th Hussars, an armored unit; and Major Alex Ramsay of British Special Forces.

It might be most instructive to investigate the finances of these individuals and ascertain if any of the four were able to buy large estates in Scotland and Ireland respectively after the war. British officers were not paid at a level that would account for such expenditures. However, had any or all of them, as stated by a US CIC report, dipped their individual or collective hands into Globocnik's loot, a trail should be clearly evident.

When the book was first published, there was no official comment from US sources even though it contained highly damaging correspondence from the Central Intelligence Agency (CIA) which clearly stated that Müller worked for the American government. This correspondence resulted in the dismissal of at least two senior CIA officials.

Most agencies had never heard of Heinrich Müller and could care less. Many believed the book to be a hoax or deliberate disinformation since their files, with the exception of the US Intelligence files at Ft. George Meade, Maryland and, of course, the CIA, contained no references at all to Heinrich Müller. The author found it necessary to explain that the former Gestapo Chief certainly did not work for the U.S. under his real name. When this obvious fact finally penetrated the Stygian gloom that seems to envelope all government agencies, there was a sudden awakening of interest.

Much of Müller's postwar career is covered in this book, and a good deal of additional information concerning the postwar years came from Karl Müller, grandson of the late *Gruppenführer,* who, like his grandfather, holds a responsible post in law enforcement.

Both the author and publisher were bombarded with letters from people claiming to be historians, stating that each and every one of them had "valuable" material on Müller which they would love to share with us. The only caveat was that they wished to look through the entire body of Müller files, which contain over 800 microfilm rolls, to "help them with research" matters. As none of them were able to answer even the simplest questions about Müller, or produce copies of even one picture or document they claimed to possess, it became the usual practice to toss these suspect, clumsy approaches into the trash.

The general goal of these ham-handed individuals is to establish the existence of the papers and then, having read them, to report back to their employers who then would attempt to replevin, or seize, the entire lot because of what is vaguely termed "National Security."

To the small handful of petulant and outraged academics who have also made attempts to visit the author, the reply is, in essence, that no academic of any kind is to be trusted with valuable papers. Academics could, and would, make copies of them and then rush the contents into print, suitably embellished and written by a favorite, and discreet, student. Showing an academic anything with which he can make money is like presenting a burglar with a ladder.

The Unmasking of the Interrogator

The basis for the works on Heinrich Müller is a lengthy interview conducted in Geneva, Switzerland in 1948. This interview was conducted, according to its contents, by a representative of the newly-created CIA but the interviewer was only identified as "Welborn II" in all of the documents. There is no specific indication in the headings of these interviews as to who "Welborn II" was, nor which American agency, if any, he worked for.

What did emerge about the persona of this man, from bits and pieces of informational asides, was that he was well-educated; a man with a background in art history; a member of the OSS operating in northern Italy during the war; acquainted with Allen Dulles, OSS station chief in Bern, Switzerland; involved in interrogations at Nuremberg; friendly to Göring; and he had a favorite uncle who died during the great Spanish Flu epidemic of 1918.

The stenographer is merely listed as "Frl. Irmgard Krieger" without further identification.

Critics of the first volume were quick to note the lack of identification of both the interrogator and his organization and stressed that this informational hole created a tremendous problem of authenticity. Had "Welborn II" been an employee of the CIA, the critics would have felt smugly safe in their knowledge that the CIA would never confirm nor deny the existence of "Welborn" nor his employment by their agency. To do so would be to make a disastrous link between the CIA and the chief of the dreaded Gestapo—a link that could have the potential of creating a publicity nightmare of monumental proportions.

The first volume was well advertised in the American media and sales were especially heavy in the Washington, DC area. In February of 1996, Dr. Frank Thayer, the author of the book's forward, was contacted by a well-known and published American intelligence specialist, William Corson. Mr. Corson informed Dr. Thayer that he had read the book with great interest and believed that he could identify "Welborn II" with considerable certainty.

Verifying this information was not difficult. Not only was the anonymous questioner uncovered, but additional work also revealed the stenographer's identity.

The interrogator was James Speyer Kronthal, born in 1913 to Leon Kronthal and Maude Ranger Kronthal. Leon Kronthal was the partner of Joseph Speyer of the New York investment banking house of Speyer and Company which had once been a banker to the Czar of Russia. This firm was founded in Frankfurt am Main in 1837 and an American branch was opened in New York in 1838. By the 1930s, this firm was a well-established entity in the New York financial world and James moved in the best circles, getting an education at the Lincoln School and later earning a BA at Yale in 1934. While at Yale, James Kronthal was a member of Phi Beta Kappa and a member of the rowing team. After graduation, Kronthal went to Germany to broker the sale of confiscated Jewish works of art. At this time Kronthal became personally acquainted with Göring. The irony of this situation is that Kronthal was Jewish but this did not hinder his sales of confiscated art or his friendly association with the art-loving head of the *Luftwaffe* and the second man in the Third Reich.

With war on the horizon, Kronthal returned to the United States and attended Harvard University earning a graduate degree in Art History in 1941. While at Harvard, Kronthal became acquainted with James Jesus Angleton, also of a wealthy family, and both of them entered the military after the US joined the Second World War.

Angleton, who later became a power in the CIA, went into the OSS and Kronthal went into the US Army Signal Corps. In 1944, Kronthal joined the OSS and became acquainted with Allen Dulles, OSS station chief in Bern, Switzerland. Dulles came from a wealthy and politically active family; his uncle was Robert Lansing, Wilson's Anglophile Secretary of State. Lansing had married Eleanor Foster, daughter of John Foster, Harrison's Secretary of State. Dulles was not a particularly competent intelligence agent; his reports on conditions inside wartime Germany were exceedingly maladroit and inept, but he did have the proper Washington social connections, as did James Kronthal.

On April 21, 1947, Kronthal was appointed as the CIA's new station chief in Bern. He enjoyed the highest approval of his superiors and remained in Bern until May of 1952 when he was recalled to Washington to assist in the expansion plans of the CIA.

On April 1, 1953, James Speyer Kronthal was found dead in his Washington home, apparently a suicide. There has been cogent speculation that Kronthal may have been turned by the Soviet KGB and was suspected of having passed information to them during his stay in Switzerland.

An interview with Heinrich Müller's son shed some circumstantial light on his father's post-war activities. He stated that after his return from a prisoner of war camp (young Müller had been a tank driver in the elite *Leibstandarte* (bodyguard unit)), the American CIC made regular checks on the Müller family home in Pasing, a suburb of Munich. Their stated purpose was to locate the recently retired Chief of the Gestapo. These visits stopped in 1948, at about the time Heinrich Müller was engaged in high-level negotiations with the CIA in Geneva. The CIC informed the Müller family that Heinrich was now known to be working with the Soviets. Following this revelation, a Russian journalist told the son that his side was absolutely positive that Heinrich Müller was in the employ of the Americans.

Müller was obviously not working for the Soviets, as numerous post-war American documents show, and in this case, Soviet intelligence was correct. Whether their knowledge came from Kronthal or whether they were merely making assumptions is not now nor will ever be known.

An interview with Mr. Corson, who knew the Kronthal family, verified many of the small, unpublished details of James Kronthal's background, especially the anecdote about the death of a favorite uncle in the flu epidemic of 1918. The material supplied by Mr. Corson, in conjunction with OSS file material makes it extremely clear that 'Welborn II' was James Speyer Kronthal, CIA station chief in Bern in 1948.

The stenographer, Irmgard Krieger, was not an employee of the CIA at the time of the interview. She was a German national, a relative of *SS-Sturmbannführer* Hans-Joachim Krieger of the RSHA and one of Müller's former secretaries who worked under Barbara Hellmich, his chief secretary. It is obvious that Müller had found gainful employment for a number of his former workers, long before he had scores of them brought to the United States under the CIA's "Operation Paperclip."

Kronthal was fluent in German, had indeed been in the OSS, was a protege of Allen Dulles who later headed the CIA, and would certainly have been able to negotiate with Müller with full authority from his superiors.

From the interviews, it is obvious that Müller enjoyed sparring with his interrogator, but it becomes equally obvious that they seemed to enjoy the game, and that Müller genuinely liked Kronthal, at one point even indicating that he would put his abilities to use should he leave the CIA.

The Death and Transfiguration of Heinrich Müller

The flood of reports concerning the fate of Martin Bormann that poured from the pens and imaginations of journalists, amateur historians and Nazi-hunters seeking publicity and funds is both overwhelming and a source of humor, but there is almost nothing published about the fate of Heinrich Müller. There were many rumors about his fate and some of them were discussed with Müller during his 1948 interview:

Q Although we have a decent working relationship with the Army CIC, we do not have anywhere near full cooperation with them. There is a good deal of information about your fate in Berlin in 1945, most of it false. Hoettl, for example…

M A typical Austrian fantasy spinner. I couldn't believe a word he said and told Kaltenbrunner and Schellenberg to sack him. Hoettl got into the Bernhard counterfeit money business and stole with both hands and his feet. What did he say about me?

Q That you had a secret bunker built under Gestapo headquarters with tunnels leading out all over Berlin. You had this built secretly and filled with food. And apparently escaped from there in 1945.

M Nonsense. How could anyone build a secret bunker under the headquarters without attracting attention? Actually, I had a Zeppelin up on the roof of the *Reichstag* and flew away in that at the last minute. Any other stories to entertain me?

Q In fact, there is some more substantive information that you were a suicide in Berlin along with your family and were identified by the Russians and buried.

M I thought you said "substantive information." How could I be a suicide and be talking to you?

Q Ah, I have you there. You had a double you shot and left lying outside along with your family.

M Not likely. And my family survived the war as I well know.

Q You had daughters?

M A daughter and a son.

Q Two daughters were mentioned. And your wife.

M And this comes from the Russians? They must have been blind drunk and cockeyed at the time.

Q They found your papers on the body.

M I burned them personally before I left. Have you seen them?

Q No one on our side has.

M Then don't worry about that. This is an entirely stupid conversation, I must say. Are you asking me if I am dead along with my daughters?

Q I am only discussing what we have been told. We don't want this to surface at this juncture and delay processing your employment.

M That, of course, is sensible. I have no idea what your unnamed informants are talking about unless the other Müller is involved.

Q Dr. Müller would be an obvious answer. Do you know what happened to him?

M No idea whatever.

Q Did you live on the Prag Street in Berlin?

M No, I lived on a number of streets in Berlin during my residence there but never on the Prag Street.

Q We are checking the Berlin Document Center to see if the other Müller lived there.

M You might develop this idea, after all. It could save all of us problems in the future if I was officially believed to be dead.

Q We had that in mind, but we do not know who might have your papers and it is probably too dangerous to rely on this.

M I said to develop it, not accept it right out of the oven.

Q We can tell them you fled to Argentina with Bormann.

M You keep bringing Bormann up to me. If I have told you once, I have told you a dozen times that Bormann is dead. Your intelligence people and the stupid journalists so love to hear yourselves talk. Actually, Bormann is on the moon living in a special colony of SS men, former Party members and pretty girls from the "Strength through Joy" Association. They flew there after they stole my Zeppelin that was up on the *Reichstag* building. If you walk around Berlin with a push cart full of cigarettes you can get thousands of eye witnesses who will swear they saw Martin waving good-bye to them.

Q You know that I am supposed to ask you certain questions, after all. These are not my questions.

M No, you aren't an idiot. From what I have heard of Mr. Wisner…

Q Now, now, let us watch ourselves. No one is perfect.

M I've been saying that for years.

Historical Significance—Reflections of the Author

A US Counter Intelligence report dated June 4, 1946 and concerning Heinrich Müller, states in paragraph three (see Appendix for a copy of the actual document) that: "Reports from the Russian Zone of Berlin, seem to indicate that MUELLER shot himself, his wife and three other children on 27 April 1946." This date has been circled with a question mark and is very obviously a typographical error. Another CIC report of May 8, 1961 (see the Appendix to volume one of this series) states that:…"SUBJ was killed or committed suicide close WWII and buried at Standort-Freidhof, Lilllienthalstr, 35, Berlin Nuekoellin. Allegedly SUBJ body subsequently exhumed for positive identification by allied authorities." On the same page of the CIC file on Müller found at Fort George Meade in Maryland, additional information is given on Müller that answers a number of puzzling questions about his purported death. Given as his date of birth are both April 28, 1900 and June 7, 1896. Also given is a home address of Prag Street 10 in Berlin.

The Chief of the Gestapo was born in Munich on April 28, 1900 and lived at Cornelius Street 22 in Berlin-Lankwitz. However, there was *another* Heinrich Müller in the RSHA, *also* an *SS-Gruppenführer* but this Heinrich Müller was Doctor Müller and had once been a high-ranking NSDAP official in the state of Hessen in 1933. He was a friend of Dr. Werner Best whom he invited to be Police Chief in that state. When Best went into the SS, he brought his friend Dr. Heinrich Müller with him. It was to avoid confusion that Heinrich Müller was called "Gestapo" Müller.

The "other" Heinrich Müller, here a SS-Oberführer.

Dr. Müller did kill himself just before the war ended and his body was subsequently found by the Soviets. The papers discovered on the body indicated that the owner was an SS General named Heinrich Müller from the RSHA, with the date of birth and home address which are both indicated in the CIC file and in the SS personnel records of the Berlin Document Center.

Heinrich Müller's son indicated in an interview with the author that his family had been notified by German authorities that the body of SS General Heinrich Müller had been buried and that papers found on the corpse identified it. Müller stated that he had been told that this body had been dug up, examined and reburied in another area. No papers were ever shown to the family and have never surfaced in the intervening years. The purported grave of "Gestapo" Müller was opened in 1963 and parts of three other people were found in it, not a reburied corpse of a single person.

Aside from considerable activity on the part of German authorities to locate Müller for prosecution, nothing was heard about the former Gestapo Chief until a tabloid article appeared in the German magazine *Focus* in late 1995. Coincidental with the announcement of the German edition of Volume I, it described how Müller had fled to the Argentine, was discovered by Czech intelligence agents, drugged, kidnapped, flown to Moscow and shot. Müller's son was supposed to have assisted in this, a statement greeted by the son with a mixture of humor, contempt and an emphatic denial of the claim.

Another important Third Reich personality has been subjected to a far greater flood of tabloid journalism over the years but in the case of Martin Bormann, the overall body of writing sounds as if it were part of a therapy program in an asylum.

It might be instructive to consider, briefly, the post-war career of Bormann, the former *Reichsleiter* and powerful Secretary to the *Führer* because it can serve as a comparison between historical writing and journalism. Creative writers assertions to the contrary, the two are not the same and the latter merely obscures the former. The basic facts concerning the fate of Martin Bormann are that on May 1, 1945, those persons remaining in the Chancellery bunker complex made an attempt to escape the underground confines of Hitler's last headquarters. Among these were Bormann, Dr. Ludwig Stumpfegger, Hitler's last doctor, Artur Axmann, leader of the Hitler Youth and others.

They emerged from the relative safety of the bunkers to witness Soviet troops fighting the defenders of Berlin. The two Soviet generals leading this attack, Marshals Konev and Chukov, had both been charged by Stalin with the task of conquering the capital, but instead, attacked each other to impress Stalin. The streets were littered with rubble and the corpses of German and Soviet military personnel, and civilians who had tried to venture out of their hiding places in search of better shelter and food.

The escape party broke into smaller groups; one consisted of Dr. Stumpfegger and Martin Bormann. Sometime around midnight, Axmann came across the corpses of both men lying by the railroad bridge at the Invaliden Street. Neither man showed any sign of violence, but Axmann had no time to conduct a through investigation. After the cessation of hostilities, the Soviets had German civilians remove the corpses in the streets and bury them as quickly as possible. A number of persons came forward later to state that the bodies of Stumpfegger and Bormann were buried on the grounds of an exhibition hall near the railroad bridge. Searches were conducted but no bodies were located.

Bormann was charged, tried at Nuremberg and sentenced to death *in absentia* and in the ensuing years, a great manhunt for Bormann was conducted, mainly in the media.

Cataloging the various sightings of Bormann would assume epic proportions; but suffice it to say that the missing *Reichsleiter* was seen in Munich, Rome, Moscow, Syria, Lebanon, Egypt, Argentina, Paraguay, Brazil, Chile, Spain, Denmark, Sweden, Portugal, Japan and Panama. He was disguised as a farmer, a Franciscan monk, an export businessman and the owner of a bowling alley in Buenos Aires. He escaped from the ruins of Berlin on foot, in a helicopter, in a boat, a floatplane and possibly even on a donkey. He fled to Denmark or the Bavarian Alps at the same time and from there began his world cruise that so occupied various persons over the years.

Dr. Fritz Bauer, a Jewish attorney and former concentration camp inmate, became the postwar Attorney General for the State of Hesse and launched a campaign to track down and punish his former jailers. Bauer was successful in locating a number of minor players but the famous Bormann was always just one step ahead of him. His favorite phrase, given at numerous press conferences was, "We are now closing in on Bormann and will have him in custody soon."

As the police will testify, whenever a particularly notorious murder has been committed, there are always a number of individuals with weak minds who come forward and confess. This is why the police always keep some details from their press releases and these details simply are not known to the spurious killers. A number of such individuals came forward from time to time to enrich the Sunday supplements and encourage writers like Ladislas Farago who claimed to have original postwar photographs of Bormann. When these proved to be fakes, Farago went on to other projects, leaving the field to Dr. Bauer and Simon Wiesenthal, an Austrian engineer who had also been incarcerated in a camp because he had the misfortune to be Jewish. Like the Attorney General, Wiesenthal was always just one step behind Bormann but the elusive man was constantly moving around, hidden in underground bunkers built by Nazi escapees deep inside various South American countries which these gentlemen claimed held more Third Reich leaders than the Nuremberg Party rallies.

Bauer and Wiesenthal were both motivated by a desire for revenge, but Bauer wished to try Bormann, and Wiesenthal was apparently far more interested in publicity and fund-raising. In the end, both they and a legion of tabloid journalists were to be disappointed. They never found a living Bormann, and their publishers, who would cheerfully print a street map of the lost continent of Atlantis with a perfectly straight face, began to look for other subjects such as flying saucer landings, plots by Martians to kill President Kennedy and Global Warming.

Although a living Bormann was never found, a dead one certainly was. On December 7/8, 1972, excavations at the site of the former exhibition hall uncovered two skeletons. They were located in the approximate area where the German gravediggers claimed they had put them in 1945. The remains were subjected to thorough testing by government pathologists and the final report indicated that without a doubt, these were the remains of Dr. Ludwig Stumpfegger and Martin Bormann. Quite naturally, journalists and other individuals with heavy investments in time or money were most unhappy about this closure of what had been a low-grade money machine.

The question arises that if Bormann had indeed been dead since May 1, 1945, who was running around the world in various guises, and positively identified by hundreds of absolutely trustworthy witnesses? Perhaps a simple explanation may be found in Müller's comment about the witnesses that could be located through the medium of a cart full of cigarettes or perhaps the person seeking his few moments of fame and bribed with a bad dinner and cheap wine at a Buenos Aires restaurant might be a more likely suspect.

Although Bormann has fallen off of the stage, rumors, backed up by more trustworthy witnesses have it that Bormann was rescued by a British intelligence team who were acting on the orders of Winston Churchill. Living safely in the English countryside, Bormann died several years ago and was buried in a secret, unknown grave in England. Martin Bormann now finds himself in good company, along with Lord Kitchener, Amelia Earhart, the Grand Duchess Anastasia of Russia, John Wilkes Booth and Elvis Presley, all of whom have been seen at various places, long after their deaths, by absolutely trustworthy witnesses.

Königsgrätz Revisited

In the first volume of this series mention was made[1] of an *Aktion Königsgrätz*. Müller comments that, "There was a plot in certain circles of the SS to remove Hitler and make Himmler the head of state. This plot was hatched by Gottlob Berger and some of the foreign SS people. All of their contacts were in the East…in Moscow."

Almost nothing could be uncovered about this alleged plot until a report from the US Army Counter Intelligence Corps (CIC) surfaced. There was only a brief mention of this intended action, but it was sufficient to establish that it was a viable factor.

To bolster the contention and support Müller's comments, the first page of the CIC report was published in the American edition of the book but not the German. The entire CIC file is included here with the commentary by the actual participants. A number of misspellings of German names and locations have been corrected in this review. The original documents may be found in the Appendix. The report is on standard American military forms, WD 341/ 1 June 1947. It is headed, "Agent Report, German Nationalist Underground (Communist Penetration)/ RE Activities in the British Zone/ RE Project HAPPINESS/11." The date is December 2, 1948 and the control number is IV-2090/11.13:

1. Reference is made to paragraph 161. Consolidated Orientation and Guidance Report, Headquarters, 7970th CIC Group, EUCOM, dated 9 July 1948.

2. Allegedly the DAHLKE Group is an armed group in the German underground and all its members possess firearms. The group is also alleged to have connections with the SED. (*Sozialististiche Einheits Partei Deutschland* - German Party of Socialist Unity, the Communist political entity in the Soviet Zone of Germany). The most prominent personalities of the group are:

1. Walter DAHLKE, HAMBURG, (L54/S55) Kielortallee 2
2. Alexander DOLEZALECK, former *SS-Hauptsturmführer*

---

[1] *Gestapo Chief Heinrich Müller, San Jose, 1995, pps 168 et seq*

3. Dr. Herbert BEER, LUETJENBURG (Ost Holstein)

4. Dr. Herta SUADICANI, BERLIN-WILMERSDORF

a. Walter DAHLKE, former Captain in a German Armored Division is now a student of law at the HAMBURG University where he is in contact with communist students. He is described as a very complicated and mistrusting person. He was recently contacted by members of the National Committee *Freies Deutschland* (A Soviet group of former German military personnel), who are said to have furnished identification and gave DAHLKE messages from a Captain who resides in the Soviet Zone. DAHLKE told a sub-source that all illegal transports of arms are brought into the Western Zones at a point between JERKSHEIM and GUNZLEBEN near HELMSTADT. The transports are camouflaged as furniture transports from LEIPZIG.

b. Alexander DOLEZALECK, former *SS-Hauptsturmführer* in the *Germanische Leitstelle* (of the SS Main Office), participated in the so-called "*Aktion Königsgrätz*" in 1944 (groups within the SS and the German Foreign Office who secretly sided with the Soviet plan to murder HITLER and replace him with HIMMLER). DOLEZALECK has resided in the Soviet Zone since 1945 and is working actively for the SED, FDJ (*Freies Deutsche Jugend*- Free German Youth, the Communist youth group with mandatory membership) and the Trade Unions. He has a leading position in SCHWERIN, and under the alias of BOMHOFF, attends to the cultural administration for the SED. He is a member of the *Deutscher Volksrat* (German Peoples' Council, a Communist organization) and participated in the meetings of this organization. On March 19 1948, he held a secret meeting with the DAHLKE Group in HAMBURG. He crossed the border illegally under the name of DORRNICK and was accompanied by a former German professional officer whose name is not known but who is allegedly a leading personality in the FDJ in DRESDEN (N52-F29). At this meeting, DOLEZALECK stated that it is his task to establish contact with illegal national groups in the Western Zones and to find a common basis for common action. Stress was also put on the *Bodenreform* (Land Reform movement of the Soviets) and Socialization during the meeting but a complete agreement was not reached. It was agreed that close contact should be maintained between DOLEZALECK, DAHLKE and BEER. Consequently, DAHLKE made several visits to DOLEZALECK in the Soviet Zone and Dr. BEER also went there in May 1948. DOLEZALECK also has the task of bringing former members of "Amt VI" of the RSHA (*Reichssicherheitshauptamt*- SD) into the Soviet Zone. When DAHLKE returned from his first visit to the Soviet Zone, he told sub source about the secret training of former German Army personnel in the vicinity of FUERSTENWALDE and DESSAU. DOLEZALECK is expected to return to HAMBURG in the middle of December 1948 for another meeting.

c. Dr. Herbert BEER was a Major and Commanding Officer of an Engineer Unit in the German Army. In 1946, he started extensive political activity and built up an organization of his many friends from both the Western and Eastern Zones of Germany. Allegedly he was imprisoned by the Soviets, NKVD, at the end of 1945 and entered the Western Zones in 1946. He is also supposed to be covering his activity by working for British Intelligence. Knowing that he is closely watched by the British, he claims that he has succeeded in fooling his British liaison about his real activity. Besides his home in LUETJENBERG (M55/N83), where he runs a translation office, he has another apartment in HAMBURG , Isestrasse 139/III.

d. Dr. Herta SUADICANI, BERLIN-WILMERSDORF, was also a member of the "*Germanische Leitstelle*" and works with BEER, DOLEZALECK, and travels between BERLIN (N53/Z75), NUREMBERG and MUNICH. When in MUNICH she resides at the apartment of former *SS-Standartenführer* SPAARMANN, MUNICH, Anglerstrasse 18. She is also very friendly with Gerhard RIEMER, MUNICH, Agnes Bernauerstrasse 86, the former *Ortsgruppenleiter* of the NSDAP in Poland. He is an employee of the laboratory of the METZLER tire factory in MUNICH and also works for BEER.

e. Gerda KIRCHNER, STUTTGART-BAD CANNSTADT, maintains liaison for BEER and he stays at her apartment when visiting STUTTGART (L49/S02).

f. Professor Dr. Rudolf SEWIG, BRAUNSCHWEIG (M53/X90), Campestrasse 7, works with DAHLKE and BEER. SEWIG is a leading employee of the Photo firm of VOIGTLAENDER and maintains another apartment in the same house as Dr. BEER in HAMBURG, Isestrasse 139.

g. Otto ZANDERER, former *Hauptbannführer* of the HJ (Hitler Youth) succeeded Reinhold SCHLOESSER as chief of the Cultural Department of the " *Reichsjugendführung*" (national leadership of the Hitler Youth) and is now chief of the Cultural and Political Department of the " *National Zeitung*" (a newspaper) in BERLIN and also belongs to the DOLEZALECK Group.

h. Dr. BEER is also well acquainted with *Generalarzt* Dr. SCHREIBER, the right-hand man of General SEYDLITZ (the head of the *Freies Deutschland* group). SCHREIBER recently escaped to the Western Zones. BEER, who is regarded as SCHREIBER's future son-in-law told Source that it was untrue that SCHREIBER, as officially reported, used the first opportunity to escape to the Western Zones when he was brought to the Soviet Zone. BEER also stated that SCHREIBER has been in BERLIN several times since 1945 and each time traveled back to MOSCOW on the "Blue Express." DAHLKE said that SCHREIBER's escape to the Western Zones was a well organized maneuver on the part of the Soviets.

i. Dr. BEER is in contact with a former member of the *Waffen-SS* (first name unknown) KOELN, LENSAHN (Oldenburg). KOELN brought two members of the RSHA Amt VI, whose names are not known at present, into the Soviet Zone where they received good positions with the Soviet Intelligence. This was accomplished with the aid of a female Russian refugee in LUEBECK, whose name is unknown.

SOURCE: F-2518-IV-G EVAL: B-3

3. (Censored entirely)

Approved: MARIE T. CLAIR ERNEST GUNTHER, 7970th CIC Gp. Reg.IV

Special Agent, CIC
Case Officer

This report on Soviet espionage in the Western Zones appears to be reasonably detailed. The purpose for including a copy of the first page in the Appendix of the American version was to indicate that there was a plan, fathered in Moscow, to kill Hitler and replace him with Himmler.

The names of the participants contained in the report were unknown, who today might reasonably be expected either to be dead or in nursing homes awaiting the final trip to the cemetery. In December of 1995, the author received a letter from Alexander Dolezaleck, Director of a private library called the *Dokumentenkabinett* located in the town of Vlotho in the vicinity of Hannover, Germany.

Dolezaleck had read the German version of the Müller book, noticed the reference to *Königsgrätz* and wrote to discuss his leadership of this action and his reasons for his participation. Dolezaleck had not seen the CIC report, which was not reproduced in the German edition, and had no idea of its existence.

In his letter, Dolezaleck stated that he had received an unsigned letter from someone inside Amt IV (Gestapo) of the RSHA warning him that he was meddling in matters that were the perogative of the *Führer* alone. He wrote that he had been head of the Planning Section (*Hauptamt "Planung"*) of the SS Main Office (*SS-Hauptamt*), Section D (which was later called the *Germanische Leitstelle,* and later the *Europa-Amt*). This section dealt with foreign volunteers in the *Waffen-SS*. Dolezaleck's letter explained that there were over 36 countries represented by his section of the SS Main Office. He stated that Müller did not understand the concept of this section and would have put him in a concentration camp had he discovered what Dolezaleck and his friends were doing.

These activities were described as the concerned action of front-line soldiers, such as himself, regarding the outcome of the war. They were afraid of another dictated peace like Versailles or Trianon. They believed in using an "inner line" between East and West as a way to increase the numbers of contacts in internal and external politics. Dolezaleck referred to this as a dangerous and risky course and he had named the project after the battle of the Austro-Prussian War of 1866 in remembrance of Otto von Bismarck's policy. Bismarck had once been the Prussian Ambassador to the Czar and was generally regarded as pro-Russian. This was, of course, before the Bolshevik Revolution in 1918. He ended the letter by mentioning that he could mail tape recordings and copies of documents to the author if he wished them.

Following this letter, the author sent a full copy of the CIC report to Dolezaleck and received a letter dated January 12, 1996 which was more specific than his first. In this communication, Dolezaleck stated that the CIC report was 90% pure fantasy and 10% misunderstanding. He claimed that he did not know Dahlke, Gerda Kircherer, Professor Dr. Sewig, Otto Zanderer and Frau (sic) Koeln. He did, however, know Herta Suadicani, who had married and was now Mrs. Schütze and lived in the city of Fulda. Dr. Beer was also known to him, but he had been dead for some time

Dolezaleck stated that the report was due to the NKVD's penetration of the CIC and, like Dr. Beer, he had been imprisoned by the NKVD for unspecified reasons in 1950. He wrote that he would search through his files for more information.

The next, and last, letter received was dated January 18, 1996 and was much shorter than the previous two. Dolezaleck wrote that he had been advised by a friend (unnamed), that the report must have been the product of a Soviet double-agent. The writer did not appear to be pleased with the contents of the CIC report. However, he supplied no specific information to refute of the charges of being a Soviet agent and addressed none of the points the CIC report had raised.

This was left to Dr. Herta Schütze neé Suadicani who wrote on March 15, 1996 from Fulda. She had received a copy of the CIC papers from Dolezaleck. Schütze stated that she had no knowledge of the Dahlke group or of Dahlke himself. She indicated that she was well acquainted with Dolezaleck and Beer, since she attended the Berlin University with them from 1933 to 1939. Schütze stated that Dr. Beer had died in 1971 and that she believed that he knew nothing about Königsgrätz. She had known Dolezaleck since 1936 when she had been in a student work group with him at the Berlin University. After her graduation in the autumn of 1939, Schütze was in the Warthegau, once a part of Poland, where she worked with the resettling of German nationals between 1940 through 1944.

In August of 1944 and until the end of the war, Schütze was assigned to the *Europa Amt* of the SS Main Office which was run by *SS-Standartenführer* Erich Spaarmann. She lived in Berlin-Zehlendorf and not Berlin-Wilmersdorf.

After the war, Schütze visited Dolezaleck at the town of Gadebusch where he was a teacher. She neglected to say that Gadebusch was in the Soviet Zone, very close to the city of Schwerin. The CIC report stated that Dolezaleck worked as a functionary of the SED in Schwerin. She also acknowledged that when she visited Munich, she stayed with Alice Spaarmann, which is consistent with the CIC report. Schütze's final remarks indicated the entire CIC report was nonsense and that she had no knowledge of any persons mentioned in it.

The reader may draw what conclusions they wish from the CIC report and responses to it from Dolezaleck and Schütze. What is important is that Dolezaleck acknowledged he was in the SS Main Office on July 20, 1944, the day of the attempt on Hitler's life. He claims that he and his friends were seeking a negotiated settlement for the end of the conflict that involved Soviet contacts. Dolezaleck wrote that he lived in the Soviet Zone and had been visited there by his former classmate and fellow member of the Germanic Section of the SS Main Office, Dr. Herta Suadicani.

Both the CIC report and Müller have specifically stated that the action in question was Soviet-directed and was run from inside the Germanic Section of the SS Main Office and the German Foreign Ministry. Dolezaleck spoke of his interest in the Russian Volunteer units raised by the Army and the SS, and the man who prepared the organizational structure for these groups was Stauffenberg himself.

Müller and CIC agents have supplied the dots, and Dolezaleck and *Frau Doktor* Schütze have merely connected them and helped to clarify an important but hitherto very obscure part of German history. Had the CIC report been included in the German version, it is rather doubtful that they would have ever written their comments and apologia.

Bloody Sunday

The outbreak of war in Europe in 1939 saw the commencement of a brutal sub-war against the civilian populations of both hemispheres— a trend which has continued unabated until the present day.

Many historians point to the Sino-Japanese war of the 1930s as the precursor of this trend and even more have singled out the Polish campaign as its inauguration in Europe. Müller's comments on this ugly aspect of history are well worth studying.

Q The problem of the Combat Groups[1] keeps cropping up and we really need to get some comment from you about this. I assume you have some first-hand knowledge of the matter?

M Of course. This actually was under Heydrich in the beginning and later the chain of command was changed. First, it was the Main Security Office[2] through the chief of the Security Police, but later it went directly from Himmler through the Senior SS and Police Leaders.[3] I was actually not in the command chain but, of course, a number of Gestapo personnel were detached for duty with these groups.

Q It is just this that I would like to address. These groups have a very unsavory reputation and your connection with them is of importance.

M I imagine from the point of view of the communists, they would have such a reputation. And, also bandits, criminals and murderers would not have found them to their liking. As I said, these groups were not under my command although I was once asked to command one. I did refuse this, not because I thought they were wrong in their actions, but because I had too many other more important things to do than to run around after these creatures.

Q Yes, but they did hunt down and kill Jews, didn't they?

---

[1] *Einsatzgruppen der Sicherheitspolizei und des SD.*
[2] *Reichssicherheitshauptamt- RSHA*
[3] *Höhere SS und Polizeiführer- HSSPF*

M They hunted down and killed the people I just mentioned to you. If Jews were guilty of these things, then Jews were also included, but not specifically because they were Jews.

Q Why should there be these armed raids on Polish territory, if not to exterminate your political or especially your racial enemies?

M If you think anyone had the time or the interest in having a wild hunt after Jews, you are sadly in error.

Q But surely in Poland…

M Yes, in Poland. What do you think was going on in Poland at the beginning of the campaign there? Tell me what you think, not that I couldn't guess.

Q Well, of course, the extermination of Poles and especially of Polish Jews is the first subject that comes to mind. These groups, and this was well covered at Nuremberg, are known to have run amok in Poland and slaughtered many people… and in Russia as well…

M Let us take things in their proper order.

Q Very well, please proceed.

M I don't see any reason for giving you a history lesson here because neither one of us really care. But, I would like to set aside some misconceptions, just to be accurate. I have said that I did not participate in those things, but I most certainly knew all about them, even from the beginning. What do you know about German relations with the Poles. Anything?

Q It is not my field.

M For a time, it was mine, so I will enlighten you a little and improve your knowledge, if not your point of view. Germany and Poland were bitter enemies after the Versailles Treaty. Large areas of Germany, areas that had been German for centuries, settled and developed by Germans, were given to the Poles by your idiotic President Wilson. I would say that Wilson alone was the most responsible for the last war, absolutely without question. He made an agreement with our government about the peace and then, when Germany was disarmed, deliberately changed it. I can see the return of the French territories, but the business in East Germany and especially Silesia was monstrous.

From the beginning, those Germans who remained in our former territory were harassed and brutalized by the envious Poles. It was so bad that the British and French observers, sent there to assist in the theft, made protests about Polish barbarity. No one paid any attention and the business went on.

In 1932 when the Poles thought Hitler might come to power, they massed troops on the borders of East Prussia and Silesia and threatened to invade us. We had a small army and could not have prevented this, so Hitler had to give way to their demands, mostly that we sign treaties favorable to them and, of course, to cease dealing with their enemies—the Soviets.

Later, after the Union with Austria, and especially after the Sudeten business, the Poles became very much alarmed that we would try to get back our stolen

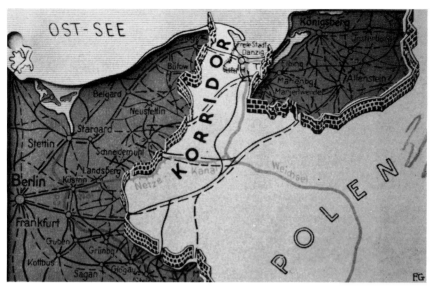

This 1939 German propaganda postcard depicts the disputed Polish Corridor which separated Germany from its eastern state of East Prussia.

land. Instead of trying to negotiate with us, they tried to threaten us. Of course, by that time, the army was much expanded and such threats meant nothing. For some reason, these idiots thought that they were a world power instead of a dwarf without legs. They went to the French and the British and insisted on having a pact with them. They defied Hitler and refused to even negotiate on the Corridor with him. Naturally, this angered Hitler who felt that of all his territorial demands in Europe, the Corridor and Danzig was the most legitimate.

Beck, their Foreign Minister, was an arrogant mule with delusions of greatness and behaved like Louis XIV. But a Louis without an army or an economy or, even worse, an intelligent population. The Poles are, without question, some of the most stupid and brutal creatures on earth...

Q Now...

M Please, let me finish. You can comment when I am through. And I said "brutal." In, I think, April of 1939, Warsaw began a campaign of terror against the German minority in Poland as a means of warning Hitler that there were potential hostages if he became too aggressive. Anyone who knows Hitler would tell you that you did not deal with him by pointing a gun at his head. They had gotten away with that once, but never again. Of course, reports of beatings, arson and killing came into Berlin, to the Foreign Office mainly, from German diplomats in Poland, and each report drove Hitler into a rage. If there had been one incident, it would have passed, but the campaign went up a notch every week until it was really impossible to ignore.

A number of the more fortunate and daring Germans escaped into Germany and brought all manner of terror stories with them. Of course, Goebbels made

31

This Polish, pre-war propaganda poster shows the anticipated, extended Polish border should they attack Germany.

A conference held on August 16, 1939 in the Berghof, Hitler's residence on the Obersalzberg. Here, Hitler revealed to his entourage his intention to attack Poland later that month. Left to right: Karl Wolff, Bormann, Gestapo Müller, Schaub, Himmler, Heidrich, Dr. Brandt, Max Wünsche, Hermann Esser and Hitler.

Ethnic Germans flee towards the German frontier as roving groups of Poles burn their homes behind them.

the best of it and the papers were full of these things. And in spite of what you might think, most of these stories were true, as we found out later.

We can skip over the actual outbreak of war now and get down to the reasons for the German behavior in Poland. We can discuss Russia later. Immediately after the war broke out on the 1st of September, the Poles in the former German districts, on specific orders from Warsaw, attacked the German minority with bestial ferocity. Women and children, even babies, were tortured and butchered in ways that I will not even begin to discuss here. I have thousands of police photographs which I would be more than happy to show you later, but let me proceed. Those Germans fortunate to escape this slaughter fled to the German lines and sought the protection of the troops. Many of them formed themselves into Self-Protection units and aided the military. When our soldiers advanced and then saw for themselves the evidence of the Polish barbarity, feelings ran very high and demands were made to round up the Poles who had committed these terrible crimes.

A German Catholic priest says a prayer for murdered ethnic Germans in Bromberg.

Now in the Sudeten area, the Security Police had sent in units in support of the occupation, and their purpose was to maintain order behind the advancing troops and also to round up anti-Hitler Germans who had fled to Czech territory and who were engaging in propaganda and occasional commando-type activities across the border. The security people were also after Czechs who were expected to offer resistance and also those who had attacked the Sudeten German minority. The Czechs were angels of mercy compared with the Poles, let me tell you.

Once the Polish campaign began, these security units were formed again, and for the same purposes as before. I knew about this from the beginning because, as I said before, the Gestapo loaned a number of its agents to assist the regular security police and I had to approve the choices and the transfers. I attended a number of conferences on this, and I was completely aware of what the goals and the purposes of these security groups were.

The discovery of the widespread slaughter of German civilians added another factor to the situation. When Hitler learned of what had happened, he went into a terrible rage and summoned Himmler and Heydrich, and later, myself, into his presence and ordered in the most emphatic way that not only must something be done to protect the Germans in Poland from such atrocities, but that those responsible must be apprehended and shot at once. At first, the military was shocked by this, but suddenly they changed their song when it was revealed that German prisoners of war had been brutally murdered by Polish military units. Eyes were cut out, genitals cut off, living people disemboweled or set on fire while still alive. Oh yes, many such incidents, and of course, the military now demanded that justice be done. And of course it was. The problem was not improved when the surviving Germans, now assisting the military as official auxiliaries, began to conduct their own counter-campaigns which were just as terrible as the Polish ones. In fact, worse I might say. It got so bad that the military demanded that such things cease and eventually these groups were disbanded, and those of military age were officially taken into the armed forces.

As for the rest, the security forces rounded up as many of the murderers as they could find and brought them to justice. There were proper courts set up, evidence was presented and death sentences handed out. This was an orderly process, unlike the revenge attacks of the German civilians.

Q I can see the other side, at least from your view, and I really do not want to see any pictures but we both know many Poles were liquidated, don't we?

M Certainly. Not enough in my view. Do you know how many German civilians were slaughtered?

Q I have no idea…

M I do. 13,000 corpses of old people, women, children and babies were identified. There were tens of thousands more who were so mutilated or so decomposed that identification was completely impossible…

Q Total?

M Over 50,000 dead, mostly unidentified. Now, do you understand the counteraction? My own opinion then, and I had seen the reports and had numerous interviews with my own men when they came back, was that we should have driven the whole lot of them into the swamps and drowned them. It would have saved time and ammunition. Jews? Actually, not many were involved in the killings. Don't forget, the Poles loathe the Jews and killed a number of them on their own without any help from us.

Seit Ausbruch des Krieges
mehr als 58 000 Tote

hat das deutsche Volkstum in Polen in den Tagen seiner Befreiung vom polnischen Joch im September 1939 verloren. Bis zum 1. Februar 1940 sind 12 857 Leichen von Volksdeutschen identifiziert worden. Zu den 12 857 Identifizierten Ermordeten kommen nach dem heutigen Stand der amtlichen Feststellungen mehr als 45 000 Vermißte, die gleichfalls als umgebracht angesehen werden müssen. Aber auch mit dieser erschreckenden Zahl ist die Verlustliste der Volksdeutschen aus dem September 1939 noch nicht im entferntesten erschöpft. Es besteht kein Zweifel, daß sich aus den im Gange befindlichen Nachforschungen noch viel erschütterndere Zahlen an Toten und Vermißten ergeben werden. Mit dieser Mordaktion hat die Ausrottungspolitik ihre Krönung gefunden, die der polnische Staat von seiner Entstehung bis zu seinem Zusammenbruch konsequent und erbarmungslos gegen das Deutschtum durchgeführt hat. In diesen zwanzig Jahren haben immer wiederholte polnische Terrorakte zahllose deutsche Blutopfer gefordert. Millionen von Deutschen wurden von Haus und Hof verjagt und den Zurückgebliebenen durch Raub ihres Landes und ihres sonstigen Eigentums sowie durch ständige Drohungen und Gewalttaten das Leben zur Hölle gemacht. Wieviele Deutsche durch diese systematische polnische Vernichtungspolitik der letzten zwanzig Jahr in den Tod getrieben worden sind, wird sich in seinem ganzen Umfang erst feststellen lassen, wenn die hierüber eingeleiteten statistischen Erhebungen zum Abschluß gekommen sind. Nach Ausbruch des Krieges sind im Feldzug in Polen zahlreiche deutsche Wehrmachtsangehörige die Opfer scheußlichster Kriegsverbrechen der polnischen Soldateska und der polnischen Heckenschützen geworden. Diese im folgenden im einzelnen belegten Tatsachen bilden eine Anklage, die in ihrer Furchtbarkeit das polnische Volk für alle Zeiten belasten wird.

The above page is from the official 1940 report on Polish atrocities committed against ethnic Germans living in Poland in September 1939 ("Dokumente Polischer Grausamkeit").

(Right) The foreign press is shown a location of murdered ethnic Germans.

Foreign doctors listen to 14-year-old Dora Radler's eye-witness account of the murder of her father and two brothers. Left to right: Dr. Espionsa (Chile), Dr. Karellas (Greece), Dipl. Ing. Santoro (Italy), Dr. Faroqhi (India), and Dr. Ohanian (Persia).

Q Yes, I know something about that. Did you know that when Auschwitz was liberated by the Soviets there were about 12,000 sick Jews your people left behind when they moved the camp personnel to the west? A really ugly story, but I had to verify it once, so I know. When the Soviets came into the camp, the guards at once began to slaughter the Jews by machine-gunning the barracks they were in. A Soviet infantry colonel told me at Nuremberg that blood was running out the doors. The guards who did the shooting were all Poles who had been hired by your people to take over the camp when they closed it.

M That I was not aware of, but it only bears out what I just told you, doesn't it? What did the Russians do?

Q Nothing at all. They didn't like the Jews either and they did nothing about it. Several Jewish officers tried to stop it but it was too late.

M And, of course, we get blamed for all that now.

Q But, you maintain that the Gestapo was not involved directly in this business?

M No, I do not. I told you we supplied a good percentage of the makeup of the security groups. I, myself, was not in the line of command although I was fully aware of what was going on, and to be most honest, I agreed then with their course of action, and I agree now. I do believe that allowing the self-defense groups to participate in actions was bad judgment on the part of the group commanders and I know that these Germans, for whatever reason, justified or not, did exceed their instructions.

Q Do you not then agree that the German authorities were ultimately responsible for the excesses?

M From a moral standpoint, yes. From a practical standpoint, no. And military and police operations are not conducted by moralists. The Old Fritz[4] said once that if a soldier started to think, he would leave the ranks at once. This does not excuse anything, but all armies engage in savage behavior from time to time.

Q Yes, but your record…

M My record? I don't think so. I told you I did not run any of these groups. Approving their actions is not an admission of guilt.

Q I recall one episode that I had to prepare a brief on for Nuremberg, a massacre of Jews outside Kiev in 1941. Weren't 30,000 Jews taken out of the city and shot by the SS?

M No. The Ukrainian police, set up and armed by the army, let me advise you, had an afternoon of fun and shot about 3,000 Jews. Yes, that part is true, but the numbers have been changed. Someone added an extra zero. The leader of the group was later shot by us.

[4]*Frederick the Great, King of Prussia, 1740-1786.*

Q What? For shooting Jews?

M Unauthorized killings. Now, I suppose you will say that because the Germans armed these Ukranians and that we were in occupation of the area, we were responsible. Indirectly, yes. I agree with you on that. And, if an American soldier gets drunk in Antwerp and rapes and kills a Belgian woman, your military is also responsible.

Q We hanged them.

M So did we. Bad for discipline—rape and pillage. But to get back to the actions in Poland, and later Russia, please note that such things did not happen in France, Denmark or Norway. There was no need for such things. These were civilized people, not Poles or Slavs. There is a difference. Since the Russians are now your enemies, why should you care how many bandits we put up in trees or shot? Your people don't care about butchered German civilians and I personally don't care about hanged bandits. If you ever have to deal with these creatures, you would come running to me asking me to destroy them. In fact, you already have discussed the Bartholomew Program with me and it amounts to the same thing, doesn't it? Only, that program is preventive, not punitive. Timing is everything in this sort of business. Be assured that I did not have any direct command or direct responsibility for the security units. That's what you want to hear, isn't it?

Q I think we will have to edit this extensively before we submit it.

M Of course. Now you sound like the Russians with your editing. When your superiors give you all these pointless questions that you have to put to me, doesn't it strike you as a waste of time? I give you this example: A lunatic is up in a building, shooting at random into the streets. Completely innocent people are being killed. The police get a man on a rooftop and he shoots the lunatic through the head. Justified? Of course. But there are always idiots who will say that the poor lunatic was a misunderstood man. Maybe his mother beat him as a baby. No one understood him and now kind doctors can't even examine his brain because a terrible policeman splattered it all over the wall behind him. Now if the daughter or son of one of these chronic weepers got one through the stomach, they would sing out of the other side of their mouth, wouldn't they?

Q I recall the verse about soldiers and God being implored in need but not before.

M You can add the police to that too.

Historical Significance—Reflections of the Author

*B*lutsonntag (Bloody Sunday) was a massacre of civilians that actually did occur in September 1939 in various towns and cities throughout the former German provinces, especially at Bromberg, but certainly not limited to that city. Extensive coverage of the killings was provided by foreign journalists who were brought into the areas by German military press units.

The *Einsatzgruppen* were not designed to liquidate Poland's three million-strong Jewish community but to act as political police behind the advancing German armed forces. The fact that their numbers were never high and that they were officially disbanded in November of 1939 would indicate that their duties were over. Rounding up and killing three million people of any persuasion would have been impossible in three months for a force of less than 6,000 police officials.

Postwar German historian, Martin Brozart claims that only 4,000 to 5,000 German civilians were murdered and that an additional 2,000 died as a result of the war.[5] The figures concerning identified victims cited here were valid as of February 1940, but the balance of the victims were so badly decomposed or scattered that an exact count and identifications were impossible.

Postwar German historians have, almost without exception, engaged in an extensive and often repulsive *mea culpa* litany, coupled with garment rending and other manifestations of social self-abuse found in those who wish to curry favor with publishers. The total lack of objectivity in their writings has left a large gap in German history. Students in the German school system find that German history ends in 1933 and begins again in 1945.

After the fall of Napoleon and the temporary return of the vapid Bourbons, it was strictly forbidden to write about or even possess a picture of the former Emperor. This official, and very often mindless repression, led directly to the destruction of the Bourbons and the eventual elevation of Napoleon's nephew to the throne of a Second Empire. It has been said the Bourbons learned nothing and forgot nothing, but this failing is certainly not limited to French monarchs.

That a large number of Poles were rounded up and shot following the massacres is beyond question. Whether or not those who engaged in the slaughter of German civilians deserved their fate is a matter for the reader to determine.

Even larger numbers of Soviet partisans were, to use a German phrase often mistranslated, rooted out by the same *Einsatzgruppen*, aided cheerfully by local Russian militias, the German armed forces and members of various Baltic and Croatian military units allied with the Germans.

The massacre of some of Kiev's Jewish population is known as the *Baba Yar* incident. Extensive correspondence exists between the *HSSPF* of Kiev, Jeckeln and Himmler concerning the killings carried out by a Ukrainian militia headed by one Berutko. Jeckeln, without direct orders, wanted to shoot Berutko. Himmler agreed with him, but suggested that the SS leader take over the militia and provide strict supervision, which was lacking under army control.

An extra zero was added to the totals at some point during the preparation of evidence to be used at the Nuremberg trials.

---

[5]*Martin Brozart, 'Nationalsozialistische Polenpolitik, 1939-45: Stuttgart, 1961. p. 47.*

Rudolf Hess and the Flight to England

A subject that has long intrigued historians is the flight of Rudolf Hess, the second man in the Third Reich, to England in 1941. His motives for the flight, his treatment in England and his death are subjects of great interest. The Gestapo conducted a thorough investigation into the Hess flight, but British files on what happened to Hess once in England and on his death are not available to researchers, nor are they ever likely to be.

Q Your people conducted an investigation into the Hess matter, didn't they?

M A very thorough investigation, believe me. Hitler was in a terrible rage about this and he demanded that he be given the truth of the matter as quickly as possible. He had Hess's aides put under arrest and wanted everyone, including the wife, interrogated without delay.

Q I think the question we all would like to know the answer to is whether Hitler had sent Hess to England to seek a negotiated peace so that Hitler could attack Russia. Is there any truth to that?

M No, none at all. Hitler had no knowledge of the flight in advance; neither did he instigate it or even approve it. He was stunned by it and realized the propaganda value it would have for the English.

Q Did Hess know about the attack on Russia?

M Yes, but Hess was not in the military picture and there, I think, lies the real reason for the flight. Hess is a mystic, like your Wallace, and was personally very loyal to Hitler. He was not a practical man at all and made no real efforts to maintain his position with regards to Hitler. As long as there was peace in Germany, Hess had no problems that he was aware of, although these existed for certain. I, of course, refer to his chief deputy, Bormann. This one was always seeking to climb up to the sun and he certainly had his connection with Hitler. But, as long as Hess was there, Bormann found his path to power blocked. You see, neither Hess nor Hitler enjoyed the detail work of the bureaucrat. I, on the other hand, am used to it and realize that it is the bureaucrat who works six days a week that can accomplish more than the brilliant politician who only works when he feels like it.

Bormann was very efficient and made life easier for Hitler, and Hess, by tending to all the small details. Of course, as both of these men depended on his activities more and more, Bormann achieved a good deal of power. But not the kind of power he wanted. Bormann wanted to have immediate and direct access to Hitler at all times. As a functionary of Hess, he did not have this, so he began to scheme to remove Hess. He could not kill him because if Hitler found out, Bormann would have had a fatal heart attack within a week or died in a car crash. No, Bormann had to find another way.

Alan Spurlin

Rudolf Hess   *Martin Bormann*

The outbreak of the war gave him his opportunity. Hitler decided to run the war himself and began to spend most of his time at his headquarters with his generals. High Party leaders were not invited to headquarters except for occasional ceremonial functions, and so Hess found himself more and more out of the picture. With him, it was not a question of power but one of personal feeling. He deeply admired Hitler and felt rejected when he was no longer able to communicate with him on a regular basis.

Q Do you think Hess was in love with Hitler?

M A good point. It had occurred to me at one time, but I think it was a mental attitude, not a physical one. Hitler had the ability to attract people to him and many of these people worshipped him, almost literally. I was immune to this personality business, but I could see the effect Hitler had on most people. He never tried to mesmerize me, and in my case, I think he felt that an appeal to my professionalism was important and in this way, he was successful. But Hess was a Hitler worshipper and was suddenly cut off from his idol by the war. Now,

Victor Lutze, Hess, Bormann and Hitler in the mid-1930's.

Bormann saw a chance to get Hess to commit some kind of an act that would close the door between himself and Hitler.

Q Bormann was the force behind the flight?

M Yes, in a sense he was. You know that I detested Bormann, but I must admit that he was very patient and he could be very subtle when he wished to be. The prize was worth the wait to him. He began to work on Hess, who was a very untidy and emotional man, and finally convinced him that he could make a great coup by persuading the British to negotiate a peace settlement with Hitler.

You must be aware, of course, that Hitler was initially pro-British and actually wanted to make peace with them. That was before the bombing, of course. With Churchill in power, there was no chance to achieve this end, as you must realize. Churchill was not a sane man and was determined to eradicate Germany forever by any means he could find and at whatever cost to his country in capital and manpower. We undertook private conversations with the British in neutral countries like Sweden and Switzerland with Hitler's consent, and actually, by his order. Their Foreign Office people were receptive. After all, Hitler was willing to make a peace treaty that took nothing away from England at all. Certainly, more reasonable than the peace treaty that Bismarck prepared for the French in the 1870 war and that was certainly more than reasonable. No, Churchill forbade any contact with us on the matter and it should have been evident to everyone in the *Reich* leadership that England under Churchill would never make any kind of a peace.

Bormann insinuated to Hess that Hitler had mentioned often in his presence that the man who could make peace with England would be worth twenty new

43

divisions. I don't know if Hitler actually said this, but it did reflect his thinking at that time.

Q Could Hitler have used Bormann to influence Hess?

M No. It would not have been necessary. All Hitler would have had to do to send Hess off to England would have been to ask him. Hitler was not that devious, but Bormann certainly was. And Hess saw this as a chance to bring a precious gift to Hitler and regain his personal position once again. I told you that Hess was not a practical man. Hitler did not reject Hess at all, but Hess saw it that way. I reviewed all the reports afterwards and it became very clear to me what had happened. But, there was no proof that Bormann had pushed Hess into this and after Hess left, he got the position and quickly consolidated it. Bormann now stood right behind Hitler and at this point, it was not a good idea to challenge him.

If I had had proof of a positive nature, I could have seen to it that Hitler knew but I did not. Afterwards, Bormann wanted to arrest everyone connected with Hess, including his wife, and put them away where they wouldn't talk but Hitler wouldn't hear of it and nothing happened. Bormann made initial problems for everyone connected with this but finally gave up and trusted to fear to keep people quiet.

If there had been no war, Hitler would have kept to his social schedules and these would have included people like his old comrades like Hess. Therefore Bormann would have had to try and find another way to get into power.

Q Then your analysis is that Hess felt himself out of the picture, was convinced by Bormann that the best way to get back into favor was to perform some spectacular deed?

M Yes. Hess was a pilot and to personally fly to England at some danger to himself and bring about a successful conclusion to a war Hitler did not want would certainly have achieved his end. We all saw the triumphal return of Prien* to Berlin after he sank the *Royal Oak* in the Scapa Flow and I think that certainly this must have had an effect on Hess.

Q In what way?

M Hess saw, of course, that Prien received a great deal of attention for his act and Hess is a person who needed recognition from Hitler. It is obvious to me that Bormann made use of Hess' insecurity to push him into leaving his post. Bormann saw Hess as an obstacle, a man who had been with Hitler since the War and someone on whose loyalty Hitler could depend. Given Hitler's personality, he would have never gotten rid of Hess because Hitler was consistently loyal to his early adherents.

So, Bormann could only rise so high and no higher with Hess in the way and then the best thing to do, short of having Hess killed, was to get him to leave

---

* Günther Prien, commander of the U47 that penetrated the heavily-guarded anchorage of the British fleet and sank the battleship Royal Oak.

on his own. Hess was unstable enough to persuade him to do this. You see, these complicated things usually have a very simple foundation.

Q You know that Hess was very brutally treated by the British. He was physically abused and they even broke his leg.

M That doesn't surprise me at all. You should see all of the papers we captured from the British murder-commandos at Dieppe. Killing unarmed prisoners, killing Frenchmen who might be friendly to us, putting poison in wells, killing children and making it look like we did it. No, nothing can surprise me about British brutality. And they put on such a face about being the saviors of liberty and democracy—and then go out and butcher the Irish or the blacks somewhere. And forcing the Chinese to take all the opium they were raising in India and turning that country into drug addicts. No wonder there were uprisings in China and that the Boxers began to slaughter Westerners in 1900.

If you draw a bill, you have to pay it one time or another. But Hess was absolutely earnest about trying to make peace with England, believe me. I have gone over all of his papers and reviewed the interviews we made with his wife, friends, aides and so on. Hess was motivated only by a desire to make peace and I am sure the British knew that when they broke his leg. Of course it was foolish because with Churchill in power, no kind of settlement could ever be reached. He bombed our cities and hoped we would retaliate, which Hitler did in time. And then he used this to get your country to help him.

But Hess is now in Spandau for the rest of his life which is a miscarriage of justice based on what I know about the affair. Then, of course, revenge was the sole motivation for the Nuremberg business and we both know that. It would have been less complicated if you had simply shot every government leader you caught rather than make up a faked trial. You have set an ugly precedent with that nonsense, believe me, and it will come home to haunt you. Suppose your country got into a war with Mexico and their partisans were all shot when captured. And this would not be a problem unless you lost the war.

Q There has been some debate about that issue and your point is well taken, but we digress from the Hess matter. Did Hess have knowledge of the impending invasion of Russia?

M Yes, he did. That was a primary worry for Hitler at the time: Would Hess tell them?

Q Apparently he did say something at the time. I understand that he was subjected to physical abuse to the point where his leg was broken. The British passed the information to the Russians, but we know that Stalin ignored it.

M What a wonderful commentary on Anglo-Saxon justice! Here is a man who makes a genuine attempt to achieve peace and he is beaten and eventually tried for war crimes and given a life sentence. Hess had nothing at all to do with the war and certainly was not involved in planning any part of it. He had nothing to do with the Jewish problem either, but he was seen as a Nazi and punished just for this. This reminds me of the fate of those Germans who tried to stop 45

Hitler and went to the British for help. Churchill simply turned their names over to my people and they died for their belief in British justice.

The Hess flight is not a mystery to anyone who knew about it. Hess was a harmless eccentric with a desire to do good and look what it cost him. I know that Bormann tricked him into it, but I doubt if Bormann realized what would happen to Hess in the end. I don't think that would have bothered Bormann, but Hitler would have had Bormann's head if he had ever found out. We can now expect to see many books about Hess from retired intelligence agents and journalists who like to eat.

Q The date of the Russian invasion was certainly known to both the British and us, you know.

M How could you keep something that enormous a secret? That's like trying to hide a cow in your bedroom cupboard. The only way we could try to conceal huge troop movements was to try to convince Stalin that this was a show to lull the British into a sense of security. Did you know that we actually printed up thousands of maps, guides and so on for the invasion of Britain? And of course left them around for Hitler haters and various agents to find. It did convince Stalin in the end and we were able to smash him flat in the first year of the campaign there.

Q Mr. Dulles was of the opinion that the Hess flight was a sacrifice to give false information to the British.

M You know what I think of the intelligence of your friend Dulles. I should tell you about the time that my Swiss friends and I were having a very nice lunch at a restaurant in Bern when one of my men rushed in to tell us that Dulles and his staff were coming for lunch. We all had to run out the back door and, how amusing, Dulles sat at our table. I kept his seat warm for him. Did you know their housekeeper, by the way?

Q Yes, I did.

M Such an efficient woman. Sold everything to us and the Russians. I think she even tried to sell the dinner plates to the gypsies.

Q There are no gypsies in Switzerland.

M Maybe she sold them to the bears at the Bern zoo.

Historical Significance—Reflections of the Author

The Hess flight has become to European journalists what the Kennedy assassination has become to their American counterparts.

All that may accurately be said of the Kennedy matter is that the American president was shot at least once while traveling in an official motorcade in Dallas in November of 1963. The only known film of the murder indicates that the official car with the President and Governor of Texas slowed nearly to a stop and then the President was fatally shot in the head from a position to his right.

On the other hand, the Governor was shot from above and behind with a smaller caliber weapon.

Beyond this, we know little. And, beyond the fact that Rudolf Hess flew a Messerschmitt 110 from Germany to Scotland in 1941, was captured by the British, eventually tried at Nuremberg and sentenced to life imprisonment—a sentence terminated by his suicide many years later—very little else has actually been released to the public.

Göring, Dönitz and Hess at the Nuremberg Trial.

In both cases, journalists have produced a large number of works on their subjects which range from the serious to the lunatic in nature. Stories about secret flights of Hess to visit the Duke of Windsor, his murder in England and the substitution of a duplicate Hess have heaped upon each other like Pilion upon Ossa.

It would seem reasonable to believe that the goal of a historian would be to look for facts and conclusions by removing irrelevant undergrowth from their subjects. William of Ockham, a British philosopher, stated that entities must not be multiplied beyond need. Reason has little to do with the writing of history, but point of view and book sales certainly do. A short chapter on the reasons for the flight of Hess from the papers of the Chief of the Gestapo, who closely investigated the case, is not as spectacular as a work that depicts Hess as a murder victim or a secret British agent.

In the same vein, the facts of Bormann's death and Kennedy's shooting are far less interesting than inventive speculations and inverted logic. The Hess case has not received the manic attention that the former have been plagued with, but as time goes on, no doubt it will.

Gertrude the Screamer

Although the great body of the Müller interviews is serious and often endlessly technical, there are occasional moments of genuine humor. Witness the following exchange about interrogation techniques:

Q Unfortunately for us, such a body of propaganda about the methods of the Gestapo has been developed that I can't see any way to rationalize it to certain gentlemen in Washington. Your name means nothing, frankly, but the word "Gestapo" conjures up images of torture chambers and so on.

M You shouldn't have started such nonsense.

Q Of course we did. Propaganda is necessary to whip up enthusiasm in wartime. You know that.

M I do, but our sessions in the Prinz Albert building were not what you think they were. We Germans are very bureaucratic and love to follow routines, and wild torture sessions, beatings, hot irons and so on are nonsense. I often said we ought to bring up the Iron Virgin of Nuremberg and set her in the interrogation rooms. Do you know about the Iron Virgin?

Q No.

M Looks like an iron mummy case with the front that opens in half. Put the victim inside and close the doors on him. The doors are full of sharp spikes that penetrate the eyes, the brain, the heart and other parts. I always thought if we put some fake blood on the floor in front of it, a suspect would be much more inclined to sing his songs to us. Unfortunately, the museum people in the Nuremberg castle refused to loan it to me and I am sure that to this day, some of them think we were actually going to use it. Besides, it is rather short... people were shorter in those days... and it would be just about right for a 15 year-old boy but not a grown man. But, we did have Gertrude the Screamer, the Mad Doctor and Horst Kopkow instead.

Q When you look at me that way, General, I know you want me to insist you explain your sly remarks. Very well, who was Gertrude the Screamer?

M A typist in our office. Wanted to be an opera singer but didn't have the least talent for singing, but my God, what a screamer she was! You see, we would bring in an important suspect and take him into a special interrogation room. Then I, or someone else, actually mostly myself because I can control myself and not laugh when I shouldn't, would start to question the suspect. When I was going over his answers, say in about the first half hour, one of my men who looked like a circus freak with a huge head and hands… a nice fellow actually but he looked like a monster… would open the door and announce that we had just arrested the suspect's wife and were bringing her upstairs. This used to frighten the suspect but he tried to put a good face on it for a while. We would install Gertrude in the office next door with some cream buns and a bottle of mineral water and Kopkow, who had a loud, nasty voice, used to start shouting threats at the wall and then he would end up beating a leather sack full of sand from a boxing gym with a big stick. My God, it sounded absolutely terrible through the door. And Gertrude would put her head back and start to screech at the top of her lungs and whimper and moan.

This was usually enough to get the suspect sweating and many just gave up and told me what we needed to know, but sometimes they were tough so Kopkow would shout out that he was going to break her fingers, one by one. What he did was to snap a big stalk of celery and then, of course, Gertrude would really begin to shriek. Of course, we told her who the suspect was and she began to call out his name and ask him to help her.

Q Oh, this is really too much.

M That is nothing at all, my friend. If he hadn't confessed by that time, Kopkow would start thrashing the bag again, and Gertrude would begin to wail like an air raid siren, and there would be a great crash as Kopkow knocked over a chair and silence. A secret weapon then came along in the person of the Mad Doctor. This man was actually a driver and quite decent, but like the other one, he looked strange—a thin face, thick glasses and hair that could never stay combed. We stuck him in a doctor's white coat, splattered it with red ink and he would open the door after the chair fell over and say to me that he thought they had broken her leg. Usually at this point, the suspect would start to blubber and go on like a stuck gramophone record.

Of course there were some problems with this. On a hot day, we had to keep the windows open and when she was in full voice, you could hear Gertrude three streets away. People must have heard her all the way to Unter den Linden. And right below us were more secretaries, and they could hear the noise, so most of them were sent home for the day. God knows what they told their families. And one time, the bloody doctor had to go down to the toilet and someone saw him—a woman clerk—on the stairs and fainted away. She fell down to the landing and broke her collar bone and we all felt very badly about that. I even brought her flowers in the hospital but I couldn't tell her what was really going on. You simply cannot trust people to be quiet about such things. I told her our doctor was a lunatic who had escaped from an asylum, gotten out **49** of the cells and had a nosebleed. The ink always looked fresh and the only real expense was the celery and the food that we had to get for Gertrude.

Q She sounds like she must have been quite fat.

M Be kind. She was comfortable. But, at least the celery wasn't a loss. We sent it down to the cook in the office canteen and it went into the soup pot. Are you quite all right? Please try not to get sick here. (Pause)

Q I am sorry but I couldn't help myself.

M You should have better control at your age. Now you've spewed coffee all over the table. That's a valuable table. Here, clean it up with your handkerchief or I will have to call someone in to do it for you. There you go. Try to be neat about it. I admit that the business has some humor about it but you seem to be hysterical. Now don't get started again on that; it's hardly that humorous.

Q The celery...

M Yes, well, I hate to see food wasted after all.

Q The images in my mind...I am sorry but I can't help it. You were so serious ten minutes ago, and then this business about...(Pause)

M I said to control yourself. What will my charming stenographer think? Gertrude...please, make some attempt at self-control.

Q Take this out of the record.

M And of course when the suspect found out that his wife was actually quite well and had been at home reading a romance while he thought our little theater group was beating her into cat meat, he was terribly embarrassed.

Q I'm...it sounds like the Ziegfeld Follies.

M What is that?

Q Vaudeville. Slapstick comedy. My God, it must have been a regular circus in there...

M Oh no, it might be humorous to you...and I confess I used to find it funny too, but mark me, we were very serious about the whole thing. It simply makes things easier if you can laugh once in awhile. Hitler liked vaudeville, you know. Absolutely loved to go to the theater and watch the dancers and the comedians. I used to have a sense of humor, I am told, but somewhere along the line I lost it.

Q I really don't think so.

M How kind of you to attribute human feelings to me.

Q Now in all seriousness, General, I beg you not to tell such stories when you meet with the Admiral's man. I can assure you that they will not find Gertrude...excuse me please...find that story funny. I am very sorry. Will not find it funny at all. Most of these people have absolutely no sense of humor, even black humor. You will put this project in jeopardy if you can't be absolutely serious.

M You mean we can't have someone in a bloody doctor's coat burst into the room waving a leg of mutton around?

Q Please…

M You see, once you get started laughing, it is hard to stop. And now the charming young lady is also laughing as well. Have more coffee and let us go on to more substantive matters, like the radio nets you wanted to know about. And the interlocking teletype systems. Just consider this a comic interlude and let us go on with really important matters. I will never say "celery" again in your presence.

The Wet World of Josef Stalin

One of the more important roles played by Stalin's NKVD was the removal of his enemies, both in the Soviet Union and abroad.

Q I think the problem we face here is that so many of the Soviet agents have used cover names.

M Not only that, but they also change their names for political reasons. For example Trotsky was actually Bronstein, Lenin was Ulanov and Stalin was once known as Dzhugashvili. But most of the changes were made by Jews who wanted to appear more Russian. This made for great confusion about the identities of various people. I had a number of very capable former Soviet intelligence people working for me and they had to make up lists with various different names for the same person. It could be very confusing and I spent as much time working out the names of the players as in trying to identify their games.

Q We have had that problem repeatedly. How often were names changed?

M Inside Russia itself, not often. For foreign intelligence operations, as often as they liked. For example, if you could identify a certain Yaroslavski as being born Gubelman or someone with the Russian name of Alexander Orlov as being Lev Feldbin you made a beginning.

Q Pash had this problem too when he was working on the Manhattan Project as chief of security. German refugees always used their real names but Russians almost always had fictitious names. They claimed this was to avoid persecution by Soviet agents in the United States, but Pash felt that most of them were themselves Soviet agents. When I was working on the Nuremberg trials, I had dealings with a number of Russians, all of whom we were sure were NKVD people, and I never knew… do you by any chance recognize the name Zaitzev?

M Oh very well indeed. One of Beria's top assassins. Only his name isn't Zaitzev; it's Leonid Fedorovich Raikhman. You had dealings with him? A professional murderer of the worst sort. He was involved, along with Eitingon, in the murder of Trotsky in Mexico, was the man who on direct orders from Stalin slaughtered the Polish officers at Katyn…

Q My God! I had lunch with him once…!

M You had lunch with me today, too. And did you like him?

Q No, a nasty and vulgar man. He married a ballet dancer…

M Lepeshinskaya. Difficult to pronounce. Russian always sounds like you were trying to spit out a mouthful of nettles.

Q I think you are right about her. I don't remember the name…

M I remember everything. What was he doing at Nuremberg?

Q Working with the Soviet team under Rudenko. He supplied many documents used in the trial. I'm afraid most of them were forgeries…

M Oh my yes, the Soviets love to fake up papers. They do this in their great public trials and have been doing so for years. Did your people know this?

Q Certainly but no questions were asked.

M And how many people did you hang with Party Comrade Raikhman's forgeries?

Q Their evidence was always the strongest, so I would assume all those executed were involved.

M And it never troubled your conscience that you were killing people by using faked evidence? You were an accomplice of Stalin's at that point.

Q This was a government policy at the time and I had no control over it whatsoever. But Raikhman's role doesn't surprise me at all.

M He was behind the attempt on Ambassador von Papen's life in Ankara as well. Stalin wanted the Turks either neutral, or on his side, and decided that von Papen needed to be removed. It went from Stalin to Beria to Beria's co-religionist…

Q Raikhman was Jewish as well?

M Almost all of the NKVD people, and the commissars and the prison officials are Jewish. The assassins of Trotsky and the NKVD killers at Katyn were too. The von Papen incident was rather amusing. The actual killers were supposed to shoot the Ambassador in public, for greater effect, and then throw down smoke bombs and escape in a cloud. Unfortunately for them, the lead assassin threw down his bomb first and was at once blown into small pieces. The second one, covered with brains, was so terrified that he forgot to shoot and was quickly caught. These were not smoke bombs at all, as you can imagine. Such loyalty to your people! Stalin wanted trouble, but did not want to take the blame for his murderous activity so the idea was to get the killers to blow themselves up, but only after they killed the Ambassador. But let us return to Nuremberg for a few moments. First, the so-called trials were not legal, at least not under your legal system.

These are called *ex post facto* punishments and even your government must recognize that you cannot try someone for something that was not illegal. Now take Streicher, for example. I admit that he was not a pleasant person. A man of gross character, I would call him, but not a war criminal by any stretch of anyone's imagination. The reason you tortured him and later hanged him is because of his magazine. Everyone knew Streicher was a terrible anti-Semite, but if that were a hanging crime, half the politicians in your country, South America and elsewhere would be swinging on lampposts.

Julius Streicher, a lifelong enemy of the Jews, who founded the infamous newspaper "Der Stürmer" in 1923. He was so corrupt and sadistic that he was tried in a Party court in 1940. It is reported that when in prison during the war crimes trials after the war, other Nazi prisoners refused to speak to him.

Q General, I don't think this is the forum to discuss what is past…

M But everything you have been asking me deals with the past.

Q You know exactly what I mean, I am sure.

M Of course, and you know what I mean. So you had lunch with the head hyena? Did you know he personally directed the massacre at Katyn?

Q No, I did not.

M Would you still have had lunch with him if you had? I know you aren't Polish, but I would think that you might have smelt the blood across the table.

Q There were a number of other people there. It was a formal meal, not a private meeting.

M Well, that's another one with a fake name.

Q Do you think that he was up to anything serious at Nuremberg? Aside from the fake papers that is?

M Who knows. Stalin conducted a whole series of political assassinations prior to that point, but what could he do in Nuremberg with a killer? Aside from killing German leaders with fake papers.

Q I was struck about how insistent they were that Hitler was dead, in public, but that in private, the Russians I had dealings with were even more insistent that Hitler was not dead and were spending a lot of time, money and vodka trying to pry information out of our side on that subject.

M We have mutual advantages here, don't we? No one wanted Hitler alive, but they all wanted him dead. I assume that if Stalin learned that Hitler was alive, someone like Raikhman would have finished him off for sure. After all, Stalin once planned to kill Roosevelt…

Q Oh come now, General, I must ask you to keep your strange sense of humor out of this record.

M I don't make jokes about such matters and you are well aware of it. As you say, this is the record. I said that Stalin once planned, or rather had serious discussions, to have Roosevelt removed. The way it was set out, I am sure it would have succeeded.

Josef Stalin

Q General, I would appreciate it if you would not just toss bombs into this and then sit back and smile at me. I would like you to at least explain what you started.

M The idea wasn't to remove Roosevelt because Stalin disliked or feared him. Stalin viewed Roosevelt as his good and very cooperative friend. The problem was one of how long he could depend on Roosevelt. There were rumors…even we heard them in Germany…that Roosevelt was very sick and was going to die. Then there was the question of succession. The Soviets were more than happy with Roosevelt and would have been delighted with Wallace as President. But Roosevelt was to be elected in 1944 and what if someone other than Wallace   **55** was his successor? Who would this be? Someone like Wallace who was entirely in the communists pocket or some unknown person? And what if Roosevelt was not reelected? Not a strong probability but certainly a possibility.

Franklin D. Roosevelt and Henry A. Wallace, a 1944 presidential ticket Stalin could live with.

Stalin, you see, was a man who looked into the future and planned for it. Roosevelt and Churchill did not. Roosevelt wanted another useless League of Nations and Churchill wanted to keep his rotten empire together. Stalin wanted security for Russia and to him, security meant buffer states between him and the West, who had invaded Russia before, and, of course, wanted also to grab all of the German industrial base in the Ruhr. Hence, his instigation of the Stauffenberg plot. Stalin felt, and of course, all of this came from my own sources through the radio "playback" system and captured agents, that Roosevelt and Wallace were known and useful tools. Churchill was not even considered by Stalin who viewed him as a crazy drunk...

Q Roosevelt said the same thing.

M Yes, and Stalin needed security and support for his expansion programs after the war. Roosevelt or Wallace would have supported these absolutely without question, but someone else might not have. And, of course, Stalin was right. Wallace was not the Vice-President when Roosevelt died and your President Truman was an instant enemy of Stalin. Your press should realize that Truman certainly kept the red flag from flying over the White House and stop attacking him as they do. But then, the press is full of Stalin-lovers, isn't it?

Q Yes, and the movie people are worse. But please, go on about the subject of killing Roosevelt. If you can prove it...

M I can if I want to.

Q Then let us have it for the record. You have given some motivation which makes sense. I take it that if Roosevelt were killed by whatever means, the succession would be safe enough?

M Wallace was a crazy man and also far healthier than Roosevelt. Yes, safe enough to allow Stalin to expand as far as he liked without interference. The specifics, and I stress that this was only in the planning stage, are when Roosevelt and his aides flew to Tehran at the end of 1943, Stalin would make an appraisal of Roosevelt's attitudes and his health and try to find out if he were planning to stand for reelection in 1944 with Wallace as his Vice-President. If Stalin felt that Roosevelt was in bad health, that was one thing, but the important business is whether or not Wallace would be in the line of succession in 1944 and 1945—the critical period for Stalin. Roosevelt apparently did not appear to be seriously ill at the time of the conference, was very cooperative with Stalin's views and indicated that he planned to run for office again with Wallace in 1944.

Stalin was now more or less satisfied with the situation, so the plan to kill Roosevelt was put on the shelf.

Stalin, Roosevelt and Churchill at Tehran, Iran. Roosevelt had initially gone to Oran on the new battleship "Iowa," from Tunis he flew to Cairo aboard the C-54 "Sacred Cow" where he met Churchill and Chiang Kai-shek and from there flew on to Tehran.

Q How was this assassination to be accomplished? At Tehran?

M Oh no, Stalin is far too clever to do things so obviously. His plan, and it certainly has technical merit, was for Roosevelt to be shot down by German aircraft on the way back from Tehran. Of course, they would be real German aircraft but with Soviet crews. The Soviets had captured a number of German aircraft, and used them for intelligence operations just like we captured a number of your aircraft and used them in a similar manner during the war. It would have been very simple to attack Roosevelt on his way back, shoot him down in flames and the Germans would have the blame. Of course Hitler forbade this kind of action. The Russians called this "wet action" by the way, but I can assure you that if we had known of the route, we would have shot him down—Hitler's orders or not. The Russians had the exact route and the time schedules, so it would have been simple to effect. Also, I understand that Stalin had an even more interesting suggestion. The Soviets had a number of American and British aircraft and one idea was to repaint these in Allied markings and "accidentally" shoot Roosevelt down. That would have caused all kinds of squabbling, especially if it was a British aircraft that did it. As I have said, Stalin was a very clever man and very devious.

As it turned out, Stalin discovered at the Crimean conference that Roosevelt was not only dying but had lost his reason and Wallace. The new Vice-President was an unknown factor and Stalin hates unknown factors. From his point of view, he made the wrong choice at Tehran.

Q You mentioned German use of American aircraft just now. You know there were rumors that this was going on during the war. Aircraft were sighted that followed our bombers on their raids and we suspect that larger aircraft, like big bombers, were used to move agents around.

M Certainly this happened. Although we never dropped bombs from US marked aircraft on the Vatican or some other such target, nor ever shot at your planes, these aircraft were used for intelligence purposes. I must tell you that as a pilot and aircraft technician, I was fascinated with some of your military aircraft. I think the best was the Flying Fortress bomber. I actually flew inside one once, and sat up in the greenhouse next to the pilot. A very fine plane, well made and extremely dependable. It was much better than our 177, which kept catching on fire. We used those for reconnaissance flights and especially for dropping our agents in England before the invasion. The other plane that was excellent was your 51…

Q The P-51 Mustang.

M Yes. A very fine aircraft. I never flew one but I have watched them being flown. Our Dora (Focke Wulf 190D) was as good, but that was for sure an excellent plane. As you can see, I can be very objective when I want to. Here were two planes that killed hundreds of thousands of German civilians, one with bombs and the other by shooting people in the streets, and I can still praise their construction, if not their usage.

Q You are certain about Stalin's interest in killing Roosevelt? You will be asked about this later, I am certain.

M I have no problems with this. I am sure the British would relate to this. After all, they killed all kinds of people in such a way. Inconvenient people. Stalin would kill his mother for bad cooking, but he would find some way to blame

Heinrich Müller in his uniform as an NCO in the Royal Bavarian Flying Corps, before he won the Iron Crosses I and II Class.

Heinrich Müller and his observer in front of his aircraft, 1918.

The first B-17 captured intact is displayed at Larz Airfield on June 12, 1943.

it on another enemy. I am sure that he would like to wipe Truman out but it would be difficult to get at him in the United States. Truman should not fly to Europe again. I am not in power anymore, but from bits and pieces I have heard from this or that source, Stalin hates Truman who began to remove all his top agents from your government and, let me say this, from the ministerial levels…you call them cabinet officers as I recall…as well.

Q Cabinet officers? You mean like the Secretary of State or Commerce?

M Or Treasury or whatever you like. Oh yes, Stalin had many friends. He used the anti-fascist bait to attract some of them into his arms.

Q I could probably make a very educated guess, but we can save that for later.

M Write it on your pad of paper and give it to me. Let us see how perceptive you are. That doesn't go on the record.

Q Why not? (Pause)

M You are wrong on one name but absolutely correct with the other two. But I notice that none of them are still ministers of state. Do you think your Truman was well-informed or fortunate?

Q Well-informed, and certainly well-intentioned.

M Complete agreement.

Q Now as far as names are concerned, I have here several lists that I would like to go over with you. I will incorporate these names into this record by giving a copy to the stenographer and one to you. If you will be so good as to look over the first list which contains the names of German and Austrian refugees, you might be able to recognize names of persons who might have had communist connections while they were in Germany or Austria. That is the first list and after you have had a chance to read it over, please indicate to me any names you might recognize. Now merely because someone might not like the government of the Third Reich is not what we are interested in.

M You are looking for communists and perhaps other antisocial individuals, I believe.

Q You might say that. Let me hand this to you now and if you will oblige me by looking through it, I would be appreciative.

M Of course.

Q Thank you.
(The following is a complete copy of the list in question)
Andras Angyal
Reinhold Baer
Max Bergmann
Peter Bergmann
Felix Bernstein
Eric Beth

Konrad Bloch
Walter Burg
Hans Cassel
Alexis Dember
Immanuel Estermann
James Franck
Rudolf Ladenburg
Rolf Landshoff
Erich Marx
Lothar Nordheim
Fritz Reiche
Marcel Schein
Klaus Schocken
Guenther Schwarz
Martin Schwarzschild
Hertha Sponer
Otto Stern
(Resumption of interview)

M Very well, I have looked at it and marked a number of names that I personally recognize as known persons with communist connections. There are five, as well, that have involvement with radical Zionist organizations. I have marked the first with a "K" and the second with a "Z". Will you want to discuss these now?

Q If you will supply us with any specific information you have on these people, I would appreciate it.

M Certainly. I note that most are German Jews and all the names I recognize are in the field of physics. Are they working for your atom bomb programs or can you say?

Q Some are, some aren't. Let us worry about that and I should say that some of the names are merely put in as a sort of control.

M I see you don't wish to trust me yet.

Q That's not the point here. You already have made a comment which shows me that you know what we want and why. You have spoken to me about a certain list you have in your possession that you are prepared to give to us. Perhaps you can state for the record what this list comprises and from whence it came to you.

M Certainly. This is a listing of Americans who we knew to be involved with Soviet intelligence. They were listed by the Soviets as reliable sources and sympathetic with the aims of the Soviet government. All of these sources have been identified by their names in various communications with Moscow. We were intercepting radio traffic, both from the United States and Canada, and these names are a compilation of both sources, plus information gained from my own interrogations. They are not in any order, either by name or by position, but of course, you will recognize, as I did, that some are very important fish indeed.

Q And you identify these as communist agents specifically?

M No, I positively identify these as very important sources for the Soviets and I know that some are, in fact, paid agents of Moscow. I will indicate which are which in the event our negotiations are successful.

Q I will have this list placed in the record.

(The following is a complete copy of the list in question)

Benjamin Cohen	Executive Advisor to the President
Adolf Berle, Jr.	Assistant Secretary of State
Herbert Feis	State Dept. Advisor on Economic Affairs
William Bullitt	Ambassador to France and Russia
Ambassador Steinhardt	Ambassador to Russia
Henry Morgenthau, Jr.	Secretary of the Treasury
Henrietta Klotz	Assistant to the Secretary of the Treasury
Anna Michener	Assistant to the Director of Research
Harold Nathan	Assistant Director, FBI
Alger Hiss	Assistant Solicitor, Justice Dept.
Nathan Margold	Solicitor, Dept. of the Interior
Louis Bean	Economic Advisor, Dept. of Agriculture
M. S. Eisenhower	Dir. of Information, Dept. of Agriculture
Nathan Golden	Chief, Motion Picture Div., Commerce Dept.
Frances Jurkowitz	Ad. Assist. Secretary of Labor
Lester Herzog	N.Y. State Administrator, WPA
Jacob Viner	Assist. Secretary of the Treasury
Boris Kostelanetz	Assistant U.S. Attorney
Nathan Strauss	Administrator, U.S. Housing Authority
Louis Domeratzky	Division Chief, Department of Commerce
Benjamin Frank Berman	U.S. Dept. of Commerce
Frances Perkins	Secretary of Labor
Anna Weinstock	Commissioner, Department of Labor
E. A. Goldenweiser	Central Statistical Board, FEA
Michael Strauss	Dir. of Information, FEA
Joel David Wolfsohn	Exec. Secty., FEA
Jacob Baker	Asst. Administrator, FEA
Harold L. Posner	Asst. Director, FEA
Abe Fortas	General Counsel, FEA (later Supreme Court)
David Saposs	Chief Economist, National Labor Relations Board
Joseph P. Lash	Ex-communist Youth Leader
Harold Ickes	Secretary of the Interior
Frieda Miller	Commissioner of Labor, New York State
Colonel William F. Freidmann	War Department, Cryptographic Division
Louis Resnick	Director of Information, Social Security

Cohen — Berle — Morgenthau

Perkins — Ickes — Jerome Frank

Samuel Dickstein	Congressman for New York, 12th Dist.
Leo Wolman	Amalgamated Clothing Workers
Vito Marcantonio	Intl. Labor Def. (later legislator, New York)
Dr. Alexander Sachs	Chief, Research Div., N.R.A.
Max Lerner	Editor *The Nation*
Jerome Frank	Chairman, Security and Exchange Commission
Harry Dexter White	Assistant, Secretary of the Treasury
Dr. Robert Oppenheimer	Physicist, Manhattan Project
Dr. Edward Teller	Physicist, Manhattan Project

(Resumption of interview)

Dr. J. Robert Oppenheimer

Q In reading over this, General, I must say that I am horrified. Of course, I recognize many of the names and I must ask you to be very certain about your identification of many of them. We have two Cabinet officers and one high FBI official listed here. You are certain?

M I am certain. Again, who were merely sympathetic, who were unaware that they were dealing with Stalin's agents and who were professional spies, will be made clear later. About three quarters of that list were actual spies by the way.

Q I think you are using this as bait, but I will send it on by cable.

M Please do so, but be sure the Soviets aren't reading your mail. A courier would be much safer these days. By the way, have you a list of the British you want to check on? I am better off with that. I can give you one very good name for your people: Victor Rothschild. Do you know the name?

Q The name is, of course, very famous. What position does he hold…and I assume this is in England?

M Yes. Very high post in British Intelligence.

Q Was or is?

M You can tell me. *Was* I am sure of but *is* I can not say.

Q Don't worry, we can find out. We don't trust the British at all, but the question is: Are they spying on us for England or Russia?

M At this point, is there a difference?

Q Actually, no, but we do need to be specific. I'm sure you understand.

M Of course.

Q And while on the subject of organizations, I have a long list of American organizations for you to look over. It's something you will have to take some time over, so we can discuss it later. I don't really think that you will be of much help here. It's a domestic matter and the FBI has already filled us in but anything you could add would be helpful. (*This list is to be found on page 207.*)

M You are doing the correct thing in tracking down these people and silencing them. We had an identical problem in Germany during the Weimar period, believe me. Soviet assassins roaming around the country, killing people at will, and a great proliferation of communist groups masquerading as intellectual assistance societies in every major city and all of them tied direct to Moscow. Did you know that when we broke into the Soviet Embassy in Paris in 1941, we found a perfect murder mill? Execution chambers, crematoria, torture rooms and so on? It looked like a charnel house in there. The Russians are brutish by nature, all Slavs are, as a matter of fact, but the communist branch of the tribe is one step removed from the caveman. The history of bolshevism in Russia…and Hungary as well…is a history of sadism, brutality and degeneracy run wild. You must know about Bela Kun in Hungary, and I know personally about the butchery in Munich when the Russians tried to set up one of their criminal "Council Governments" there. You would have to experience the insanity and criminal brutality to really understand why I loathe these scum and have made it my life work to root them out and destroy them. Working for you is not business with me. I look at it more as virgin territory to cleanse of filth and degeneracy. When you had an extra atom bomb, you should have dropped it on Moscow instead of the Japanese. One was enough with them, but the other would have incinerated the sewer rats of the Kremlin in a second. You will regret not having done that.

I told you once that Stalin will not invade you as long as he has a state within a state in Washington. We both know he had that when Roosevelt was on the throne, but now that he has lost the center of power, look for his trained rats to burrow deeper into your government and society and try to rip it apart from within. The professional Soviet agitator, and your country is full of them disguised as labor leaders, intellectual activists, writers and film producers, will find any opportunity of getting a toe in the crack. They will play one group off against another, degrade public opinion of the government, attack the system by many different means. Their most important goal is to discredit your system and then put their own filth up as a perfect antidote to that which they hate. And if these broken down creatures have their way, they would institute a reign of terror in your country that would make the one they had in Russia look like a church choir outing in the country.

And while we are on the subject of hostile foreign activity in your country, don't disregard the British. They may be morally and financially bankrupt, but they still hate you, and I know they spy on you as a matter of course. I don't think they will ever forgive you for financially raping them at the beginning of the war.

Q I think you are overstating the matter here. They needed help and we gave it to them, but of course, these bills had to be paid…

M Oh yes, and were. One of the conversations between Churchill and his Ambassador in Washington covered his views about how Roosevelt had broken the back of the Empire. I will give you a copy of that for evening reading. I hope you get as much pleasure reading it as I did six years ago. To get back to our original discussion, I will give you a list of all the top Soviet intelligence agents and their different names. That, I think, your people will find most interesting. And I will look over the list of groups this evening. We will both have some interesting reading, I believe.

Q I think you like to disillusion me, General.

M No. I like to confront you with reality once in a while.

Q Enough said on that.

Historical Significance—Reflections of the Author

With the collapse of communism in Russia, as opposed to the United States, an increasing amount of information and documentation has become available to historians and researchers. Great care has to be taken, however, to consider the source of this information because the descendant of the dreaded NKVD, the KGB, has been reorganized but still maintains the security of its own files. Documents from this source are to be considered as extraordinarily suspect insofar as accuracy is concerned. This agency, which supplied carloads of faked documents for Stalin's murderous purges, is still in the business of preparing counterfeit papers to suit whatever needs might arise. Foreign journalists pay large sums in hard currency and are given boxes of papers for research and eventual publication, just as the Stasi sold the counterfeit Hitler diaries for much needed foreign currency.

In the area of early communist organizations and history, much of the information is considered harmless historical background and is often released without the doctoring and fabrications found in papers relating to more current events. Anything relating to assassinations, high-level Soviet agents in foreign countries, Soviet agendas of subversion and aggression and their intelligence contacts with foreigners in sympathy with the aims of the former Soviet Union are certainly not available. A thick file on Lee Harvey Oswald has been displayed, but never opened to anyone, and other files on such political personalities as Willi Brandt, former West German Chancellor, and US President William Clinton are not for public consumption. Although at least one American intelligence agency firmly believed that Roosevelt's chief advisor, Harry Hopkins, was in the pay of the Russians, no file on Hopkins, who spent considerable time in direct contact with Stalin, is even admitted to exist by current Russian officials.

It should be noted that the Soviet intelligence agencies kept extensive files on anyone of interest to them. Records of persons known to be hostile to their aims share the same locked archives as files covering those known to be sympathetic to or cooperative with Soviet ideology and intentions.

Post-communist Russian intelligence agencies have made a healthy profit selling stacks of counterfeit papers to journalists. Most of these papers were forged during the Cold War and deal with various individuals at high levels in the Third Reich. Military plans, diaries of the prominent, correspondence dealing with such matters as the slaughter of civilians and so on were cranked out by the forgery factory in the KGB and sequestered until they were needed for propaganda campaigns. When the Soviet Union disintegrated, Germany was no longer an ally of the United States to be vilified but was, instead, a wealthy potential trading partner against whom these paper weapons were not needed.

Even with the release of former Soviet files, no one should be surprised about the internal and external programs of murders and assassinations ordered by Stalin and carried out by his immense cadre of ideological killers. Although it was far easier to liquidate Polish prisoners of war, internal dissidents, uncooperative Ukrainian peasants and potential sources of rebellion in conquered territories, Stalin's NKVD (which changed its title to KGB after Stalin's death but not its aims) found ways to kill dangerous opponents outside the borders of the communist empire.

White Russian leaders in Paris, exiled Leon Trotsky in Mexico and inconvenient foreigners were shot, poisoned, hacked to death or kidnapped and dismembered inside Soviet diplomatic missions in hidden rooms set aside for this purpose. Unlike Roosevelt and Churchill, Stalin had a much clearer view of his own goals and his massacres and assassinations had a far more pragmatic basis than mere revenge and killing for its own sake.

Müller's comments about the duplication of Soviet agent messages sent from the United States and Canada to Moscow is of considerable interest in current times. US intercepts of Soviet radio traffic were purported to be extremely difficult to decrypt and were termed the Venona Project. The allegation has been made that the US National Security Agency, one of the best equipped and effective agencies in the world in the area of interception and decoding and its predecessors in this field, have labored for over 30 years to break the Soviet agents' coded messages. The statement has been made that only fragments have been decoded in all that time. The fact that the Germans intercepted and decoded identical messages, sent in a different code from Canada, is not mentioned, but a reading of it makes it very clear why the hitherto unfathomable delays have occurred in the release of Venona material, because these US intercepts shows the degree and extent of Soviet penetration of American top-level intelligence, military and political circles. The material is shocking in the extreme as the names of some of the leading luminaries of the Roosevelt New Deal are encountered. The delays in releasing Venona appear to be more in the nature of political damage control rather than code complexities. The top secret atomic bomb program, the Manhattan Project, was compromised and Soviet agents were either in place in or had close contact with very high-level persons in the Roosevelt Cabinet, OSS, FBI, Treasury Department and War Department.

It appears that Roosevelt himself, though not a communist, had no difficulties in utilizing their services both to maintain his presidency and assist Josef Stalin, his closest ally in the war against Hitler. The OSS was so infiltrated with avowed Communists that Harry Truman disbanded it as quickly as he could when he became President in 1945. Cabinet-level personages suspected of working for Stalin's agents were quietly retired and a very discreet shake-up was instituted.

That the Roosevelt Administration was filled with Soviet sympathizers and actual agents is well known. The many lists compiled by Müller, some of which have been reproduced in this work, reflect the names of many prominent Soviet *sources* but in all fairness, a distinction must be made between a source and an agent.

A source could well be a person sympathetic to the Soviet system, a US government official who was merely cooperating openly with a wartime ally, a high-level Roosevelt Administration personage who was acting as an official conduit between the President and the Soviet government, or even a name stuck into a report by an ambitious Soviet agent to impress Moscow with his contacts.

In reviewing material released by the US National Security Agency on the Venona project and comparing this with far more extensive material intercepted by the Germans during the war, it becomes evident that actual agents in place are never referred to by their actual names but are given code names while sources, whatever their ideology, are almost always identified by their own names. Closer reading of the German and US intercepts indicates that often a source would be turned into an actual agent and at that point, a code name would be used in transmissions. However, Soviet agents were not noted for their intelligence and even these disguised entities are easily identified in the texts by addresses, positions or reference to previous input.

The legacy of Stalin's army of spies is with us today, and fear of their exposure is a motivating factor in the timorous release of information to the general public.

The Coup D' Etat in Russia and the United States

Müller was considered to be one of the foremost experts on the political and intelligence structures of the Soviet Union. He had studied communist history in great detail and had an understanding of it unmatched in US intelligence circles at the time of his interview in 1948. His views on Lenin's seizure of power in 1917 by a brilliant *coup d' Etat* are coupled with his suggestions about how such a coup might be conducted by Stalin, or anyone else for that matter, in the United States or another democratic society.

M The question about the methods by which Stalin might fatally disrupt your society is certainly a germane one, and if we study the methods by which the communists have achieved power in various countries, it is easy to understand how they can suddenly come into power. And having come into a possible precarious control of the state apparatus, how they will consolidate their position.

In 1917, and this was the most important lesson that Stalin learned, the Menshiviks or the moderates under Kerenski, were in power in Petrograd. Lenin, just returned from exile in Switzerland, wished to come to power himself, but Kerenski was in a powerful position in the capital. He had all the powers of the state, the military and the police in his control and also had physical possession of all the key areas of Petrograd. Lenin was afraid for his life and fled to Finland first and then later returned to Petrograd where he hid in the suburbs disguised in a terrible wig.

The real revolution, and I suggest that your people make a careful study of this, was not carried out by Lenin, the man of words, but by Trotsky, the man of action. This man was a brilliant, unstable Jew who saw at once the means by which the minority and generally distrusted Bolsheviks could seize power from the conservative to moderate Menshiviks. While Lenin and his friends drew up battle plans calling for a genuine mass uprising, Trotsky planned to seize power by a coup using no more than a thousand men. And these, to be used against over 20,000 loyal and armed troops, police and so on, all in physical possession of the city.

Lenin's plans would have led to disaster because they were entirely based on the current concept of revolution. This was embodied in the Utopian nonsense of Marx who always dreamed of a mass rising of the lower classes against the upper ones. These things simply do not happen and Marx was an intellectual babbler with no grasp of reality. His co-religionist Trotsky, on the other hand, instantly saw how to accomplish this seizure of power and this was by using a small, well-trained *corps d' elite* composed of shock troops, technicians and the like. What Trotsky did was to select the key targets for control, send his men out in small groups into a city filled with deserters, frightened workers and so on and in the confusion, get them to infiltrate into these key points. They made no attempt to seize them but merely to do a military style reconnaissance.

When Lenin was eagerly planning his mass rising, one day and without telling anyone, Trotsky and his men struck at the establishment, seized the key points and let in Lenin's ponderous units—something they could not have done themselves against a well-organized defense.

This done, Trotsky then presented Lenin with the city and eventually, the whole of Russia. I stress that Trotsky was a very dangerous man and his idea is the greatest importance in the study of how to either perform or defend against the only form of the coup that can work quickly.

Q Would this small group be effective in a western country?

M It would be effective anywhere, especially in a well-ordered and law abiding country, because the citizens are trained to trust their establishments and when they fall, have no idea at all what to do. The bees lose their queen and the hive has no defense.

Trotsky was like a valuable tool in that he could perform these deeds, but in the long run, Lenin was much more successful and later, Stalin even more so, because he is not a vaporizing intellectual, in love with his own words but a practical, deliberate Georgian peasant who proceeds slowly and carefully to gain his power and especially to consolidate it. Trotsky tried a coup on him, as you may remember, in 1927, but Stalin crushed him entirely by methods that are typically Stalin and again, ought to be studied carefully.

Stalin was a strategist and Trotsky was a tactician, purely stated. How Stalin blocked this *putsch* is instructive. He worked in the shadows while Trotsky worked in the open. Stalin spied and plotted while Trotsky orated and plotted. Stalin carefully got his people into position, especially Menjinski, head of the G.P.U. or the secret police. This was his masterstroke because Menjinski was able to establish a secret telephone network to compliment his antidote to Trotsky's secret army. This was his own secret army that always kept one step ahead of Trotsky and his friends.

With this force in place, Stalin then proceeded to stir up public animosity against the Trotsky faction and remove any popular support from him. This proved to be very simple for Stalin. Trotsky was a Jew, as were almost all of his supporters. Stalin merely unleashed an anti-Semitic movement which in Russia is always present, against the plotters. Trotsky did not help his cause by leaving Russia to help direct revolutionary activities in the West.

In his absence, Stalin began to isolate his allies, remove them from prominent positions and then move against Trotsky who was removed from his post as head of the military. As you know, Trotsky was a genuine hero of the early revolution because of his successful fights against the White Armies and very popular with the active revolutionaries. However, like Röhm, Trotsky wanted perpetual revolution and anarchy which he seemed to revel in. Both Stalin and Hitler could see that the citizens soon grew weary of constant struggle and yearned for peace and quiet. Stalin played on that wish as well.

When Trotsky made his move in November of 1927, Stalin's own shock troops had taken a leaf from Trotsky's book and occupied the key areas of Moscow with small groups of their own trained experts. A demonstration in Red Square was quickly broken up and Trotsky forced to flee. That was the end of that and as we know, Stalin tracked Trotsky down in Mexico and had him murdered, both out of revenge and to prevent his brilliant enemy from ever attempting such business again.

It is not the bombastic Lenin or Marx to worry about but the brilliant Trotsky to watch. Such coups are entirely possible anywhere, even in your peaceful country.

Q Could you enlarge on your statements on that score? Be more specific?

M With pleasure. Certain conditions must exist before a really successful coup could be launched. A sudden decline in the standard of living which leads to distrust of the bureaucracy, which in turn leads to the bureaucracy launching repressive actions against the unhappy citizens. If this repression, or perceived repression, is coupled with a weak leadership at the highest levels, the public becomes frightened, unhappy and demanding of change. Bureaucracies are not responsive to genuine public unhappiness, as we both know, and their response to what start out as loud complaints and can escalate into minor acts of sabotage or resistance, is to increase their methods of control. The leadership becomes frightened and demands more and more police who antagonize the people even further.

There will be outbreaks of civil disobedience—quickly stifled, clandestine newspapers, small meetings of disgruntled citizens and then the anticipated repressive measures. Religious agencies will become involved against the government, who will make a cardinal error and attempt to repress them as well. This will anger neutralists who will side with the churches and at some point, someone, some group, will seize power by a coup.

Q You are suggesting a communist-led coup here?

M No, not necessarily. If the communists are not directly involved, a right-wing coup is the best assumption. The public wants a return to stability and only a dictator can supply this. They will willingly surrender the authority to him if he will assume all responsibility. He will do this and order will be restored. This happened in Germany but I should tell you here, that rather than repress the people in general, Hitler was clever enough to present himself as their defender against the forces of darkness from within and without. The communists and their Soviet masters were very real menaces, but the Jew was only an enemy in Hitler's mind. Anti-Semitism did help unify the country, but in the end did far more damage than good. I speak in a purely professional manner at this point. Had we demonized only the communist, all well and good. Most Germans well remembered the communist risings in 1918 and were terrified of them. These people made far better unifying factors than Jews, believe me. Hitler's disaster was to let his personal prejudices become a policy of the State.

But to return to your question: A seizure of power can come from either political extreme, left or right. I have some views on how this could be accomplished in your country if you have any interest…

Q Oh, certainly proceed.

M The fewer numbers of actual plotters, the better. Secrets are very hard to keep and we would be dealing, in theory at least, with a government that was looking for such things. A few key military units, preferably elite ones, in proximity to the capital, a few key units specializing in communications and you have a successful coup. First of all, how is the news controlled in your country today?

Q News? It isn't controlled at all. We have newspapers and radio stations in every large city and most are independent. We do have some chains, like the Hearst people, for example, but they do not control the news. The radio stations, true enough, are owned by the major networks. But they can't make a coup.

M No, but they could support such a coup in the critical early hours of its birth. These organizations could keep the people quiet and make the job of the coup leaders easier until they quickly consolidated their power. Of course, they wouldn't do this as a knowing of any plot at all. Their participation would be based on ignorance and faith.

Q This is not very realistic theory, General, as I am sure you are aware. The press is not controlled by the state as it was in Germany.

M Oh yes, it certainly is. It always is. Not to such a great degree or extent as you might think, but it is controlled. The public get all of their news from the papers and from the radio, correct? And pray tell me where do these groups get the news that they print or put out over the airwaves?

Q They have reporters of course…

M All over the world? In every city in the country?

Q No. The reporters are responsible for the local news…

M I know that. I mean national news. Where does that come from, please tell me?

Q There are news services that supply stories…

M And of course, there you are. The news services supply material to their clients by wire, do they not?

Q Yes.

M How many wire news services are there and where are they located?

Q Most of it comes out of New York and I think there are ten or so major services. We have the Associated Press, United Press, Scripps-Howard and so on. Far too many to control.

M And if, for some reason, these services went out of business or were combined so that there were only, let us say, three? Not impossible over a period of time. And then all one would have to do would be to send armed technicians into their main sending stations and put out just the right kind of news at the critical moment. You don't need to subvert newspapers and radio stations if you control their news, do you?

Q Interesting concept. And the rest?

M If the coup leaders have a justification for their acts, the public will not react at once and then the process of coordination can begin. Of course there must be a common enemy against whom the new government will ruthlessly proceed to bring law and order back to the people whom they serve. And it would be incumbent then to find a means to improve the economy so that salaries would rise a little and make the grumblers happy. In our country, we used the Jews as an enemy and in your country you would use the blacks and the Spanish. I have seen long reports about the Belle Isle riots in Detroit in 1943 and the riots against the Mexicans in California. Very eager killing went on in both cases. What did they call the Mexican problems? Some stupid name that I have forgotten.

Q The Zoot Suit riots. The clothes the Mexicans wore were called Zoot suits. Very long coats, short pants and flat-topped hats. Distinctive and rather crude.

M The enemy identified. And these attacked white sailors at a navy base and then there were riots in which many Mexicans were killed or beaten. Correct?

Q Yes, and both the black problems and the Mexican ones were sat on by the Government at the time.

M Control of the press, perhaps?

Q In context, yes, but national defense measures…

M An example for you to consider.

Q It was necessary to maintain harmony on the home front, General…

M And necessity knows no law, isn't that right? Shall I enlighten you further about how a coup could be carried out in your country?

Q Continue. But it would be preferred if you mentioned the means by which communists could come to power.

M Both the extreme right and the extreme left are both horns on the same goat but we can call the coup-makers communists if it pleases you.

Q It would please my superiors a good deal more.

M We are talking about making a coup here. I have simplified things and your country is very large and diverse. Lenin would conceive of your farmers from the dust bowl making a revolt or the workers in the automobile factories or the coal mines doing the same thing. He would have to wait until Hell froze over if he was depending on such diverse and unwieldy allies. No, intellectual idiots like Lenin and Marx are certainly dangerous in the long view, because they appeal to the feebleminded and justify their anti-social behavior, but the Trotsky types are the most dangerous to the immediate safety of the state.

The foundations of any revolution or mass movement are supplied by men of ideas and words, but the actual machinery is turned on and run by men of action and these are always the most dangerous. Watch people like this and if it appears that they are beginning to move in the directions I have indicated, either lock them up as a precaution as I did, or kill them, whatever suits you the best. You could always follow our night and fog program in which we quietly picked up such creatures and made them utterly vanish into a camp, never to be heard of again. This causes panic and uncertainty in their followers and you can always put it out that their leader has gone over to the other side and informed on everyone. That, too, causes panic and panic leads men to rush to you to confess in order to save their skins.

I wouldn't worry too much about the various left wing imbeciles in your country, the ones that Roosevelt let creep into his government. These creatures can be watched carefully and dealt with in various ways if they do more than blabber to students or fellow idiots. Watch the man of action carefully. And note that very often the man of words can be effectively seduced from his revolutionary path by paying attention to him and praising him. These worms suck up praise and eventually become harmless. No one paid any attention to Marx in the beginning because he was a man of no sense. This made him angrier and he became even more shrill in his denunciation of a system that treated him like the sham and poseur that he really was.

Another problem can arise that I should mention to you, and that is that in developing a secret police to combat these menaces, one can place too much power in their hands and place too much reliance on their honesty. The Imperial Russian secret police became a state within a state, fabricating plots against the Czar and against the government in order to gain more power and killing those on their own side, both to remove rivals and prove that there actually was a menace to fight. I had to watch this tendency in the Gestapo, but I ran the bureau myself and did not indulge in such dangerous practices. The SD, however, began to slip into this mode and we had to keep a close watch on it to prevent trouble. They interfered in foreign policy, forged British and American money…which they spent on themselves…and engaged in all kinds of ventures well outside the scope of their duty.

By enlarging the police forces to protect yourself, you run the danger that they will eventually decide that they are better suited to run the country than the politicians. Although Stalin has a firm grasp on Soviet policy, if and when he leaves, the secret police will for certain begin an expansion program, convincing Stalin's heirs that they alone can protect them. Eventually, the NKVD will run Russia to suit its own needs and not those of the state. And believe that terrible corruption will grow and spread.

Democracy or not, you will have the same problems in your country if you give too much power to an agency designed to protect you. Your FBI has become much larger chasing German spies that did not exist and now one can see that they will become even larger chasing communists and other perceived enemies of the state. And your own agency that is designed to function in foreign countries can become dangerous to the state when your intellectuals decide that they know more about the actuality of foreign policy than the leaders of the state and begin to secretly push their own programs.

Q You are getting into a dangerous area, General, and you know it. At the present time, I personally cannot see this encroachment by our agency, or the FBI either, into the executive sphere. I think you have had too much experience with more devious European modes and I would suggest that you keep such ideas to yourself outside of this room and also read more contemporary American history so that you can better understand our national psyche.

M I have already done a good deal of reading on the subject, and believe me, I know much about your country. What makes you think that you are any different from any of the rest of us?

Q Well, for example, our country is not an aggressor nation. We do not invade and conquer our neighbors and engage in an endless series of wars for nationalistic ends.

M Oh come now, don't treat me like a young college student. You are perfectly aware of American aggression just in this century alone. I will give you a number of examples and you can tell me if I have done my reading. We could discuss the war with Spain, because that happened just before the beginning of the century. Why not? You made war on Spain, used the pretext of a battleship sunk in their waters, seized Cuba and Puerto Rico, attacked a Spanish fleet in Manila that was totally unaware of the war and slaughtered it, sent troops into Nicaragua and Haiti, attacked Mexico, both across your borders and at Vera Cruz, sent troops into China and looted the Imperial City, sent troops into Russia in 1919, seized the kingdom of Hawaii, seized Greenland and Iceland from the legitimate government of Denmark, and Roosevelt and Churchill planned to invade the neutral state of Ireland and establish bases there during the last war. Churchill especially wanted this because he loathed the Irish and wanted an opportunity to kill more of them. The only reason this didn't happen is because Roosevelt decided that the Irish vote in America was too important to his re-election plans.

There are other incidents to mention but most of this came from your history books and, with the exception of the Irish invasion, are well known. Now, do you want to argue with me?

Q This is a question of interpretation, General. The Spanish war came about for a number of very complex reasons and our occupations of Haiti and other

Latin American countries was solely to establish a safe, democratic government.

M Ah, these are the precise reasons Hitler and Ribbentrop gave for their invasion of Yugoslavia, Greece, Crete and our attempts to support a nationalistic rebellion in Iraq. The exact same reasons without a question. We are wrong, of course, and you are right solely because we lost the war and you won it. Stalin's excuse for seizing Poland, the Baltic states, Hungary and Roumania are precisely the same in every respect. That makes no one right, of course, but people in our situation had best not throw dung at each other because we will both become covered with filth. Do you agree?

Q You must not talk in such a way to those who wish to use your services. I suggest that you use the rationale that you are a non-Nazi, Catholic conservative that would like to place his expertise in fighting communism at our disposal.

M I am not a fool, of course. This is not a public conversation, and I am sure that if I took such a line with you, I would be dismissed as a fool or an idealist, which is the same thing. I have learned my lines as well as you have and naturally these comments are private. Now, shall we proceed to discuss more about the coup I was talking about?

Q Yes, that subject is of great interest. As I have been talking with you, I have made notes and perhaps you could prepare a private study of the mechanics of such a coup for me. I would most particularly be interested in the mechanics of such a plan, rather than in the reasons for it or, for that matter, the political nature of those would conduct such an operation or their motives.

M I shall be tactical rather than strategic. That's what you want, no doubt. Your superiors might want to file it away in the event of future need, if I am not in error. Ideology has no part in such things, at least from my point of view. But please do not lecture me that a coup might not be necessary in your own country at some time. We can make educated guesses about the future based on the present and past, but no one except God can see the future. I will keep everything tactical just for you.

Q And for yourself, as well. We do agree on that, don't we?

M Certainly.

Q And there is one other subject that I would like to discuss with you. That is the subject of weapons in the hands of private citizens. You permitted this in Germany?

M We did, but there were many restrictions to owning firearms and all had to be registered with the local police. We did not have many firearms-related crimes in Germany, aside from the communist insurrections after the war.

Q How do you feel about keeping weapons of any kind out of the hands of the public?

M We had no trouble, but we did have control. Are you having such problems in your country?

Q Not at present, but there has been some suggestion that we might establish a stronger control over guns. Right now, the laws are very lax. Would you say that an armed public could be a dangerous public?

M That's an obvious statement. I would assume that the danger would lie not so much in the weapons, but in the attitudes of those who might use them. Are you referring to criminals or political groups? Communist fanatics should certainly not be allowed to be armed, but a man who likes to hunt or someone who wishes to keep a gun in the house to defend himself or his family against criminals is another matter. Of course, if the police are functioning properly, honest citizens don't need to defend themselves with guns. But you Americans have a history of violence and anti-government behavior. Revolutions, civil wars, riots and so on.

Q Well, in the time just before the Revolutionary War, we had armed militias throughout the colonies. These were basically people in remote areas who banded together to fight the Indians. They were armed and used to drill. During the Revolution, most of these groups were taken into the army.

M We had such groups in Germany. I think their danger lay more in their lack of proper training rather than in any menace to the government. Most of these small farmers and businessmen would support the government and essentially be of a conservative nature, correct?

Q In those days, yes. Of course, our country has become settled and urbanized, but one still finds quite a few militant farmers out in the countryside.

M And you want to disarm them? That probably wouldn't be very wise. With your national inclination to rebel, the farmers would shoot back.

Q That really isn't what the problem is but perhaps you have given me another view of it.

M As long as such people are potential supporters of the government and willing to act as a physical support for it, or to supply at least partially trained personnel in the event of a war or internal disturbance, they should be encouraged and officially trained. We have found such people very helpful to us in our past. Citizens taking an active part in the defense of their country should be encouraged…and controlled.

Q But there is a danger in this.

M What kind of a danger? Criminals should be controlled, of course, and taught that their activities will not be tolerated. When Hitler came to power in 1933, crime was out of control in Germany. Brutal crimes like robberies, beatings, killings, rapes, and so on were very common. The first thing he did was to set up camps to reeducate these vicious predators and then fill them up with professional criminals. A year or two working in a quarry or digging out swamps had a wonderful effect on most of them. The next time, they could serve four years and so on. I am quite in favor of such a program and I will tell you that crime nearly vanished during the Third Reich because of our attitude towards the anti-social elements.

Of course, your liberals would run around, screaming with rage, if you tried to do something like that in your country. Did you have in mind raising new volunteer units to fight the criminals? Not a good idea at all. Leave such things in the hands of the police. If the police can't deal effectively with criminals, your country will find itself in serious trouble and then the home guard units could be used.

Q We called them "militias."

M We had the same term. The concept is acceptable, but only in times of need. A stable society does not need such groups, but in an unstable one, many citizens would feel threatened by their government's lack of protection, and no doubt, form such groups. And, of course, if the government were left wing, they would fear such private armies very much because of the inherent threat. Of course, these part time soldiers would have to be disbanded and disarmed so that they could not be the nucleus of a rebellion. If it hadn't been for the assistance the central government in Berlin received from volunteer *Freikorps* and various local self-help citizens groups in the fights against the communist seizure of power in 1918, the whole country would have fallen under the control of Moscow.

I would say that the question could be answered by considering the loyalty of any such organization to the government. A stable, conservative government would naturally receive the support of such movements, but a repressive radical national leadership would be their ultimate target and such an entity would at once wish to disarm them.

Q I suppose it all depends on whose ox is gored in the final analysis.

M I have some paperwork on the *Volkssturm*[1] which I can give to your people to study.

Q Much appreciated. We do seem to have wandered a bit from the path. You were going to be tactical with me.

M Yes, you were interested in the seizure of power, weren't you? From a theoretical point of view, of course.

Q Of course.

Historical Significance—Reflections of the Author

Historical events are very much like a child's kaleidoscope. It is possible to identify all of the shapes and colors of the bits of glass contained in the toy, but when they are placed in a mirrored tube, no one can accurately

---

[1] *The Volkssturm was an organization raised in the last months of the war that consisted of armed civilians, trained by the military and controlled by the NSDAP. It proved to be very effective in some areas and worthless in others. Much of their usefulness depended on motivation, training and equipment.*

predict the exact patterns that will emerge when the tube is rotated. Historians can recognize the factors and forces that create change but can never predict exactly when or how they will combine or what the effect of these combinations will be.

The coup, a seizure of power, has been a part of history for as long as man has been an organized social animal. The determined will attack the complacent, sometimes with success, and as often with failure. That which was successful in a disorganized and demoralized Imperial Russia might not be at all successful in another country at another time. Müller points out with great truth that the fanatic activist, Trotsky, is far more dangerous than the intellectual activist, Lenin. The former make coups while the latter discuss them...endlessly.

The interest expressed by Müller's interrogator in the former Gestapo chief's knowledge of the tactics of the *coup d'Etat* might well be idle curiosity or could equally well indicate that a practical knowledge of the techniques of seizing a government were of interest to individual members of the same government.

In 1948, there was no reason why anyone involved in the American intelligence community would have any interest in conducting a coup against the Democratic Administration of Harry Truman. Such an act might have had some appeal during the Roosevelt era but that was over and the United States was gearing up for, at the very least, economic warfare with the Soviet Union.

Intellectual curiosity was more likely the reason for the emergence of the subject, but the continued discussion about the bearing of arms by non-military citizens is much more interesting. The concept of the citizen army in the United States had its roots in the rural militias of the colonial period, when small communities, far from urban areas or standing garrisons, needed to protect themselves, their families and their holdings from attacks by hostile Indians. These militias grew in strength and eventually viewed the British Army as a more serious enemy.

That the first government of the United States viewed the citizen-soldier or the militiaman as an important implement of defense is reflected in the Constitution where the subject is specifically addressed.

Although Müller spoke in the abstract when he referred to the hostility of an administration bent on public control to the dangers inherent in the existence of armed citizens, times change and often what was abstract comment fifty years earlier can become reality.

In one of his dinner table conversations, Hitler once said that the purpose of the police was to protect the citizen, not to intimidate him. Müller's comments about the danger inherent when the police can no longer protect their charges certainly have recognizable validity fifty years after he made them.

No coup or popular rising has taken place in times of relative stability. It is only when the great middle-class awakens to find itself and its institutions under attack and undefended that the thought of self-defense becomes valid. Violent upheavals do not begin without warning. Before a volcano erupts, there are nearly always ominous signs of the impending disaster and very often, clear though these indications may be, they are ignored out of the fear of radical change found in the complacent throughout history.

Trotsky very clearly recognized this fear of change and took swift advantage of it when he seized power in Russia. By the time the public was aware of what had happened, it was almost too late to react and by the time the population, most of whom were only interested in survival and creature comforts, might have reacted, the militants were in power and increasing their control on a daily basis.

A conservative government might be dull but it does not, in general, attempt to exert control over its citizens, other than to maintain law and order. A radical government, on the other hand, cannot feel safe in its power until is has established an ever-intrusive control over its people. Control of weapons is certainly a prime goal for such an entity and this would work in tandem with discrediting, and eventually destroying, any institution that might be able to mount an attack on it. The first target would be any religious group who might find a moral, and hence religious, fault with its goals or techniques. The second target would be any other organization that could conceivably organize against it.

In a monarchy, the people have little choice over the succession of rulers and a good king with a short reign can easily be replaced by a bad one with a long reign. In a republic, malfunction and mendacity are correctable at the ballot box. If this safety valve is shut down, an explosion will certainly result. Thus, Müller's discussion of the importance of the press, or media, as a means of public control has complete validity.

News can easily be controlled by those with the desire and ability to do so. Governments can exert great influence over nearly any media entity through their power in the granting of licenses or their control over entree to official information. By a *de facto* control over the reporting of news, an administration bent on complete domination can accomplish the implementation of their goals with relative ease, given a receptive and passive audience.

Faked opinion polls and heavily slanted pro-administration reportage might have had a strong effect on this audience when there were no other sources of information. But, with the advent of alternative information sources, such as the computer, the photocopier and the facsimile machine, propaganda is far less able to influence, dominate, and control public perceptions.

The concept of civil unrest is always abhorrent to the entrenched entities which comprise the leadership of the political and business factors of an urbanized and stable society. These individuals belong to the Order of St. Precedent whose motto is "Look Backwards," and whose watchword is "That Which Has Not Been, Cannot Be." Trotsky and his ilk well know how to utilize such blindness.

The Trials and Tribulations of
the Duke of Windsor

One of the most discussed events of the 1930s was the abdication of England's King Edward VIII in 1936. The official reason given for the abdication was the King's infatuation with the American divorcee, Wallis Simpson. At that time, a divorced woman could not become queen but there were other reasons behind the drive to force Edward to abdicate.

Q You once spoke of papers or files you had on the Duke of Windsor. How extensive are these files? Are they originals or filmed copies and could we look at them?

M They are extensive. A number of papers are original. Many are on film and, of course, you can look at them. I said "look," however, not "take away."

Q The Duke is no longer a figure of any importance except in society, but there is some interest in his connections with your side before and during the war.

M It was intended that the Duke become an object of interest before and during the war. The Duke's real power ceased the day he abdicated, but Hitler considered him a person that could be used to create a certain impression with the British. The Duke was forced off the throne, not because of his lady friend but because there were powerful people in England who viewed his pro-Hitler attitude with real anger and some fear. Crystal Night had not happened yet, but it became very obvious to Jewish groups both in England and your country, that their co-religionists in Germany were being mistreated and forced out of the country. I would imagine that this created quite a bloc of anti-Hitler persons in the British banking and finance community. Couple this unpleasant anti-Semitism with Hitler's barter system that bypassed the British banking system with its high-interest international loans and you can understand the anger and fear directed at the new King. He didn't help matters at all by his pro-Hitler statements and the machinations of his German relatives. After all, the Windsor family had been Saxe-Coburgs until the 1914 war and were related to all the ruling families of Europe.

Q The Battenbergs changed their names to Mountbatten at the same time, as I recall.

M Oh yes, that was another matter. The Battenbergs were left-handed relatives of the Prince of Hesse. You see, Prince Alexander of Hesse married a Jewess in the 19th century and the family could not allow their descendants to be Hessens so they created the title of Battenberg. That's why I called them left-handed Hessens. If I recall, the current head of their house married the granddaughter of Ernst Cassel, the banker of Edward the Seventh. Also a Jew. But the Mountbattens are not important at all, although they too helped push their cousin off the throne and for the same reason that the London bankers did. The Simpson woman was only an excuse. The new King was as feeble-minded as the rest of the family and could barely speak. If it wasn't for his wife, I doubt if he would have enough sense to remove his clothes before he took a bath. I must say that I have very little regard for royalty. They mostly seem to be inbred imbeciles who marry their cousins and produce children with the intellects of chickens.

Q The Queen is Scots.

M Yes, and a change from the idiots. Her uncle, by the way, was in touch with us before the war and was even more interested in Hitler than the King. A bit of history for you to chew on.

Now to get back to the Duke. Although as King he had very little actual power, he could and did see all the important political dispatches and could and did pass much of this on to our ambassador in London. I don't think you could consider this as treasonable but was, from the King's view, helpful to his German friends. We, of course, were most helpful to him, but rumors that we pushed the present Duchess into his bed are nonsense. In the first place, the Duke preferred soldiers, and in the second, I doubt if he and the Duchess ever slept together. From observing them and from reading many pages of reports, it appears that *she* was *his* husband but not in a sexual sense.

I met both of them at a reception in Berlin in October of 1937 and actually had an interesting conversation with the Duke. The wife, of course, could not speak German, but the Duke spoke it fluently, if a little stilted. He was actually a good and entertaining conversationalist and she was sitting near him, staring very intently at both of us. Someone had told the Duke that I was head of the Secret Police and he wanted to ask me some questions about the British Secret Service. The Duke felt that after his departure from England, he was constantly under surveillance by one agency or another, probably MI 6. This, of course, was true and I discussed this with him. It was not easy for the British to keep up with him in Germany because we watched their agents as closely as they watched the Duke. Of course, we used that too, and I will explain this a little later.

I found the Duke to be reasonably intelligent but not entirely normal in that he seemed to be obsessed with his rather masculine wife and quite confused in his mind about the forces that compelled him to abdicate. I was under orders

On October 22, 1937 the Führer received the Duke and Duchess of Windsor in his house on the Obersalzberg.

At an afternoon reception in Dr. Ley's home, the Duke of Windsor also met with Dr. Goebbels.

An den Fuehrer und Reichskanzler.

Beim Verlassen Deutschlands danken die Herzogin
von Windsor und ich Ihnen aufrichtig fuer die grosse
Gastfreundschaft, die Sie uns gewaehrt Haben und fuer
die vielen Moeglichkeiten, das zu sehen, was fuer das
Wohl der schaffenden Deutschen getan wird.

Wir nehmen einen tiefen Eindruck von unserer Reise
durch Deutschland mit und werden nie vergessen, mit
welcher Aufmerksamkeit wir von Ihren Beauftragten um-
geben worden sind, und eine wie herzliche Aufnahme wir
ueberall gefunden haben.

Besonders danken wir Ihnen fuer die schoenen
Stunden, die wir mit Ihnen auf dem Obersalzberg ver-
bracht haben.

EDWARD

23-X-37

The Duke of Windsor's thank-you letter to Hitler.

To the Führer und Reichskanzler,

　　Upon our departure from Germany, the Duchess of Windsor and I wish to most sincerely thank you for your great hospitality which you have shown us and for the many opportunities to observe what has been accomplished for the welfare of the German people.
　　We take with us a deep impression of our trip through Germany and will never forget the attentions shown us by your representatives and the overall heartfelt reception we have received.
　　We especially wish to thank you for the beautiful hours we spent with you on the Obersalzberg.

Edward
23 October 1937

from Himmler, once he found that the Duke wished to have a talk with me, to be very careful what I said. I was told that the Duke was a valuable tool and not to frighten him but to convince him that we were his real friends. That was not difficult to do because that is what the Duke really believed, so I gave him just some small background information to confirm his suspicions.

His closest associate, one Bedaux, had been on our side in 1914 and had been engaged in espionage in your country then. Later, there was a falling out with him because of some embezzlements of our funds, but then we all kissed and made up.

Q I know about him. We had him killed during the war in an internment camp. Too dangerous and he knew far too much about certain things.

M I knew that. Were you involved in that?

Q No, not personally, but one of my superiors was and he told me later.

M You people are so indiscreet after all. But then, so was the Duke. In 1937, the Duke had no access to state papers and was not wanted in England anymore. The new Queen hated him for pushing her dim-witted husband onto the throne and there was very bad blood between the brothers after that.

Q You have such a negative view of the British.

M You know that I have an even more negative view of the Soviets, but to be polite, I have said very little about your country except to discuss your habit of hanging black people, the slaughter of the red Indians and a few other small matters. At least in your country, if you get an idiot elected as President, you can always throw him out after four years. Of course, Roosevelt would still be in office if his brain hadn't given way.

Q Roosevelt was very popular in some circles.

M Certainly, and especially in Moscow. Now the Duke was an albatross around the neck of the British and I am sure they would have killed him if it wouldn't have been such a scandal. And they did watch him like an eagle watching a hare.

Q You said Hitler used him. Can you explain that?

M Certainly. We were reading British agent radio traffic and decided that, as the situation heated up in Europe, the British were afraid that we might invade them, and that we would use the Duke as a figurehead King to maintain order in England. That being the case, we played on that piano for quite a while. The Duke and Duchess were received in Germany with much pomp and ceremony. Why, when their train pulled into the Berlin station, there were only a few minor officials from the British embassy on the platform, but an entire regiment of our top people in full uniform. Oh yes, the Duke and his wife were given the special treatment with receptions, visits to various leaders and so on. This infuriated those in England who had forced the King out and naturally they began to whisper and chatter to each other in their clubs that we were planning to put the Duke back on the throne someday and his wife next to him. In those days, I had little direct contact with Hitler, not like later. But Himmler explained the matter very clearly when he said that the *Führer* was using the Windsors as a card to be played when the time came.

Q And the time came when the war broke out?

M Yes, that is when the Windsor card was played, along with others. You should understand that Hitler was not anti-British at all. He admired England for her achievements, and in fact, did not want war with her at all. He felt that after the Polish campaign was over with such brilliant and obvious military success that England and France would negotiate with him. All he wanted was to be left alone and had no intentions of attacking either country. This was not to be and it became very obvious that no negotiations would ever be possible, especially with Churchill in power.

Q I am sure Churchill did not want to see the defeat of England or loss of her territories.

M I am sure he did not, but then Hitler had no interest in taking anything away from England or France either. He only wanted to call a halt and decide if he would have to move against Russia or not. So to force the British to the table, he went to great lengths to plan—obviously plan—an invasion of England. From a military standpoint, such an invasion would have succeeded but would have had no practical point to it. Shipping was massed in channel ports; fake stories were spread in neutral capitals about this invasion; and we even printed up thousands of operational maps and books for our troops that we leaked to known British agents and unfriendly diplomats. At the same time, we were instructed to make it appear as if the Duke would be our puppet ruler in a defeated England, and this we did. It had some effect because the royal family was making serious plans to flee to Canada. The King wanted to go at once but his wife held him back. As I said, she is a formidable woman, but then, of course, she is not a drooling Coburg cousin.

Q There have been stories that the Duke supplied your side with valuable military information he obtained while attached to the staff of the British forces in France. Comment?

M Yes he did. He supplied very important information about troop positions and joint British-French military plans. This was very vital material and permitted our successful breakthrough by Sedan in 1940. However, the Duke did not give this material to us. He went on leave to Paris and told Mr. Bedaux everything. The Duke was that way, you see. He had been raised in a hothouse with absolutely no contact with the real world and as heir to a powerful throne, felt above politics and most people. He could not understand the interaction of people and duplicity was certainly not one of his characteristics. When I spoke with him in 1937, the Duke simply had no guile at all with me and in a sense, I rather felt sorry for him because he would never be able to understand the world outside the walls of Buckingham Palace. I have known a number of lesser royalty in my career and most of them were impractical people with no knowledge of anything except court gossip and protocol.

Mr. Bedaux went straight to Holland, then neutral, and told them everything at the Embassy. In that sense, the Duke was not a traitor to his country but a totally inexperienced man with a strong anger against his family for their slights to him. To my knowledge, he never gave military information to us nor probably would ever have done so. The Duke was not anti-English, only outraged about his treatment. We were told to call his wife "Royal Highness" although this was forbidden in England. This pleased both of them very much which, after all, was the idea. And that was made public which further enraged his enemies at home.

Q And these papers prove all that?

M I would say so, although an unfriendly person might take matters out of context and make a case that the Duke was a Nazi. He was not, of course, but he was very pro-Hitler and, one could say, very much pro-Third Reich. The other thing is that the Duke did not like Jews at all and they obviously did not like him. But, they were far more clever than he was and knew how to stay carefully in the background when weaving their plots.

You must understand that if I were a Jew, and especially a Jewish banker, in England in those days, I, too, would be angry and frightened about a pro-Hitler king and certainly would want someone else on the throne. What they finally got was a human nothing on the throne and a maniac as his prime minister. In the end, the war destroyed their financial empire and I suppose our forging of their money didn't retard the progress. Most people never think very far ahead in the end. Even if the King wore a swastika around his neck and had a picture of Hitler over his bed, he had no real power in England and would certainly have been blocked from any adventures of a real pro-German nature.

Q There has been some speculation about the Duke's final days in Spain and Portugal. Belief that you were going to seize him or that he was going to go to Germany so as to await the cross-Channel return.

M That was the idea, of course. We did contribute to this heavily, but I know from the top that Hitler never had any intention of invading England and that the Duke was only a pawn on the board. Since there was to be no invasion, there was no real need to have the Duke in the meat locker to drag out when we needed him. But the British believed we were going to invade and the British believed our planted stories that we were holding final negotiations with the Duke and acted on these beliefs. Basically, the British government warned him discreetly that if he didn't go to the Bahamas as Governor, they would kill his wife and so he went. That was a relief in Berlin because if the Duke had fled to Germany, what in God's name would we have done with him? Put him in an old castle like the Belgian King and listen to his stream of complaints about the food and the service?

Q You know that the British went to great trouble to get as many of the files as they could find after the war. A grand hunt after all that material. We had some and gave it to them and so on.

M Did you ever see any of it?

Q We copied everything, even though Eisenhower forbade it, and I once looked at some of it. I would say you were correct when you say it could be taken several ways.

M I personally don't care about the Duke one way or the other, but in my professional opinion, he was only a vain, foolish man who was angry but certainly not any kind of a deliberate traitor. An accidental one, perhaps, but not deliberate. His sun has long set in any case and the field is now open for the journalists to speculate in.

Q The British become so obsessive and secretive about such simple matters that I don't wonder that everyone connected with them sees conspiracies around every corner. Latrine rumor, as we used to call it, credits the Duke with being a Nazi spy but, on balance, I suspect you are right.

M Of course, I am right. Naturally, if I were ordered to prepare a paper for Hitler that said the Duke was a suspected communist, I would do so without hesitation. And don't raise your eyebrows when I say things like that. I am sure you, and especially your Mr. Dulles, have done the same thing. You say what you are told to say and forget everything else. Isn't that correct? But in private—in private—we say what we really think, don't we?

Q I would say so. But, not to be offensive, are you always truthful with me?

M When it suits both of us, quite naturally. I mean, my comments on Windsor have no other motivation than to recall my impressions. You aren't going to arrest him and there is no more Hitler for him to support so his bad judgment will pass into history suitably embellished to suit some third-rate author and his publisher.

I rather wonder what someone would do about my history? I would be depicted as a monster who rushed around Europe pulling out old women's toenails with a hot pincer if the wrong person decided to discuss my activities. I can just imagine a communist writer discussing me in print. You ought to make some notes and do a flattering work on me. I might give you the Czar's cigar box if you did. On the other hand, if you even mentioned my name outside of your office, they would be dragging the lake to try and find you. Or at least you would go to a very unpleasant Canossa indeed and have to stand on the ice with your bare feet until you froze to the ground. Popes and conventional wisdom have the capacity for great cruelty.

Q I would much rather write about Monet.

M Well, you can have Monet. Give me Dürer. Now, is there any more curiosity about the Duke?

Q Not on my part. But there are those who would like to review your files on him. He was forbidden entrance to the United States during the war, you know. Hoover was involved with this, but Roosevelt ordered the ban.

M What, in God's name, could the Duke and Duchess do in your country?

Q I can't discuss that here.

M Now here, you want all kinds of information from me—information that will take me a considerable time to locate—and you won't mention why the Duke was forbidden to come into your country.

Q It's nothing important. Churchill asked Roosevelt to keep the Duke and his wife out. He thought they might say things about him if he were away from the strict control he had in the Bahamas. Nothing more than that.

M You see how simple answers are in the end? Then we have finished with the Duke and the Duchess and we can stop now for some coffee and rolls.

His Majesty King George VI, Edward's brother.

Edward, the Duke of Windsor, wearing the uniform of an Admiral of the Fleet while in the Bahamas.

Right: The Duke and Duchess in the library of their temporary residence in Nassau.

Below: The Duke standing in the midst of portraits of his predecessors as Governor-General of the Islands.

Historical Significance—Reflections of the Author

Like the postwar delvings into the true meanings of Rudolf Hess' flight to England and his subsequent career in British custody, the abdication of Edward VIII and his subsequent career have occupied the careers of a number of historical journalists.

The tendency to seek new and sensational material on historical figures far overrides the actual necessity to remove any such material from the subject and attempt to find the root causes of events and personalities.

Both the Duke and Duchess of Windsor have been accused of being traitors to England, supplying the various agencies of the Third Reich with vital information and even offering to rule in a conquered England as Hitler's regents. An extensive search in official German files captured by the Allies does not prove these points, but then concealing or destroying embarrassing proofs would not be unrealistic on the part of English authorities in an attempt to protect the reputation of the Crown. However, the Müller papers contain duplicate copies of most of these released documents and none of them reflect that the Duke or his wife were traitors or active Nazi agents. Müller's comments about the Duke and his relatives, while pungent, would also tend to confirm that the Duke was a puzzled and angry man and that his wife was bitter and ambitious.

Churchill's often and loudly proclaimed cry that Hitler was going to invade the Mother of Parliaments was a successful attempt to secure American aid for a war he wished to lead to a brilliant triumph. These trumpet blasts may well have moved the Anglophiles in the United States, but they fell on deaf ears in the White House. Roosevelt was most willing to supply Churchill old weapons and decrepit shipping, but only if these were paid for in hard cash—preferably gold bars. When England was filled with America's old surplus weaponry and stripped of all her assets, Roosevelt consented to the Lend-Lease program.

Müller contends that Hitler did not plan to invade England and that the Duke was part of a deception to convince the British that he was serious in the execution of these plans. There has always been controversy about Hitler's plans to invade the Soviet Union and like the putative invasion of England, the question revolves around his motives.

Stalin would have been a genuine danger to Hitler had he decided to move west, but England was essentially a spent force after her ejection from the Continent in 1940. An all-out attack using most of the German armed forces directed at England would have left Hitler's entire eastern territories completely vulnerable to a Soviet attack, and such an attack would have quickly smashed Germany to pieces. There was no chance that England could attack Germany, except by air, and their initial air raids were pathetic in their results. A British attempt to seize Norway was countered by a successful German attack, and from the British point of view, had the disadvantage of establishing a strong German military presence close to their North Sea borders.

A German invasion, in all probability, would have been successful and extremely costly in manpower and equipment, but there was no military or political need for such an operation. All of Hitler's interest lay towards the east, not across the Channel, and in retrospect, Müller's offhand comments backed with his specific knowledge of the working of his former employers make more sense than the thesis of the Triumph of the Righteous Few over the Evil Many.

Charles Eugene Bedaux was a shadowy, secondary historical figure with connections to the German secret service, the Duke and various American interests. Bedaux was an efficiency expert whose timesaving programs made him a hated figure to American labor. Suspected of being a German agent during the First World War, Bedaux later settled in France, purchased a large chateau and acted as host and confidant to the Duke and Duchess of Windsor. He was arrested by the Americans in Vichy North Africa at the end of 1942. A number of compromising documents were taken from him at the time and he was flown back to Miami by US military intelligence personnel and turned over to the Justice Department. He was later alleged to have committed suicide, but there is strong reason to believe Bedaux was murdered to prevent him from revealing highly embarrassing contacts between US authorities, to include President Roosevelt and the Vichy French, whom Roosevelt warmly supported as legitimate representatives of the French government in the French colonial departments of Africa.

The Fall of Mussolini

The Italian Duce was Hitler's first ally, although before Hitler came to power, Mussolini tended to ridicule him in private. In point of fact, very few people outside of his own circle ever took Hitler seriously until it was far too late to correct their oversight. The Duce was an intellectual, a skilled politician who had once been a socialist who went on to form the Fascist movement in Italy and who had the misfortune to govern Italians. As the Second World War progressed, the Italian public, the senior members of the Fascist party and the House of Savoy watched with dismay as the Italians lost their colony in Libya, were the subject of Allied air attacks, suffered heavy losses of manpower in Russia and were increasingly threatened with invasion. Both Müller and his American interviewer had first-hand knowledge of the situation in Italy—one of them prior to the fall of Mussolini and the other, after the fall.

Q The Gestapo, I understand, had inside information about the dissatisfaction in Italy before Mussolini fell from power.

M Correct. But not only the Gestapo, but almost all other German agencies such as the Foreign Office, the *Abwehr*, the SD and so on. It was obvious that there was considerable resistance to the idea of Italy remaining in the war and also growing dissatisfaction with Mussolini. By 1942 he was 60 years old with chronic stomach trouble, which was probably hysterical in nature…

Q Hitler had the same problem, didn't he?

M Yes, he did. Morell, his doctor, told me that he could not understand how Hitler was still alive what with the pressure he was under. Hitler had to run everything and the work load was enough to kill most people. I think the same applied to Mussolini, but there was more because he was aware that his leadership wanted to get rid of him. Hitler, of course, supported him and Mussolini began to feel that a strong German presence in Italy could prevent a coup. On the other hand, it was very obvious to me, at least, that the Italians hated us and that such a presence could have a negative effect. This animosity, by the way, goes back to the German victory at Caporetto in the 1914 war when the Austrians called us in to support them against the Italians. We crushed them terribly at that battle and humiliated them completely. They never forgave us for that.

Q They were not the best soldiers, after all. I recall the antiquated Greek Army holding them off for weeks in 1941…

M The Greeks finally surrendered to us…to Sepp Dietrich as a matter of fact…and I know that Hitler genuinely respected them and was furious that Mussolini attacked them when he did. It threw his timetable in the east off, and he much preferred the Greeks to the Italians anyway. No, they were not the best of soldiers. Down in the Balkans, they would either kill off the local people without mercy or join up with them for some looting. It would have been far better for Germany if Italy had kept out of the war and remained neutral. Still, there was the possibility that Italy might change sides without notice.

Q Napoleon once said that if the Italians ended up on the same side they started with, they must have changed sides twice.

M A perceptive man. Italian himself, wasn't he?

Q Don't tell that to the French.

M In my experience, you cannot tell anything to the French, but I would certainly prefer them as military allies to the Italians. They are good soldiers and don't judge them by their performance in 1940. They had no real heart for that war, and the British dragged them into it, and then left them behind to pay the consequences.

Q To get back to Mussolini, give me your views on your own observations about the collapse of fascism.

M It vanished in a second like a puff of smoke in the wind. Twenty one years and gone in an instant. Shows you the impermanence of things, doesn't it? Observations…The party high-command, especially Dino Grandi, were opposed to Mussolini for years. They were opposed to the war from the beginning as was the King and his circle. And I really cannot blame them for their attitude, but once Italy had committed herself to our side, we couldn't just let her go. There would be an invasion of the country and we would have to fight on another front then. Better to keep the Italians in the war, regardless of their feelings, so at least theoretically they would support us. But as it was now obvious that they had lost their holdings in Africa and were being bombed, any real support for Mussolini vanished quickly. Most of the plots to remove him and make peace were centered on their King. That one I know something about. A very small man, secretive and not to be trusted at all. He and his circle hated us and were just waiting for the chance to throw Mussolini over and surrender to the Allies. They didn't have to worry about the Russians invading them so the choice was simple. The British were very close to the King's circle and had been trying to bribe them out of the war for some time. Churchill himself, was involved in this. He had done this in the 1914 war, after all, and hoped to do it again. There were certain letters…

Mussolini, Hitler and the Italian King, Victor Emmanuel III, review troops during the Führer's state visit to Italy in 1938.

Q Oh yes, when you are finished here, we can talk about those. Did you get them by any chance?

M No, did you?

Q No. We certainly tried hard enough at the end. We thought Mussolini had them and that is why he was shot. Please go on.

M You know we seized the records of the Italian Foreign Office, but a good number of significant documents had been hidden away before we got there. I must say this here: The Italians were absolutely treacherous to us, to each other, to Mussolini and so on. The monarchists wanted the Duce out to guarantee the continuation of the reign of the House of Savoy, the fascists wanted him out so that they could continue in power and the Army supported the King. In October of 1942, Himmler went to Rome to see for himself what was going on. Hitler asked him to do this, and Himmler had a nose for plots—being constantly engaged in his own. Maybe he hoped to pick up some pointers for his own coup—who knows? I went to Portugal about that time and my information about the visit was second-hand. Ciano, the Foreign Minister, showed up at the station with a big reception and many false smiles and pledges of loyalty. Himmler was not stupid, but from his comments afterwards, some made to me, he was as bad as Marshal Kesselring who refused to believe the Italians would break their word to him about a unilateral surrender.

And our people in Rome were not the best, after all. Dollman of the SD was a fairy art dealer who was thoroughly Italianized and whom I loathed. Kappler was adequate, but Carnaris was engaged in all kinds of duplicity with his opposite number in Italy, constantly urging him to throw Mussolini out and make a separate peace. I told you that Himmler had a hard time making up his mind on anything. After Mussolini fell and we had to finally occupy Italy, we had little or no support from a people who viewed us as the cause of their country being a battlefield. The real trouble, however, came from the communists who proved to be as vicious as ever. They set off a bomb in the via Rasella in March of 1944 and killed over 30 SS soldiers coming back to their barracks from a shooting exercise. There was real hell to pay over that incident. Hitler demanded reprisals, which under international law, he could do. Civilians attacking military units could be punished for this. Hostages, mostly jailed communists, were taken out at a ratio of ten to one and shot by Kappler, acting on specific orders from the top. Even the Pope made no objections to that because, as you know, Pacelli had been the nuncio to Germany during the years of the communist terror in our country and had an absolute horror of them. I once had an audience with him, along with others I might say, and his views were very firm on that subject. So 300+ of the bandits were driven into a quarry and shot.

After that, Rome was much quieter, but there were more problems with communists further north.

Q Do you know about the Red Star Brigade? I had some dealings with them when I was in the OSS.

M Where were they?

Q Up near Bologna, but in the mountains. Monte Sole. Marzabotto.

M Probably not. There was, as I recall, a major uprising in that area in September or October of 1944. It could have been a Red Star unit.

Q A communist named the Wolf, *El Lupo*, ran it.

M I don't speak Italian. German for sure, even Prussian, English, of course, when I have to, and some Russian. Such dramatic names. "The Peoples' Brigade for Minsk" that had a handful of terrified peasants, fanatic communists and young boys. Thirty people in all. You knew these people did you? Why ask me?

Q Allegedly thousands of Italian civilians were slaughtered by the SS there in late 1944.

M People were being slaughtered everywhere then. Frenchmen and Italians were running around after we left the occupied areas, butchering each other over old debts, for political reasons, over the ownership of a cow, and so on. I think if there had been such a killing, I would have heard of it and I do not recall it. That doesn't mean it didn't happen, but so many dead we would have heard of. Did you know Mr. Wolf?

Q We did liaison with them and supplied them with arms…

M Which they will now use against you or the Italian government, which is the same thing.

Q I don't think so. The entire unit was wiped out by combat troops.

M Good for our combat troops. If you expect me to weep, don't wait too long. You know my views on all the banditry. Now, all of these criminals will turn on American troops and stick knives into them in the night and you will be coming to us for advice, if not help.

Q Why do you think I am here?

M Yes, I think that is obvious. Anything more about Mussolini?

Q I understand he was willing to retire after Skorzeny rescued him from the mountain top.

M Certainly. His heart wasn't in it any more. And, Skorzeny almost killed him by climbing into the plane when it took off from the landing strip. Otto just had to say hello to Hitler and get his Knight's Cross.

Q Considering his end, it would have been better if Mussolini did die then.

M I told you the Italians were treacherous, didn't I? Hanging him up in the square like a dead cow. What were you going to tell me about his papers?

Q Ah yes. The OSS was very active in northern Italy and we were under specific orders from the highest authority to seize Mussolini and try to locate these documents which were from Churchill. The specific orders were to first locate the papers and then kill Mussolini out of hand. Both Roosevelt and Churchill hated him.

M By then, Roosevelt was dead.

Q Yes, but Churchill wasn't and we both have had discussions about him, haven't we?

M Yes, we have. And you caught him?

Q No, we were working with a communist partisan group who made the actual seizure and we took over the search for the papers and didn't find them. We told the communists to kill him as quickly as possible along with everyone else they captured with him and let them keep any gold he had.

M Women too, I suppose.

Q Those were our orders.

M Rather barbaric.

Q Not at all. That was war…

M Not at that point, not at all. Do you shoot unarmed old Italians and women because some lunatic politician orders it?

Q Haven't you done the same thing?

M Not personally and not in that manner. And you didn't find any papers, did you?

Q No, we did not.

M Then you killed them all for nothing.

Q We should go on to other things. Your people didn't find these papers, did you?

M You asked me that before.

Q But did you?

M I cannot remember a thing about that, after all.

Q General, you remember everything. I'm certain you remember every address of every house you ever lived in, the license plate number of every car you ever owned, all of your telephone numbers and even the birthdays of your pets.

M Now you flatter me. I do remember many things but not everything. Convenient loss of memory is an attribute I recommend to you. We will not discuss the Duce and his papers again, because I cannot help you at all. Since you lived in Italy and seem to enjoy the Italians, perhaps I can have my cook prepare a nice Italian luncheon for you one of these days.

Q It would be nice if we had the papers.

M It would be even nicer if we went on to other matters. Are we quite finished with Mussolini?

Q Perhaps a few more questions about the shootings in Rome. What did you know about this at the time. I mean, who issued the orders for it?

M It went out, the orders that is, from Hitler to the City Commandant of Rome, a *Luftwaffe* general, and as well from Hitler to Himmler, and from him to the SD in Rome, which was Kappler. Did I know about it? Certainly I did. I told Himmler we might as well round up all the communists in Rome and add them to the total, but he disagreed with me over this. I think I used to frighten Himmler at times, because I know he believed me. Himmler was a schoolmaster: proper, pedantic and always right. If he had taken my advice, Italy would be a good deal more stable now, wouldn't it? Or am I offending you, a man who used to supply the communists with weapons and probably ate greasy sausages with them around a campfire. Just like the Boy Scouts, wasn't it?

There were orders out, as you may know, to shoot any Allied liaison personnel we captured while fighting these monsters. And we did exterminate a number. Down in Yugoslavia, quite a few ended up as worm restaurants. If you play with such fire, you will be burnt. The Italian garrisons on some of the islands in the eastern Mediterranean not only surrendered to the British but offered to help them fight us. When we re-took these islands, like Leros and Cos, we treated the British we captured as legitimate prisoners of war but we shot all the Italians, including at least one Admiral.

Now I do have some knowledge about at least one of those episodes because I was deputizing for Himmler for a short time when I got a telex from down there about this. I clearly recall my response which was just this: "Shoot the lot at once." Am I shocking you? You look distressed. Did you have too much to eat for breakfast? I suppose what we did was terrible but if you did it, it was quite permissible and even laudable.

After Dieppe, we interrogated many of the Canadian prisoners that were captured and when I learned about the orders of the commandos, such as killing shackled prisoners or any civilians who got in their way, I strongly minuted Hitler that something should be done to rid ourselves of these criminals. That is not warfare but plain gangsterism, and as far as I was concerned, should be punished at once by shooting the culprits on the spot. Hitler agreed in principle and issued an order about this. In, I think, October of 1942, he ordered that commandos, but not legitimate war prisoners, were to be shot on capture. There are rules of warfare, after all, codified and practiced by civilized people. At least people used to be civilized. Most of this viciousness started in 1870 when the Communards in France began to shoot at German soldiers while in civilian clothes. They were promptly shot for this, as soon as we captured them. I should point out that it is illegal for civilians to fight soldiers and has been for some time—"Red Brigade" or whatever grand name you choose to call it.

When Hitler wanted escaped British prisoners of war shot during the war, it was done but not by my people, and I objected strongly and said that it was the right of a prisoner to try to escape. The *Reichsmarschall* agreed with me, but Hitler was not to be swayed, and that was that. The SD did the business. That I found objectionable, but of course, there was nothing at all I could do about it. And if Roosevelt ordered Mussolini murdered, along with the women, you obeyed your orders as well, didn't you? Of course we lost the war in the end.

As to Mussolini, I think in the early 20s, he certainly did improve the lot of the Italians and was the man of the moment, just like Franco was in Spain. Both countries were in a chronic state of upheaval, all caused by a lack of a strong central government and constantly agitated by communists. Still, compare Spain with Italy, and Franco with Mussolini. The one refused to be dragged into a war on the German side, which would certainly have resulted in an Allied attack and terrible destruction. From a pragmatic point of view, Italy should have remained neutral. Mussolini was envious of Hitler and wanted military glory, something killing blacks in Ethiopia did not give him. If he had refrained from falling on a beaten France like a jackal or keeping away from Greece, maintained Italy's neutrality and her standard of living, he might now still be in power instead of being hung by his heels from a gas station. Would your people have invaded Italy? The country is not good for invasions, what with the mountains, and no one invaded Spain. Of course, the Spaniards are much more formidable soldiers than the Italians, but it was not tried. It wasn't the moral issue, after all, because I know for a fact that both Churchill and Roosevelt were seriously considering an invasion of neutral Portugal, Ireland, the Azores, the Canary Islands and who knows what else. Morality had nothing to do with their restraint. Logistics did.

No, if Mussolini had kept out of the war, Hitler would have been angry, but Italy would have been spared the horror of air raids, attacks on civilians and the destruction of great works of art. Besides, many of our allies were less than useless at the front. The Swedes, Danes and Walloons were first-class soldiers, **99** but it was the Italian collapse at Stalingrad that led to the disaster and you know how they were thrashed by the British in Libya. They lost their colonies totally, whereas if they had not gotten into the war, they would probably still have them and be the dominant power in the Mediterranean. Now, they are gone forever; the British have lost their power, and no longer matter, and that area is too far away for your people to seriously bother with. There is a vacuum there and one wonders who, or what, will fill it? The British defeated the communists, or rather Stalin, in Greece so perhaps not the Russians. Perhaps the Jews will become a powerful state but, because of their numbers, more possibly the Arabs. Especially if they have some kind of a religious revival. The new Jewish state might just provide the impetus for that and I do not see any good coming from such a revival. Remember what happened the last time the Mohammedans burst their confines.

I know that Churchill had been in touch with Mussolini, trying to buy him out of the war and I completely accept your comments about orders to kill the Duce to recover the papers and silence him. Mussolini was a man of character and I have met with him several times. I did not have a bad impression of him as a man and his end was repulsive. Still, consider those who killed him and draw your own conclusions.

Q I hope that isn't aimed at me.

M Not personally, at all. I had the communists in mind. You may have encouraged them, but I doubt it. No one ever had to encourage a communist to murder people.

Mussolini, Claretta Petacci (his mistress) and two cohorts hang in the Piazelle Loreto, Milan, on april 29, 1945.

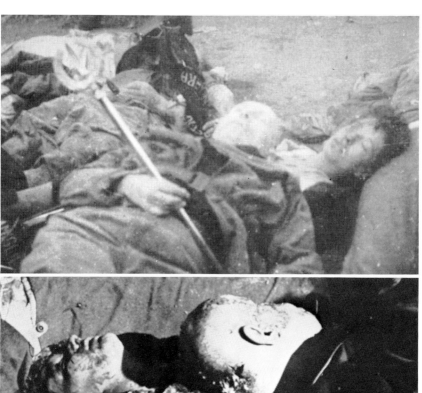

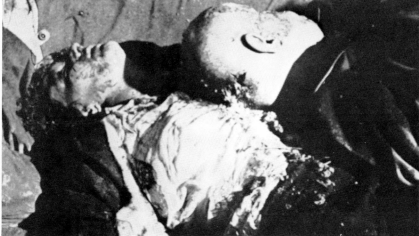

Mussolini and Petacci in a Milan public square after their execution by Italian partisans.

Historical Significance—Reflections of the Author

The shooting of hostages following the bomb attack in the via Rasalla has been the subject of limited outrage on the part of anti-German writers since the end of the war, but the facts concerning this incident and the partisan battles in northern Italy are essentially as Müller mentioned. The so-called "Red Star Brigade" that was operating in the mountains of northern Italy attacked the withdrawing German Army. These actions were countered by Field Marshal Kesselring, the German commander, who sent military units into the area to crush them. In the bloody fighting that followed, almost all of the Brigade and a large number of civilians were killed. Of course, most partisans did not wear uniforms which might have given them some immunity from summary execution if caught, and German units found weapons and explosives hidden in the small stone farmhouses that dotted the area.

There has been considerable speculation about the purported communications from Churchill to Mussolini. Churchill hoped to bribe Mussolini out of the war as the British had done during the First World War. After the fall of Mussolini in 1943, German officials including the Gestapo, descended on various Italian government centers in Rome seizing what incriminating papers they could find. From a catalog of their findings, it appears that the Churchill communications had vanished entirely. It was suspected that Mussolini had kept these as insurance in case he lost the war, but his murderous end indicated that Roosevelt and Churchill were more interested in killing him than in recovering any incriminating papers he might possess. None of the documents Mussolini was known to possess at the end have ever surfaced, and it appears that the Allies did not find what they were looking for. If Müller had his hands on them, then the documents would be in his files, along with many other historically significant papers—papers which would certainly be valuable to historians.

Weapons Old And New

Most of the chapters in this work consist of excerpts taken from a very long and complex transcript. The following section is taken nearly intact, and while its course shifts and changes, it is of such interest as to preclude taking interesting sections for study and dissertation. The subject is one that is concerned with unconventional means of warfare and how these means are considered and utilized by governments without regard for their morality or consequences.

Q The issue here is one of the use by the Germans of poison gas during the war, or rather, a possible intended use. We know about the nerve gasses, of course, but there is a question about possible SS research into destructive agents.

M Such as the atom bomb?

Q Yes, such as that. Have you any first-hand knowledge of such research, who was involved in it, and what might have been produced? We know that while your scientists were working on the atom bomb, you were far from bringing it to fruition.

M Not necessarily so. There were several projects on atom bomb research going on simultaneously. At one point, I think it was about 1943, the SS did set up its own research center into this. I had something to do with the security there and have a layman's knowledge. Our people had progressed further than the Army had, and there was some hope that a working weapon could have been developed, say by late 1945. Whether or not this was possible, I am not positive, but I do know our program was quite a bit ahead of the other ones. One of the reasons for this is the interception and decipherment of radio messages sent by Soviet spies in your country to Moscow concerning this business. If you know where to look and what to look for, radio messages can be intercepted. Reading them is quite another matter. There were a number of levels of codes. Some we had broken and others were a one-time type of encoding that was extremely difficult to break.

A spy ring operating out of Ottawa in Canada also sent messages to Moscow and many of these we could read. These fools often sent identical messages so that by tracking backwards, we could discover what was in the more complex codes. We didn't get everything, but certainly enough to keep my office informed as to your progress on the bomb.

I know this information went to our research people and not to the rivals, so then I can say that we were certainly aware of what you were doing and were able to save an enormous amount of effort in experimentation. On the nerve gasses, I have some knowledge, but then so do your people.

Q Oh yes. We got actual specimens, and the working papers, so there is no great interest there. Aside from these, was there anything more that you might have learned of?

M The nerve gasses? Tabun, Sarin and Soman are all I know about.

Q Were you actually planning to use these?

M That was the intention at the time. We knew that you were planning to gas us and we were preparing to use these on you if we had to.

Q I don't think the United States was planning to use poison gas at all during the war. In fact, Roosevelt threatened you with retaliation if you did do so.

M Nonsense. We discovered that you had shipped a great deal of mustard gas to Italy in 1943 to use against us. You know that is true. The *Luftwaffe* blew up one of your cargo ships in an Italian harbor just before Christmas and the gas shells exploded and killed thousands. We knew this as soon as it happened and the decision was made to use the nerve gasses if you made even the slightest attempt to gas us. Don't forget, Hitler had been gassed in the 1914 war and had strong feelings about this. You held your hand, after we warned you of the consequences, and so did we.

Q To get back to the atom bomb for a minute: Do you have any information in your papers about the SS project? Who was involved in it? We have many of the scientists from other projects, but there has always been a question if we got them all. And did the Soviets get some of your people?

M I would have no way of knowing any of that. I was involved with security only and not specifically kept abreast of the development. I had some knowledge based on confidential reports from Gestapo agents involved in the security aspect but not official scientific ones. I would say we came close enough. I can look, and I know we have data on the personnel in this program, if that is what you want.

Q Absolutely. This is the ultimate weapon, of course, and we are most concerned about Soviet developments. We know that the Manhattan project was riddled with Soviet agents…Pash uncovered a Soviet ring in 1943 but Roosevelt forbade any interference with it. His stated reason was that he didn't care about pro-Russian sympathies of the refugees working on the project and felt that arrests and disruptive investigations might hinder the project.

M Even after he had been informed that Stalin was getting information?

Q Even so.

M Either Roosevelt was a fool or he was acting deliberately and I suspect the latter.

Q Well, there is nothing on paper, so all we can do is to speculate at this point.

M There is seldom anything on paper, is there?

Q Not on such matters. A universal situation, I assume.

M Oh yes, in Germany too. Much was said, and often nothing was written down. I recall that at one point, it came to my attention that the army was using typhus as a means of cleaning out their camps of Soviet prisoners of war.

Q On purpose? Or were they letting typhus have its way and not trying to do anything about it?

M I first thought it was that, but then Dr. Grawitz[1] mentioned to me in early 1942 that the massive outbreaks of typhus in the prison camps for Soviets were not an accident and that he had some concern that this could spread outside these camps. Which of course it did as many Soviet prisoners were sent to camps, mainly Auschwitz, to work. They took the disease with them and it decimated the camp, killing thousands of inmates and disrupting the work production fearfully. There was a great deal of concern on the part of the SS.

Q A deliberate infecting of prisoners? Are you sure?

M At this point, I am sure, but I was not convinced for some time. We had no control over the army camps, of course, but we did have so over our camps and we badly needed workers for our economic system. To see them die like flies at the first frost was a terrible blow. And of course once I was certain that this was being systematically done, it had to be kept quiet because if it got out, there was a very good chance that your people would take revenge on us. Of course, on the other hand, since it was only communists, perhaps not. Or Roosevelt might have become angry specifically because of this and ordered retaliation against our population or even against our own prisoners of war.

I have always said that this sort of business is a double-edged sword. We know that Roosevelt was planning to dump anthrax into our water system and that is another reason we let him know about the nerve gasses. There are very ugly sides to war, especially in these times.

Q Well, I recall that American soldiers left smallpox-infected blankets out where the Indians could find, them and since they had no immunity to that disease, they died in huge numbers.

M Oh, your country is no stranger to such things as spreading infectious diseases, as I learned in 1944. There was a conference in Berlin in, I believe, May to discuss the possibility of using bacteria as a weapon against our enemies. Typhus was mentioned specifically as was the so-called double blow virus that

---

[1] *SS-Gruppenführer Ernst-Robert Grawitz, head of the SS medical service and a friend of Himmler's. Committed suicide in 1945.*

your own people developed during the 1914 war. Oh yes, and of course used. But then, you see, it got out of control and instead of killing the Germans, who had surrendered by then, it turned back on you and nearly everyone else.

Q What in the name of God are you going on about? I haven't the faintest idea what you are saying.

M I thought you must have known. During the conference, which I attended along with Himmler and others, an army doctor of general officer rank, explained in great detail about how some of your scientists developed what he called the "double blow" virus with the intention of using it on us in France. You never did use it because the war was over before you could, but somehow the virus got out and into your own troops, and from there it spread all over the world.

Q Are you talking about the Spanish Influenza by any chance?

M So it was called then, I believe. How many died then? Twenty million people? It spread all over the world.

Q I had a favorite uncle die of it. I really can't believe a word of this, General. Have you any proof?

M Locate a *Generalarzt*[2] Schreiber and ask him about this. He knows all about it because he was in the United States after the war and got this from American military medical personnel. Believe me, Schreiber is quite respectable and I personally questioned him about this.

Q I beg your pardon, General. Please let us stop here for a minute. I have some knowledge of Schreiber and I cannot discuss this with you now. Do you have notes of this discussion and was he actually involved in spreading any diseases?

M He must be working for you from the expression on your face. Yes, he had originally some knowledge of the typhus epidemics and made some minor problems about this, although he was not involved. He was spoken to sharply about this and became much calmer. Later, he was involved in such business but from an advisory capacity only. He was, after all, advising us on this. It was his contention, and I agreed with him fully, that a disease like this double blow or typhus…

Q I am sorry to interrupt you but could you explain the term "double blow" to me for the record. I assure you I have no knowledge of this at all, and I know someone would like to talk to you about Dr. Schreiber at some point.

M I am not a doctor, you understand, but the "double blow" referred to a virus, or actually a pair of them that worked like a prize fighter. The first blow attacked the immune system and made the victim susceptible, fatally so, to the second blow which was a form of pneumonia. One, and two, and there the victim is, flat on his back, dead. And that's what some of your people wanted to do to us. And there was a British scientist whom Schreiber told me actually developed

106   *²A medical officer in the German army with the rank of General.*

it. I don't remember the name now but I have it somewhere. Now, you understand why such things are insanity. These things can alter themselves and what starts out as a limited thing can change into something really terrible. Oh yes, Schreiber was involved in the plague down in the Balkans as well. Aren't medical men supposed to save lives and not take them? This is not the forum for morality, is it? Of course it never has been. You had an uncle die? You were acquainted with the results of sick minds at first hand, weren't you?

Q I do not want to think about any aspect of this, but I suppose I must ask you if this program, the one you just mentioned, was ever put into practice other than in the Balkans?

M No. But the typhus got into the camps, as I said and it came from lice. The Russians and the Poles are full of lice and cramming them into unsanitary camps only made the disease spread. I don't know if the army stopped their cleansing process at some point but the infection lived on, and when we shipped Auschwitz inmates to other camps, like Bergen-Belsen, the disease flared up again. You know that the German camp guards rarely went inside the camps for that very reason and the internal management of the camps were entirely in the hands of the inmates. It was our fear that typhus and the pest[3] would somehow get out into the civilian population and finish off what your terror bombing started. We managed to slow down the spread by taking all new arrivals, shaving off their body hair to get rid of the lice, fumigating their clothes and storing them and giving them new clothing, and treatment with medicated soap. That's why all camps had the delousing centers where Zyklon B was used. Old Morell[4] got Hitler to let him issue some anti-lice powder to the soldiers which was useless. It killed nothing, but it made Morell very rich indeed. The cyanide disinfections had to be used as a backup, even at army facilities. And typhus did spread to Germans, but we managed to limit this by very strict hygiene and regular delousing with something other than Morell's magic powder.

I am sorry about your uncle, of course, but you can blame your own people for that.

Q I will look into this. Have you any idea where this was started?

M Schreiber mentioned a fort in Kansas to me as where your people thought it got out of control.

Q Ft. Riley?

M It sounds right. I will dig all this out and let you know. Why are you using Schreiber?

Q I never said we were.

M I think so. I think some person in your government wants to find a way to start a disease in Russia and destroy your new enemies. I would advise against

---

[3] *Bubonic plague.*

[4] *Dr. Theo Morell, Hitler's personal physician.*

such things. In the first place, it would kill many Germans and I am prejudiced in their favor. In the second, it will get out of control. There are no customs police at borders to prevent the disease from spreading as it likes. The biter will certainly get bitten.

Q I don't think anyone is actually planning to do this, but you understand the need to have a contingency plan in place.

M I have never heard of a new weapon that some idiot can't wait to use. If it exists, someone will eventually use it. You should have dropped an atom bomb on Stalin and saved yourself a good deal of trouble. Of course, I tell you he will not attack you, but I am sure your people must be aware of that. May I make an observation here? Based on my long experience in such things?

Q Of course, General, but I will not be trapped into making admissions about who might or might not be working for us or why.

M These are such friendly conversations, after all, and you are such an idealistic and sincere person that I would never even try to trap you. Why far from it. I am inspired by your inner purity and now that I have finished my lies for the day, let me make a few comments. If Stalin invades Europe and drives your troops out, you feel that you ought to be able to retaliate without turning Europe into a pile of worse rubble than it already is. A little disease here and there would wipe out Stalin's hordes and leave everything intact. Besides, a small bottle of germs is so much cheaper than an atom bomb, isn't it? Why you can hold more soldiers in your hand that Stalin could possibly command and you don't have to feed them, clothe them, or supply them with weapons and munitions.

On the other hand, my idealistic and sincere friend, the threat of war and the perceived need for rearming and maintaining a huge, standing military force does wonders, in the short run at least, for the economy.

As you know, I was one of those who pressed Hitler to fight to the end and I was absolutely opposed to any negotiated peace with either you or Stalin. I would have had no problem if we set off an atom bomb in Washington, but using microbes is criminal irresponsibility.

Q Suppose you had the bomb? Just one bomb, let us say? How could you have bombed us? We had captured all your forward air bases and I doubt if you had aircraft capable of reaching us.

M Oh, we had one or two, but from what I learned, that wasn't the means by which we would have attacked you with an atomic weapon. That is, if we had one. For example, very late in the war, the choice would have been to attack Moscow or Washington. London was nothing anymore, of course and not worth the bother of a bomb. The argument was made, in my presence, let me add, that your country was the supplier of war material to the British and the Soviets and an attack on you would not cut the weed off at the ground like an attack on Moscow, but rip out the roots as well.

You ask about delivery? An aircraft? At that time we had a new U boat, the

Type 21, that could travel easily to your shores entirely underwater with no chance of detection by your forces. How easy it would be to travel up a major river and push the bomb out into the water with a timing device. Very simple indeed. Now where would be the best place to lay such a terrible egg? Washington? New York? One was the seat of power, the residence of the President and all the top military officials and the other, a major port and banking center.

The decision was not mine but I would hold for Washington, perhaps at a time when the President was making a speech to your legislators. Don't they have that once a year? I recall…

Q State of the Union address.

M Why of course, I forgot that. One minute the President is making a good deal of noise and the next, they have all gone to heaven in a mushroom-shaped cloud. Now, you see, that would be a military act, wouldn't it? I mean you did it to the Japanese, twice, and therefore, you have established a precedent, haven't you? Of course, this is just an exercise in theory because the war was over. We had no bomb, and the President died before he could do any more damage to the world.

Q There are sides to you that are not particularly pleasant, General.

M Oh my. Please don't say such things to me. I might cry myself to sleep tonight. I should think that a conversation just like this one, or the ones Himmler and I had with Schreiber and his people go on every day in Moscow and Washington. The only difference is, of course, that we lost and, therefore, we are wrong.

Q But you say you were opposed to germ warfare. Not a moral issue with you?

M Perhaps to some degree. Then, we would be as guilty as you when you burned down Dresden. If it worked, then it would not have been wrong…at least from our point of view. My real objection is not so much a moral one but a practical one. Sometimes the two are actually compatible. Such things spread, and many millions die, and what is even worse, one of these victims might be you. That is surely a reason to ponder, isn't it?

Q We seem to have wandered a little far afield here, General. You will make a serious effort to locate the names of the scientists engaged in an SS project to develop atomic weapons, will you not?

M Of course. Whatever would you want with them? You already have a bomb.

Q We don't want the Russians to get them, if they are still in Europe, and perhaps someone might have additional information to give us.

M It is not a problem at all.

Q I would appreciate it if you would refrain from discussing bacteriological warfare outside of this room. This is a subject that you would not normally be associated with and it is highly sensitive at this point in time. I mean that you   **109**

are essentially a policeman and not a scientist and we would have far more use for your services than, shall we say, the Air Force or the Army.

M As you wish. Besides, my knowledge is not technical at all, but it wouldn't take a genius to develop deadly viruses. My personal opinion is that only a fool would even think about trying to use them. The Italians brought poison gas to the blacks in Ethiopia, and I recall that I was told that Hitler viewed this with disgust. But after all, Mussolini was an ally and blacks are not important. They may not view it that way. A Greek said that while boys kill frogs for sport, the frogs die in earnest.

Q I know the quote.

M You should consider the meaning of it. No, I know nothing about such nastiness, and I would want nothing to do with it, believe me. I have no files available that could help you in this.

Q Are you certain?

M Oh yes, very certain indeed, and on that, let us discuss other matters. What else is in your little book there?

Historical Significance—Reflections of the Author

It has been said that no general staff ever developed a new weapon that they did not fully intend to use. Although Hitler was strongly opposed to the use of poison gas, having been a victim of it in the 1914 war, German scientists developed terrible nerve gasses during the Second World War that were never used, but were certainly loaded into standard artillery shells for possible use. After the war, these shells were dumped into the Baltic Sea and it is only a matter of time before the metal casings corrode sufficiently to permit an enormous amount of lethal gas to escape, wreaking havoc on the Baltic states and parts of Poland.

Bacteriological warfare has been practiced in the past as witness the comments about infecting Indians with smallpox, and no doubt it will be practiced in the future. But Müller's comments about the inability to control its spread should constitute the greatest reason for not utilizing it. Information has emerged in the 90s that during the Cold War, US military agencies have experimented to one degree or another with such substances, using their civilian population as guinea pigs. A number of outbreaks of diseases such as Legionnaire's Disease and AIDS have been suggested by reputable epidemiologists as highly suspect in origin but as official governmental agencies strongly deny these allegations, such suggestions must be entirely discounted.

The case of *Generalarzt* Walter Paul Schreiber emphasizes the US government's interest in the development of bacteriological agents for field use. The official German records show that Professor Dr. habil Walter Schreiber was born in Berlin on March 21, 1893. He served in various posts in the German Army including Chief of the Department for Science and Health at the Medical

Corps Headquarters of the German Army. Prior to 1939, Schreiber had visited the United States to study U.S. Military medical techniques in February and March of 1927. During the war, he had problems with the Gestapo because he raised objections to the development of and experimentation on Soviet prisoners of war with various bacteriological agents. Schreiber was eventually warned against further protests and returned to his duties. He was a specialist in communicable diseases and authored a work in 1944 on the plague in south east Russia. Schreiber was the senior medical officer of Berlin, captured by the Russians, and worked with them until 1948 when he escaped to the West.

After extensive debriefing, Schreiber, his wife and son were brought to the United States under the CIA's "Operation Paperclip" on September 8, 1951, and he was attached to the USAF School of Aviation Medicine at Randolph Field, San Antonio, Texas. When Schreiber's wartime activities were discovered by the media, he had to leave the United States.

An Explosive Career

Müller's professional career was highlighted with bomb explosions.

M I do not consider myself to be an explosives expert in any sense, but over the years I got quite an education on the subject, believe me.

Q The July 20 business, for example?

M Yes, that too, but there were others. I was heavily involved in the "Hindenburg" business in 1937.

Q I thought that was an accident. Static electricity.

M No, it was a bomb. Oddly enough, both your government and ours tacitly agreed that an accident was the best official solution. Actually, that was before Crystal Night and we did cooperate with your investigators on the scene, or rather they allowed our people to go over and assist them. Very discreet at the time.

Q I have traveled on a Zeppelin before and I genuinely loved it.

M I too, although I found it very hard to adjust to. I was used to a different kind of flying, but I agree that the experience was one not forgotten. Too bad the airship is a dead issue. Of course, if your government had given us helium, the disaster would never have happened.

Q How do you know it was a bomb and who was responsible?

M To the first question: Because that was the official but private conclusion, and as to the second, I admit no one knew. There are educated guesses, for sure, but nothing conclusive. From the beginning, Hitler did not want it to be sabotage and we had to conduct our investigation accordingly. There had been bomb threats before, you know, and the Gestapo was responsible for searching the luggage of all passengers boarding the craft in Germany. For this reason, I had some initial interest and once the tragedy happened, we had to go over our information to see what we might have known about passengers and crew.

There are some interesting factors involved in the business. How much do you know about it?

Q Nothing other than the ship caught fire just as it was landing.

M Then I should educate you. The *Hindenburg* had been threatened before and we instituted a rigorous search of luggage in Germany. The ship, on the trip in question, ran into some very heavy weather with stiff headwinds that slowed her down by almost twelve hours. She was supposed to arrive in America and dock about six in the morning but instead was delayed to the point where she was only able to put down at six in the evening. The twelve hours I mentioned. Now we were able to interrogate the German nationals who had been on board, including the passengers and crew. And all of the evidence from the officer's in the control car and from the crew, inasmuch as they had specific evidence, was that there was a small explosion inside the ship down inside by one of the huge gas cells. Not an explosion on the top of the ship. I mean, you saw the fire break out above, but the fire started down inside the ship. There were three men in the tail and two were absolutely positive about the source of the initial explosion. The officers confirmed also that there was no loss of gas registered on the control boards and that the landing was perfectly normal up to the point of the explosion.

This 1936 promotional poster shows the Hindenburg over the New York skyline.

Your people and ours went through the wreckage and could find nothing significant in the way of bomb parts or timing devices, but many people had carried off souvenirs, and the fire was very hot so a small timing device could easily be overlooked, stolen or destroyed. After all, a destructive device on such

Death of the Hindenburg.

an airship did not need to be large or very powerful—only powerful enough to rip the gas cell, which was made of treated cloth, and start a fire. A few ounces of powder, a battery and a detonator were sufficient. I could put such a device in my coat pocket and you probably wouldn't see it, and of course, we didn't strip the passengers who were boarding. No, I went through all the evidence and even talked with the ship's designers so I am satisfied that a bomb destroyed the *Hindenburg*. Of course for political reasons, it was better to call it an accident.

This I can say: I firmly believe that the bomb was planted in the ship before she left Germany. *Hindenburg* was not full on the way over, but she was sold out on the return trip. That is where I had the best clues as to what happened. Now, follow along with me: She was twelve hours late as I have said. I am sure that a crew member or a passenger could have gotten up inside the ship and put the bomb where it would go off, but I cannot believe that anyone would be insane enough to want to stay on board when the airship blew up. If someone embarking in Germany had planted the bomb *before* the delay occurred, I am positive they would have had time to go back and retreive it before it went off. I don't think anyone would want to be burned alive that way.

So, if we take that as a starting point, let us go on to the next point: If the bomb was planted in Germany, the planter would not know in advance that the ship would be twelve hours late. These airships were very reliable and quite on time, give or take an hour or so. But she was twelve hours late after all. Now if all had gone as expected, the *Hindenburg* would have landed around 6 A.M., disembarked her passengers, refueled and reprovisioned, and made ready for the return flight—no more than a few hours for this, and off she would have gone. Only this time, she would have had a full complement of passengers— mostly wealthy Americans bound for the Coronation in London. I said I was able to interview all the German passengers on the fatal flight that survived, but I could not get at the American survivors, so that leaves a gap. But still, the timing is what is really important.

In theory, had she not run into unexpected headwinds going to America, the *Hindenburg* would be back out over the Atlantic with a full house when she blew up—probably no survivors and absolutely no evidence. After all, when she burned, it only took a minute or so before she was gone, so over the ocean with no ship traffic in sight, and possibly no time to send out a distress message, it could have gone down as one of the mysteries of the sea.

If this were the plan, why put the bomb on board in Germany, hoping to destroy the ship when coming from America? Why make it look like the sabotage came from your side, not ours? That might indicate some plot in Germany aimed at your country, but there was no reason for this at that time in history. Many of your citizens did not like Hitler, especially the Jews, but the real problems between the two countries had not yet heated up. And a plot by the Jews would not want to blow up Americans, but the evil Nazi passengers.

I did get and examine very carefully, a list of those who were slated to take the return passage and most were wealthy Americans, as I have said. We had **115** enough cooperation with your law enforcement agencies to indicate to me at least three possible subjects whose death might be of value to someone else. It would have to be someone who had connections in Germany and who could have a bomb put on board with a clockwork device set to go off when the *Hindenburg* was on her way back.

Q A question here: You said a clockwork device. Are there such things that could be set for two or three days?

M Of course. We had just such a device called the J-Feder 504 that could work up to 21 days. We used that to blow up the Naples post office in 1944. A small device that I could easily hold in one hand and still have room for a good cigar. It could be set to, let us say, sixteen days, five hours and three minutes. Isn't science wonderful?

Q Who were the suspects?

M Not important at this point. Personal gain was the main motive, as I believe it, not political objections to the swastika. The insurance policies would, in some cases, have a caveat about acts of terrorism negating payment. It might have been instructive to compare the passenger list with such policies and, of course, consider relatives or spouses who could benefit by such a sudden tragedy. Lost at sea and never found.

Q In America, there often is a period of waiting. Seven years.

M I'm sure there would be something found to prove the ship had blown up. Some wreckage on the water, a few bodies or pieces of bodies. I'm sure enough to convince anyone that the passengers were all well-done and either at the bottom of the sea or in some shark's belly. It was all speculative anyway. And, of course, I could be wrong in my opinions. Here, we are dealing with opinions and observations and not forensic facts. The "Burgerbräu" blast was another matter. But initially I still was in error.

Q Now this I would be interested in. The one in 1939?

M I didn't know that there were two such explosions.

Q I'm sure you know what I mean. The attempt on Hitler's life in Munich.

M I thought I might have missed some event. Well, we can talk about it if you wish. What do you know about that business? It might save me some time here.

Q Nothing official, but I did hear that there might have been more to it than a single assassin working alone.

M You heard with great exactness. I meant for you to give me your version of what happened on November 8, 1939.

Q Hitler was addressing a group of his old stalwarts in a Munich beer hall, left early, and a bomb went off, bringing down the roof just over where he was standing. Your people thought the British were behind it and kidnapped Best and Stevens from Holland, tried the man who claimed to have placed the bomb and that's about it.

Hitler speaking in a Munich beer hall on November 8, 1939. Moments after an early departure a bomb went off killing eight and injuring 62.

M Yes, clear enough. Many people have questioned Hitler's early departure and his short speech that night…he often went on for hours…but I know for a fact that he had just reset the date for the offensive in the West and was determined to go back to Berlin and keep up with events there. It was the weather, after all, that was holding him up. I, too, had some doubt about this quick speech but I satisfied myself at once about this. He flew down to Munich from Berlin, but because of the chronic bad weather, had to schedule his special train to take him back. Now, the railway system could accommodate this special but there had to be schedules…there was, after all, regular rail traffic to consider…and the best opening was such as to make him cut his speech short. And then, as you say, the bomb went off ten minutes after he left. Much confusion.

I was called in along with other high ranking police officials, and Munich was in turmoil, believe me. You see, Hitler's security in the beer hall was under the Party. In his headquarters, it was under the Army, and when traveling it was under the RSD (the State Security Service). This was a group of very professional police officials, mostly Bavarian, who were constantly around him and who were commanded not by Himmler but by Rattenhuber. And he was answerable only to Hitler and no one else. They were, indeed, professional but neither this group nor the Gestapo who was also involved in Hitler's security, were allowed inside the building where the bomb was. Of course afterwards, I was able to get this matter cleared up and then both my people and the RSD were jointly responsible for security.

After the explosion, a border guard station, also under my control on the Swiss border, seized Elser and discovered he had documents connecting him with the outrage. Elser claimed he worked alone, and Himmler was in a terrible state about this because Hitler was absolutely certain the British were behind it. The SD had been playing with the British Intelligence in Holland, pretending to be Hitler enemies so as to get information from them and this convinced Hitler that the British were involved. The two senior British agents were kidnapped and I personally questioned them. I must say that I believed them when they claimed they knew nothing about the attempt, but Hitler did not. I was positive that Elser did not work alone and I was very severe in my interrogations of him. Finally, he managed to convince me that he had indeed made the bomb and placed it in the hall, simply because he actually built a replica of it in front of me. I kept this on my desk in Berlin for a time to remind myself not to be so quick to come to conclusions.

But in the end, oddly enough, Hitler was quite correct: The British were, indeed, involved in the attempt but not through their regular intelligence agencies.

Q Are you certain? Did you get the entire story out of Elser? And what happened to him?

M He was not tried but kept on ice in Dachau and in the last weeks of the war, I had him shot. He did work with the British, although he didn't realize it at the time. The reason I had him shot was because the man who acted as a middleman between him and the British was a Gestapo agent from Munich. Oh yes, don't look so startled. That's why Elser went away in the end. I knew that Elser had been unemployed for quite a long time yet seemed to have plenty of money for travel, lodging and food. I wanted to know where that had come from and he kept talking about a friend. He didn't know the friend's real name but he did recall that he was staying at a lodging in the Munich area and that his friend knew the owner.

The owner did not recognize the false name Elser had been given but eventually recalled who the man was. A great shock to me when I found out it was a man who had been in the Gestapo but resigned to go into military service. This, of course, I could not let get out, as it would do my reputation no good whatsoever so we tracked the man down and I had him seized when he came home on a special leave I arraigned for. Such a surprised man after all! He wet his pants when they grabbed him and shoved him into the car. Oh yes, and I had a nice, friendly chat with him. After I told him in great detail what I would have done to him, he began to admit what had happened. He had committed some indiscretion a few years before and somehow the British had heard about it. He was approached and more or less forced to give assistance. It was either work for the British or risk his misdeeds coming to my attention. Perhaps I should explain this: The man was involved in sexual matters with a very young girl. That, of course, is a criminal matter in Germany as it is in most civilized countries. Of course, as head of the NKVD, Beria can rape anything female over the age of three and get a promotion out of it, but elsewhere, in civilized countries, such things are viewed with disgust. If I had learned of this criminal misconduct, I would have turned the miserable monster over to the Criminal Police with a strong recommendation to have him shortened by a head. I confess that this is a personal prejudice entirely. A man in my position often has to deal with repulsive creatures in order to get information, but I assure you that debauchers of small children are too much for me to stomach. You might say that I personally feel that insects like that should be exterminated on the spot, but even in Germany, to shock you, we had courts and a legal system. No, this former Gestapo person, I think, was far more afraid of what I would do to him if he were exposed than the danger in working for the British. There was a British official in Berlin who wanted to kill Hitler and he was in a position to set this in motion.

Q This was official? I mean the British authorized this assassination plot?

M No, they did not. In fact, they were apparently completely opposed to it but our man decided to do it anyway. You keep jumping up and down in your chair there, so let me calm you by telling you it was a Colonel Mason-MacFarlane, the British military attaché in Berlin!

Q God, I knew him in Italy. He was involved with the Italian surrender and he was a perfect, obstructionistic ass. The man wrote documents to the Italians that were in direct opposition to official policy and did it deliberately. I met him once and he was a thoroughly arrogant and probably unbalanced man. The General was commandant of Gibraltar and a friend of Churchill.

M Commandant of Gibraltar was he indeed. He was there when Sikorski had his fortunate accident, wasn't he?

Q Yes, he was.

M Well, by the time we found out about your General friend, he had left the country under his own power. I assure you, diplomatic immunity or no, had I discovered the connection, he would have gone home in a box with a lot of his pieces missing. He was a cripple, as I recall, and a missing leg or two wouldn't make much difference.

Q I must say, you are most bloodthirsty today, General. Did you have raw meat for breakfast?

M No, an omelette, coffee with double cream, two fresh rolls and fruit preserves.

Q What happened to the Gestapo man?

M The unfortunate child-rapist was told that we would not put him in jail for the time being, but that he must stay in Munich where he would be kept under surveillance. One winter night, he decided to cross the Isar on the bridge by the National Museum. Two of my men came towards him from one side of the bridge and two were right behind him. It was snowing very heavily and no doubt he observed that he was not alone, so I assume that is why he suddenly leapt over a high parapet, crashed through the ice on the river below and drowned in the water before we could rescue him. What a tragedy indeed. They found him in the spring down by the dam when he warmed up a bit and began to bloat. There was an article in the paper about the soldier on leave who had a tragic accident. I had a hand in the writing of the article but I did not send flowers to the funeral. It would hardly have done to prosecute him and then have his connection with the Gestapo come out, coupled with child-perversion and high treason, now would it?

Q Probably not. Were there any other accidents like that?

M Six, all together, all connected with this business. Two heart attacks, one street traffic accident where a bicyclist was run over by a large truck, one suicide…no two suicides, and one person who fell into the Ammer Lake and was never found. I suppose you will blame all of this on my breakfasts, won't you?

Q I was only making a small joke with you.

M Do you disapprove of my attitude on child-rapists?

Q Good Lord no, of course not.

M There are predators in society that should be taken away quietly so as not to excite comment and put to death without notice. You can comment all you like about legality and decency, but it certainly is not going to change my opinion. I do have a problem with determining which is worse: child abuse or high treason. I think we should simply kill the lot of them in a private mine shaft somewhere and let the devil decide the issue later.

Historical Significance—Reflections of the Author

The destruction of the Zeppelin *Hindenburg* was generally believed to have been sabotage, although never proven. Germany's official explanation of the explosion…an accident. Germans could not admit that one of their most prominent national symbols had been destroyed by enemies of the state.

Müller's comments regarding the attempt on Hitler's life in November of 1939 are important since he was in charge of the investigation. He initially felt that the British were responsible or somehow connected, mainly because Hitler believed this, and Himmler was determined to prove the *Führer* correct. Müller's repression of a former Gestapo officer's involvement and his removal of both the middle-man and Elser is consistent with his determination not to be disgraced by the actions of a former subordinate. Although Heinrich Müller had a cynical sense of humor, this extract clearly indicates how ruthless he could be when he found it necessary. In the 1990s, Müller's draconian punishment for child abuse would have more supporters than critics.

Colonel (later, General), Noel Mason-MacFarlane wanted to assassinate Hitler and attempted to convince his superiors in London to allow him to proceed with his plans. London, however, refused permission. In a post-war interview, Mason-MacFarlane revealed that he had planned to shoot Hitler with a high-powered, telescopic rifle during Hitler's birthday parade on April 20, 1939. He stated that he had an unobstructed view of the tribune from the

Colonel Mason-MacFarlane (right), along with the military attachés from Russia and France, on the reviewing stand during the 4-hour birthday parade.

lavatory window of his apartment house. Mason-MacFarlane, a man of contentious disposition and who took delight in causing mischief wherever he went, certainly was engaging in wishful thinking in the matter of the April assassination because as military attaché he had been standing on the reviewing platform with all the other military attachés during the entire four-hour parade.

The General proved to be most uncooperative during the final negotiations for the Italian surrender to the Allies in 1943. Whether or not he proved more cooperative with the strong anti-Sikorski feelings of Winston Churchill is open to conjecture. He was, indeed, Governor of Gibraltar when the troublesome Polish leader met with a most convenient aircraft accident while taking off from the Gibraltar airfield and wrote later that he had doubts about the legitimacy of the crash. Whether this was mere conjecture or indicative of more specific knowledge was not indicated in his private journals.

Andreas and Bernhard

Müller financed his flight from Germany and his new life in Switzerland by diverting funds from hidden SS bank accounts—accounts designated by Martin Bormann and other high officials for their own post-war use. Some of this money had come from the SS industry's office, which used unpaid concentration camp labor, and even more of it came from the successful German forging of British currency.

M In a sense, my investigations into the corruption that was growing in the higher levels of the SS as the war went on proved to be my salvation in the end. Others were putting away enormous sums of money for their survival in the event the war ended against us…as it became more and more evident that it would. The money was kept, mostly, in special accounts in the *Reichsbank* and some more of it was sent to Switzerland for safekeeping. Now, my contacts in Switzerland kept me abreast of this and I knew exactly how much was in the Berlin accounts. When I made my move, and one had to wait until just the right moment, I was able to clean out most of what was in Berlin and a good deal of what was in Switzerland. The Swiss have informed me through my people, that everyone wants to get their hands on the honey pots, but you won't get much in the end. You should stick to trying to find Globocnik's horde and stop bothering the Swiss. A few millions here and there are unimportant and, of course, most of those who hid the money here are dead or in prison. I know your people are interested in the remaining funds; after all, we had to leave *something* behind to keep you happy.

Q This will eventually need to be addressed, you know. We can use that money and there is no reason letting the British have it, although they could certainly use it now. And at least one Jewish group is starting to make noise about this, although at this point in time, no one is paying any attention to them.

M Eventually, someone will. I thought I would mention something interesting to you. The communists, as we know, have seized power in Czechoslovakia. They threw Masaryk out of the window, and then the new government did a most strange thing with all the armaments in the Czech arsenal.

Q Oh, for God's sake, General, let us not get into that business now.

M I need to show you that the game is still on after all. Yes, I see you know about what happened. Wait until Comrade Josef finds out that these wonderful communists stripped the new country of its weapons and sent all of them to the Zionists! But then you know which group made up the leaders of the coup, don't you? Comrade Josef will have them all shot just as soon as he finds out, won't he? No doubt someone will tell him—some kindly person who has his best interests at heart.

Q Do let us get back to the money question.

M For such a well-educated and absolutely correct young man, you certainly display a distressing interest in money. I keep hoping we can discuss religion, philosophy and enlightenment, but instead you seem interested in assassinations, stolen art, hidden money, and so on. You sound like a Swiss banker in his cups. Nevertheless, let us go on about money and we can only imagine how many Czech Zionists will get it in the back of the neck—the famous "Russian Kiss."

Historical Significance—Reflections of the Author

The root cause of all warfare is economics. Whether it is the seizure of a weaker tribe's grazing land or the destruction of a rival power's production capacity, war, to elaborate on Clausewitz, is a logical extension of political and economic aims. War launched against an unpopular head of state or a political system is war commenced solely for economic gains; the common rationale of a holy crusade is merely window dressing for popular historians to postulate.

The hatred engendered against Hitler by the American and British official propaganda machinery before the outset of World War II was due more to the success of Hitler's barter system than to his personal dislike of Jews or threats to putative democracies in Central Europe.

Stripped of her colonies and gold reserves after the First World War, Germany had to incur massive, interest-bearing loans with both the United States and England to pay for needed imports. When Hitler came to power, he paid off the existing loans and instituted a barter system in which, for example, Germany would trade locomotives to Argentina for their beef and wheat. Previously, both countries had borrowed money from international banks at high-interest rates to pay for their respective imports.

The barter system, therefore, represented a serious threat to international banking interests which complained loudly and effectively to their respective governments, demanding intervention and relief. Many economists referred to a boycott of German products, which was instituted in the United States and England, as economic warfare, as indeed it was. The British were past-masters in creating economic warfare and experts in ruining the currency of their rivals by flooding the marketplace with counterfeit currency. During the American Revolutionary War, the British dumped so many counterfeit Continental notes into the economy that American currency became virtually worthless, and the phrase, "not worth a Continental" became common. Angered by French support of the American Revolution, the British counterfeited adulterated gold French Louis coins.

As a means of economic retaliation against Napoleon for his support of a French-dominated continental system which excluded England, the British counterfeited French assignats and franc notes. Napoleon retaliated by forging British currency. Later in the same century, the US federal government forged Confederate money in huge quantities.

The Soviet forgery of American currency in the 1930s, on the other hand, was not designed to destroy the US economy. Rather, the counterfeit gold certificates were manufactured to pay their agents. Since many of these agents were highly placed and expensive members of the Roosevelt Administration, Stalin's experts concentrated on the manufacture of $100 gold certificates. As the duplication of official US banknote paper was a problem, smaller denomination bills were bleached and over-printed.

At the outbreak of World War II, economic advisors to the leaders of England and the United States urged their respective governments to forge German marks and flood the international market which would cause a collapse of confidence in that currency and, therefore, create tremendous inflation in Germany. The British did counterfeit German military scrip but used the blank reverse for propaganda messages. These were scattered by aircraft over Germany where their impact on the population was nil, but the impact on German leadership was considerable.

Exactly *who* in the Third Reich initiated the program for the counterfeiting of British currency is not known. One man, Alfred Naujocks, an *SS-Sturmbannführer* (or Major) in the SD, has taken credit for the inception of the plan in 1940. Naujocks was a longtime acquaintance of Reinhard Heydrich, chief of the SD and it was Heydrich who initially authorized the reproduction of British pound notes. The initial code name for the operation was "Andreas."

Alfred Naujocks, a SD officer credited with the idea of counterfeiting British currency on a large scale.

It has been stated that the original purpose of "Andreas" was to falsify pound notes and drop them over England to create economic havoc. However, a more believable scenario, and one supported by period documents, is that the SS leadership envisioned the possibility of raising funds for their organization.

The SS was an official branch of the NSDAP and its funding came from the Party coffers, although the *Waffen-SS* drew on government funding for much of its military requirements. One of Himmler's best assets in this economic struggle was his complete control of the KZ (or concentration camp system). Based on the institutions introduced by Lord Kitchener in South Africa during the Boer Wars to control the civil population, the KZ system encompassed a wide spectrum of inmates, ranging from professional criminals, communists, and political opponents of the government, including Jews and other ethnic and religious groups.

At the beginning of the war, there were 21,300 concentration camp inmates, housed in six camps. During the course of the war, the total number of inmates rose to over 400,000 lodged in an enormous network of camps scattered throughout Europe and the East. SS General Oswald Pohl and his deputy Richard Glücks organized a huge, free labor pool which would provide a major source of revenue for the SS. It was this system of forced labor that the SD turned to when "Andreas" was superseded by "Bernhard." The "Andreas" attempts to forge British notes floundered in technical problems and contributed to personality conflicts within the RSHA.

"Bernhard" was named for the new head of the scheme, *SS-Hauptsturmführer* Bernhard Krüger of the SD. Krüger, born in Reise, Saxony on November 26, 1904, was a specialist in forging documents and was assigned to Section VI F4 of the RSHA where his section assembled a large library of foreign documents of all kinds which were copied for intelligence operations.

SS-Hauptsturmführer Bernard Krüger who was in charge of the second plan to counterfeit British currency. He was chosen because of his knowledge of the forgery process and the machinery needed.

The proper paper was nearly impossible to initially produce since, unlike the original, it did not properly fluoresce under ultraviolet light. Also, a proper numbering system proved extremely difficult to develop. In 18 months, **125**

"Andreas" had only produced a half-million pounds worth of counterfeit notes, many of which, however, were authenticated by the Bank of England when submitted by unsuspecting Swiss banks. Personal rivalry between Heydrich and Naujocks created so many problems that "Andreas" was eventually terminated.

The second project, "Bernhard," began only after Heydrich was assassinated by British agents in the summer of 1942. At that time, *SS-Sturmbannführer* Hermann Dörner of the RSHA began to assemble a team of specialists from the ranks of concentration camp inmates. This initial cadre was originally constituted at Oranienburg concentration camp north of Berlin, and on August 23, 1942, it was permanently established at Blocks 18 and 19 at nearby Sachsenhausen camp.

Major Krüger promised his inmate workers good housing, better and regularly served meals, no physical abuse, tobacco, newspapers, good clothing, and packages from outside sources. Most importantly, he assured them of survival. In return, he required full cooperation in the counterfeiting projects and the maintenance of strict security.

By the end of 1942, the 200-pound-pressure Stentz Monopel Type 4 press was moved to Sachsenhausen from its former location in the Berlin forgery center. Aside from the manufacture of the highest quality intaglio plates, the most important factor in the production of undetectable counterfeit pound notes was reproduction paper. British notes were printed on a high rag content paper and manufactured by the Portal, England firm of Laverstoke, which had been producing this paper for the Bank of England since the first quarter of the 18th century.

Paper used in the production of American currency was a 17- pound bond manufactured for the US Treasury by the Crane Company. As the SD turned its attention to the counterfeiting of American currency in 1943, the same German firms which duplicated the Portal paper, Spechthausen and Schlichter, and Schall, successfully duplicated the Crane paper.

The counterfeit paper for pounds had to have not only the correct texture and appearance, but had to be properly and exactly watermarked and fluoresce with the exact shade as the original paper. The Germans solved the latter problem by a careful analysis of water used in the preparation of the original British paper.

The actual manufacturing of the pound note plates was preceded by a thorough study of thousands of original examples of the British pound in German hands. The Bank of England had 156 identifying points on their plates and the forgers were able to duplicate every one of them.

Copying the lettering and numbering of the original currency presented few serious problems to Krüger's experts, but the vignette of Britannia, common to all denomination pound notes, proved to be extremely difficult to copy— a similar problem which had occured with the portraits on American currency. On the pound notes, the vignette consisted of a crown-surmounted wreath enclosing a seated Britannia holding a spear in her left hand and a floral spray in her right. However, constant reworking eventually produced an exact copy.

The correct numbering system for the pound notes was developed by German mathematicians, and the numbering system for the US bills came from American published sources. As the British used German-made ink for their currency, this aspect of the project presented no problems.

The first run of counterfeit pound notes inspected by senior officials at the RSHA in Berlin was declared a technical success, but lacked the overall visual appearance of original, circulated currency. This was solved by the addition of Soloman Somolianov, a highly competent forger, to the Sachsenhausen crew. Somolianov, a Russian Jew, specialized in the forgery of British pound notes and was successful in adding the proper patina of age to the new pounds and later, US dollars.

An example of a counterfeit 20 pound note which was detected and marked "falsification."

After the notes had been printed and aged, they were sent to the RSHA and *SS-Oberführer* Walter Schellenberg, head of Section VI of the RSHA and SD foreign intelligence, distributed the British pounds to various outlets—many of which are still officially unknown.

For many years the old rhyme, "A Pound's a Pound the World Around," recalled the preeminence of British currency throughout the world. The final product of "Bernhard" had been tested by passing it through the Swiss banking system and through them eventually pronounced genuine by the Bank of England. Armed with these bonifides, Schellenberg's agents glutted the world's currency markets with over 300 million British pound notes in denominations of 5, 10, 20, 50 and 100 pounds, in varying degrees of perfection.

First-class quality notes that defied any detection were used to purchase gold, jewels and safe currency through neutral banking systems, while lower quality notes were used for less exacting customers such as Tito's partisans from whom the SS purchased huge amounts of weaponry supplied to the Yugoslavs by British and American clandestine services.

In early 1943, full-scale production of US currency began at Sachsenhausen. First, the $100 gold certificate was printed, followed by the $50 and $20 dollar silver certificates. Although specific information on the amount of US bills counterfeited by "Bernhard" from 1943 has never been released by the US Treasury Department, a conservative estimate based on German documents and other information puts the overall total at $50 million.

As the Soviet Army approached Berlin in 1945, the unit at Sachsenhausen was moved to Mauthausen in the Ostmark on March 12, 1945 and again on March 21, to Redl-Zipf, north of Salzburg.

Finally, on April 24, Krüger ordered the prisoners transferred to Ebensee where they were liberated by the Americans. Krüger had kept his word to the inmates and at one point, in November of 1943, had secured official permission from Berlin to award twelve War Service Medals and six War Service Crosses, 2nd Class without Swords, to more deserving counterfeiters. They were permitted to wear their decorations inside the camp area and since most of them were Jewish, the attitude of the camp commandant can only be imagined.

The liberated "Bernhard" people were free to follow whatever course they chose. There is reason to believe that a number of them continued their artistic endeavors but under different management.

Soviet and American intelligence agencies were extremely eager to locate Bernhard Krüger. Their interest had to do with American dollars.

As retreating SS units threw huge sums of counterfeit pounds into Austrian lakes and streams, the acres of floating and waterlogged notes put an effective end to the usefulness of the once-mighty British pound. It is interesting to note that not a single American bill has ever been identified as a counterfeit of the Sachsenhausen project.

The Soviets and Americans were eager to locate not only the finished US bills but the plates and paper as well. Since the "Bernhard" people and their baggage fell into American hands, the Soviets ran a poor second in the race. They only managed to locate some of the workers but none of their products. Neither the plates, paper, nor German documentation relating to the counterfeiting of American money ever officially surfaced. It is noted that large sums of dollars suddenly appeared in the Mid-East as funding for various US intelligence operations in Lebanon controlled by Haj Amin-El Husseini, the Mufti of Jerusalem. Many of the funds were in $100 dollar gold certificates.

The Germans were not the only country to liberally finance their intelligence agencies and assist their countrymen in building personal fortunes through the use of counterfeit currency. The basic difference is that the Germans did not manufacture their own currency.

This form of economic warfare has certainly not ceased with the downfall of the Third Reich. The Iranian government has, by all serious accounts, been forging nearly perfect US $100 bills which have circulated throughout the

A small portion of the British counterfeit notes recovered by divers from Austria's Toplitzsee.

world and caused the US Treasury Department to issue newly-formatted bills. The US Treasury Department will eventually recall all outstanding older bills and carefully inspect them before making exchanges.

In 1984, over 2,000 extremely rare, nearly mint condition, ancient Greek silver coins, dating from 465 BC, were unearthed near Elmali in Turkey. The horde of coins, in violation of Turkish law, quickly circulated into the international marketplace, and many coins sold for huge sums of money. Discovering that their national treasures had been looted, the irate Turkish government forced the return of most of the horde through legal and diplomatic means. The British Museum inspected some of the rarer specimens and concluded that the *entire* collection had been recently manufactured at the Bulgarian State Mint in Sofia by that country's intelligence agency to raise much-needed Western currency. Following this revelation, the value of rare Greek coins toppled as quickly as the British pound had fallen in 1945.

The irony of the "Bernhard" operation is that their 5 pound counterfeits are now worth more on the collector's market than they were during the war.

The Gilding of the Lily

Governments, like individuals, are chronically in need of money to operate. This funding comes from diverse sources in the main taxes raised from the population. But in a democratic state, these funds are controlled and accountable. It would be, as it is in the United States, quite acceptable for the government to loot the Social Security and federal pension funds until all that remains to the eye of the beneficiaries is a hollow facade, only awaiting a strong windstorm to collapse. However, it is another matter entirely for a government to make a profit by selling illegal drugs to its own citizens, as only one example. Clandestine agencies are always loathe to disclose to the custodians of public funds the reasons for which their budgetary needs are required. Other, and less public, sources have to be tapped. Here we have an example of how such matters are conducted on the highest levels.

Q We have discussed this before, General, but I would like to return to the subject again. That is, of course, the money in the special accounts here. The money...the loot if you will...that was put away by prominent Nazis here in Swiss banks.

M Including my own funds, I presume?

Q No, no, of course not. I mean money belonging to Göring and others.

M He is dead, naturally, but there are heirs. His wife and daughter survived him.

Q I am sure that there are heirs, but it is not acceptable that this blood money be given to relatives of prominent Nazis.

M At least I was not a prominent Nazi, after all. You will have to take all this up with the Swiss. They control the bank accounts, not I.

Q But, you once said that your agency kept a watch on such things...

M I said that it was illegal for German funds to be sent outside of the country. The Finance Ministry oversaw such matters. We did assist in several areas, I admit, in watching this area.

Q But you knew that money was flowing from Germany into Swiss banks, didn't you?

M Yes, of course my agency did.

Q But if this was against your laws, couldn't you have stopped it?

M Money, especially large amounts of it, has its own life and its own power. Do you believe that if I discovered Bormann was hiding money in Switzerland that I could have the money seized and him arrested? Nonsense.

Q Understood, but you did know about all of this, didn't you? Didn't you get some of this money once?

M I made certain, fortunate acquisitions before it was transferred to this country. Getting money from a Swiss bank is almost impossible once it gets into it. Before, not after.

Q The point here, General, is that you do have records of such transactions—deposits, account numbers and individuals, don't you?

M Anything is possible.

Q Hypothetically, if you had such information, could we have it?

M Why?

Q Obviously, so we could get the money away from the Nazis.

M What Nazis? They are either dead or in jail.

Q These are ill-gotten gains, General, and don't belong to these people or their families.

M Behind all great fortunes lies a great crime.

Q That's not original and not true.

M Right on the first point, but wrong on the second. Never mind. All of this is going nowhere anyway. The Swiss are not going to let you poke about in their banks on a wild hunt for their clients' money and you know it.

Q But if we had specifics, we might be able to...shall we say...persuade them to relinquish this money.

M And, you would keep it safe in Washington? Protect it carefully against theft?

Q Better there than here. In theory, something might be done. If you work for us, would the incentive not be greater to assist us?

M It might be if the incentive were big enough.

Q Anything is possible.

M It always is. But remember this, I live here with permission. I will not antagonize my hosts by turning your hordes loose on their sacred banking system.

Q Naturally you will leave here...

M I know that, but I own this house, and I might like to come back. It would have to be done in such a way as not to turn the Swiss against me. You understand that I hope.

Q We all have hope.

M There are billions of Swiss francs in various secret accounts as you know. Some of these billions were deposited there by prominent Nazis, but a lot more came from other sources. For example, many foreign businessmen keep money in Swiss banks to facilitate European business transactions or perhaps to avoid taxes in their countries.

Q What about the money from those who fear persecution or confiscation in their own countries?

M Yes, too...I suppose that as well. But on the one hand, you talk about the blood money of the Nazis and on the other, the sanctified money belonging to their victims. Is that not true?

Q Money is money.

M Yes, it is. As I said, billions of francs worth of it. Are you considering money deposited here by Jewish refugees who were fleeing Hitler? And Hitler, of course, because he had money here, but his enemies...

Q Victims. His victims.

M Social Democrats, communists, and perhaps Jews too?

Q Yes. Money in general.

M Be specific. Money only related to the activities of the Reich? Is that correct?

Q Yes, of course. We could not justify seizing the funds of a South American dictator, for instance.

M Very well. Then monies made in connection with, shall we say, dealings with the Reich or within it, would be legitimate goals for your agency or government? Is that correct?

Q Certainly, certainly, just exactly what I meant. Absolutely.

M To the big Nazis and their enemies, cannot we also add the names of their friends? I mean the friends of the Reich, those who profited by their relationship with it?

Q Certainly. Any Nazi Quislings or foreign agent of the Reich would be deemed recoverable.

M You don't think very far down the road, do you? You know something about banking, my friend, so be a little careful here. There has to be some surgery here or the patient will bleed to death.

Q I don't follow you.

M You very often don't, do you. Never mind. Some of those who profited greatly by their association with my government and put their profits in the safe

Swiss banks would not like you to take their money away. And, you would not be able to do this. They would make such a noise that the entire project would be blown away in an instant and you with it. You would either end up dead or inspecting penguin shit in Antarctica.

Q We know how to pressure the friends of the Nazis. Exposure is one means....

M Oh, for God sake, use your head, man. All the time your press and President was screaming about the wicked devils in Berlin and all during the war with us, many people on your side were reaping huge rewards by dealing with us. And before the war as well, after Crystal Night when the press was yapping and wailing about our wickedness, how many of the yappers were sneaking about the back alleys, making money with us? You want examples? Certainly, I will give them to you. Sir Henry Deterding of Royal Dutch Shell dealt with us throughout and put huge amounts of money in Swiss banks. Do you want to take his money? After all, before you bombed Ploesti oil fields, you had to work out with us which refineries not to bomb. And in Cologne, the safest place to be in a bombing raid was the Ford factory. Ambassador Kennedy made millions during the Czech crisis on the stockmarket on specific information we gave him and got more millions in I.G. Farben stock. Mr. Watson from your IBM company dealt with us regularly, even during the war. Why my entire surveillance system depended on parts made available to us from IBM through Swiss sources. And, while the Ambassador kept away from Hitler, Watson received a high decoration from Hitler personally. And what about your General Motors people? I can tell you to the penny how much money all of these people stuck away like hamsters in the banks here. Are you going to seize their money too? I think not. The Rothschilds and the Weiss people also had money here. Are you going after them? They dealt with us...but of course because they had to. Still, it could be considered blood money in the end.

Q Now General, we both know that there are always some areas that we cannot explore. You know what I mean.

M After we take out British, Swedish, Swiss, American, and other businessmen, we only have left the evil Nazis and their victims. Surely you, from your own point of view, would not want to loot the victims as well?

Q Who can prove what came from where? We cannot get too holy about all of this, can we?

M You can't because you are greedy. And all of us lust after one thing or another, don't we? It might not even be money. Things more forbidden?

Q Like stolen art?

M I can respond to that with a comment of my own, but we can leave it there. You know what I mean. Read Marcus Aurelias on the subject of envy. You know, in the 19th century, there were a number of paintings made that showed the unwanted guest at the wedding feast.

Q I know what you mean...

M Yes, the radiant bridal pair in the foreground, their faces full of love and trust in the future and right behind them, the grinning skull of death in his black robes. Death at the feast. All of this greed is for nothing. They still uncover pots full of gold or silver that someone buried in the fields to keep it safe. I don't notice clouds of banknotes floating around in heaven, do you?

Q You keep twisting away from the point.

M You want the money from the evil Nazis and their saintly victims too. You know that there are additional millions you can't touch but so what?

Q If all these victims are dead, what difference does it make?

M There are heirs.

Q But suppose they didn't know about the money and never made a claim?

M The Swiss tell them nothing, and unless they have the proper codes, they could get nothing at all. This proves not a thing and you know it.

Q Claims have been made and paid.

M Some relatives knew and what is more important, could prove that the money in certain accounts belonged to them. Not all Nazis, of course, but some too got their funds to finance a new life in South America or elsewhere. Most of this money belongs to Jews, as you know. If they survived the war, they no doubt got their money to take to America or England but if they died, then you claim it for them. Correct?

Q Can it be done?

M Anything can be done. Talk to the Swiss about it, as I said.

Q We have and they tell us nothing. They will not search records and will only be of assistance if we can supply names and numbers.

M So there you are, up against a stone wall. Shall we discuss other matters of real importance to both of us?

Q No, the money is of real importance right now. You spoke about names and numbers. I am certain...Washington is certain...that you have this information, at least a good deal of it. Could you assist us in this matter? Materially assist us?

M Ah, "materially." If I had this information, I myself could persuade certain Swiss to release the funds, but we must have an agreement here.

Q Of course, whatever you think right.

M If I think of it, it has to be right. Very well, are you authorized to negotiate?

Q You know that. We have gone through all of this before, General.

M I propose that I can help you. I will not supply you with the numbers of any bank depositor here in Switzerland, but I can give you a list of names and...most important...the sums of money in the accounts. No Americans or British of prominence will be included. Agreed? Yes, agreed. Then I myself will enter negotiations on your behalf to get this money which will be divided as follows: To you, one third of the total; to the Swiss bankers, one third; and to me, one third...

Q That's quite impossible. We cannot give you a third of anything and besides, your mathematics is in error. Three times thirty is ninety, not one-hundred. You meant thirty-three and one-third, didn't you?

M No, I made allowance for an additional ten percent. That money can stay in various accounts so the Swiss can, as an example of their great character, give it back if and when.

Q Will the Swiss do it?

M They won't have much choice in the end but we must be diplomatic, mustn't we? Always leave an escape route for a man to use, or he might become desperate and do foolish things.

Q Ten percent?

M It shows compassion to all.

Q I know you could help on this and if the division is acceptable elsewhere, would you do it?

M I should prefer to leave this country, by aircraft if possible, before it is over.

Q We can do that. You have to go back to Berlin anyway to get at your files. That could certainly be done.

M It must be made very, very clear to the Swiss authorities that your government is behind this. They would throw me in jail and deport me at once if this support were not there and I made such an approach. It would be a violation of my agreement with them.

Q That would be the least of our worries.

M I have quite a bit of art in the banks here and if I do this, it would have to be moved to the United States. Perhaps a branch of the Mellon bank would do as a depository. Should we discuss why I would choose this bank?

Q There has been quite enough provocative material here....

M We could walk privately in the garden after dinner and I will show you exactly how provocative I could be if you wish.

Q I rather don't think so. We agree in principle, don't we?

M I think we do. But with all that money, the skeleton is still a guest at the banquet.

Historical Significance-Reflections of the Author

It has long been suspected, and with justification, that the members of the Swiss Banking Association (SBA) had control of billions of Swiss Francs hidden in various secret accounts. Swiss banking laws make it very difficult to obtain any information on these accounts and the bankers steadfastly refused to give inquirers, be they heirs or government agencies, any information concerning accounts in their banks unless presented proof of deposit, to include code names, numbers and amounts deposited.

After the German defeat in 1945, some funds belonging to prominent Nazis were turned over to various outside agencies, but Jewish refugees families were not as fortunate in their quests for family funds sequestered in neutral Switzerland.

The question of hidden funds was complicated by the fact, as Müller pointed out, that many American and British businessmen who had had wartime dealings with the Third Reich also had such hidden accounts and it was obvious that a full-scale disclosure on the part of the SBA could have very serious financial and political repercussions in a number of countries.

The plan proposed to Müller by Kronthal in 1948 was implemented in the later part of that year and by the terms of this agreement, monies from the accounts of prominent Third Reich officials and businessmen were seized quietly and turned over to Kronthal's agency in the proportions Müller demanded. The transactions were conducted almost entirely by a certain Herr Rudolf Stottlemeier, one of Müller's numerous aliases, and the monies went into a *Sonderkonto* or special account in the ponderous name of "Swiss-American Commercial and Banking Consortium" with the funds from the wholesale lootings kept in the Credit Suisse, Zurich.

Drained of their assets were any accounts identified as belonging to dead or jailed members of the Third Reich, Jewish depositors known to be dead and against whose funds no claim had been made up to 1948, various German companies, such as I.G. Farben, that were no longer in operation and occasional foreigners who had dealt with the Third Reich but were now known to be dead and against whose deposits no inquiries had been lodged.

It is not to be believed that once these accounts had been cleaned out, the SBA would leave any paper trail behind and the ten percent balance Müller mentioned was left in the event that monies had to be released.

In 1996, official American documents, released under the Freedom of Information Act, an act that has proven to be a double-edged sword to all concerned, the "Operation Safehaven" file. This file has proven to be of great value to Jewish groups, such as the World Jewish Council, in forcing the reluctant Swiss banks to release information on accounts held by Jewish depositors and to return funds which have been verified.

Press accounts have disclosed that the Swiss have located $32 million in these accounts—money that will be released either to the heirs of the depositors or to various Jewish organizations.

From Müller's papers, lists of depositors have been pieced together along with their code names, if known, and account balances. Also in Müller's files are lists of other depositors, including foreign businesses and individuals, obvious refugees or those wishing to keep their funds in a safe place during the *Sturm und Drang* of the 1930s and 1940s. Like those in far earlier times who buried their gold and silver in the woods to avoid rampaging and looting armies, by 1948, many of the depositors were dead or missing. Considering the low risk of disclosure and the huge amounts of money involved, Stottlemeier had very little problem in convincing the Swiss Banking Association to cooperate with him, especially when they became aware of the degree and extent of his specific knowledge.

The following list includes only inhabitants of the Greater German Reich and does not include the holdings of Heinrich Müller which included seven various accounts, a number of safe deposit boxes and vault holdings of various items of looted art, compromising documents and other items of value and interest.

This list is not in alphabetical order, nor compiled in order of account balances. Biographical material is added where known.

Reichsbank funds: Main account held under the name of Otto Gruber.
223,892,000 SF (Swiss Francs).

Hermann Göring: Main account held under the name of Medici.
25,000,000 SF
(Suicide in 1946.)

Adolf Hitler: Main account held under the name of Wolf.
188,457,332 SF
(Vanished in 1945, presumed dead.)

Ernst Kaltenbrunner: Main account held under the name of Schönthal.
1,238,492 SF
(Head of the RSHA, executed 1946.)

Walther Funk: Main account held in the name of Hoffmann.
8,000,000 SF
(Minister of Economic Affairs, President of the Reichsbank, sentenced at Nuremberg and died in 1960.)

Hjalmar Schacht: Main account held in the name of Engel.
321,000 SF
(President of the Reichsbank, replaced by Funk, died 1970.)

Joachim von Ribbentrop: Main account held in the name of Henckel.
1,500,000 SF
(Foreign Minister, executed in 1946.)

Oswald Pohl: Main account held in the name of Schiffmann.
17,581,000 SF
(SS General and head of the SS Industries, executed in 1948.)

Josef Terboven: Main account held in the name of Bock.
722,000 SF
(A former Gauleiter and later High Commissioner in Norway. Suicide reported in 1945.)

Hans Frank: Main account held in the name of Richter.
15,820,000 SF
(Governor General of Poland, executed in 1946.)

Schickeneider: Main account held in the name of Stahl.
3,800,000 SF
(Head of Ruhr Steel combine. Date of death unknown.)

Various members of the Krupp von Bohlen und Halbach concerns: Main account held in the name of Hugelmann.
136,932,000 SF
(German industrialists.)

Fritz Thyssen: Main account held in the name of Kohler.
16,000,000 SF
(German industrialist, early Hitler supporter, later fled the country, died 1951 in South America.)

Kurt von Schröder: Main account held in the name of Westbank.
2,100,000 SF
(Nationalistic bank head from Cologne, date of death unknown.)

Emil Kirdorf: Main account held in the name of Goldmann.
11,600,000 SF
(German industrialist, died in 1938.)

Albert Speer: Main account held in the name of Oswald Kronberg.
830,298 SF
(Architect and later Minister of Armaments, sentenced to imprisonment at Nuremberg, died 1971.)

Alfred Rosenberg: Main account held in the name of Fischer.
4,000,000 SF
(Minister for Eastern Affairs, executed in 1946.)

Martin Bormann: Main account held in the name of Edelmann.
128,477,921 SF
(Hitler's Secretary, died in 1945.)

I.G. Farben Industry: Main account held in the name of Gomez.
900,000,000 SF
(Major German Chemical combine. Broken up after the war. Heavy stock holdings by such persons as Joseph Kennedy and various prominent Swiss citizens. Kennedy stock holdings returned eventually after John F. Kennedy became US President.)

Martin Mutschmann: Main account held in the name of Handwerk.
750,000 SF
(Former Reichsstatthalter in Saxony, reported dead in 1948.)

Herbert Backe: Main account held in the name of Walter Bauer.
250,000 SF
(Former Reich agricultural leader, suicide in 1947.)

Philip Bouhler: Main account held in the name of Speck.
250,887 SF
(Head of Hitler's Chancellery, suicide in 1945.)

Leonardo Conti: Main account held in the name of "Lugano Arbeitsgemeinschaft."
1,620,000 SF
(Head of National Health Service, suicide in 1945.)

Franz Xavier Schwarz: Main account held in the name of Olsen.
8,175,000 SF
(Treasurer of the NSDAP, died 1947.)

Wilhelm Zangen: Main account held in the name of Beckmann.
22,876,901 SF
(German industrialist and banker. Some of these funds were returned to Zangen after the war.)

Friedrich Flick: Main account held in the name of Corvinus.
350,116,256 SF
(Leading German industrialist. Funds partially returned to Flick prior to 1948.)

These deposits alone total over 2 billion Swiss Francs of which only $32 million have been acknowledged by the SBA. These figures do not include funds belonging to non-Germans so the total of sequestered funds that were deposited by refugees, mostly Jewish, and Allied businessmen could very well run to three times that amount. Given that it is doubtful that any records remain in Swiss hands indicating which accounts were closed out, it is equally doubtful if anywhere near a full restitution will ever be made.

How much stolen art is still hidden in Swiss bank vaults is completely impossible to determine. Not included in this list are large amounts of German, Vichy French and other national gold holdings, some of which are specifically known to have been transferred to Switzerland before the end of the war.

Although the Swiss professed neutrality, they had no problem allowing enormous amounts of tainted money into their country while at the same time, the government in Bern officially sealed their borders to terrified Jewish refugees attempting to flee the Germans who invaded France in 1940. Unlike Stalin who ordered his border guards to shoot down any fleeing Polish Jews attempting to enter Soviet territory in 1939, the Swiss merely had their border guards turn the Jews away. In either case, the effect was the same.

The involvement of the Swiss government and their banking system with Third Reich monies is reasonably well known. What is not widely known is the role played by other neutral banks and financial institutions in hiding and converting German assets, before, during and after World War II.

In a US State Department report of 1947[1] it was estimated that after World War II the Germans still controlled about 750 German subsidiaries in

[1]*Department of State Bulletin Volume XVII No. 421, Washington, 1947.*

Portugal, Spain, Switzerland and Sweden and their assets in these countries amounted to $27 million in Portugal, $90 million in Spain, $250 million in Switzerland and $105 million in Sweden.

The Swedes became significant players in this field after World War I when many German companies, who manufactured and sold items of a military nature which were forbidden by the Versailles Dictate, sought the cover of neutral nations such as Holland, Switzerland and Sweden to continue with the building of submarines, aircraft and military hardware.

The most significant Swedish banking house which was involved in the concealment of German assets was the Enskilda Bank, which was controlled by the Wallenberg family. This family started in the banking business in 1856 when André Oscar Wallenberg founded Sweden's first privately owned bank, the Enskilda Bank, and the Wallenberg family eventually grew into the most powerful and influential family in Sweden. During World War I, the family acted as representatives for various German firms and after the German defeat became even more active in assisting German industry conceal the true ownership of various overseas holdings which also included extremely valuable industrial patents.

During the course of World War II, the neutral Swedes sold iron ore to the Germans, constructed naval vessels in their shipyards and sold the Germans an enormous number of vital ball bearings used primarily by the military. Although the Swedish companies producing these bearings were partially owned by German interests, the Swedes purported that they were the sole owners of the factories involved and produced reams of spurious documents to aid their claims.

The allies were furious with Sweden but were unable to halt the flow of strategic war material to their enemies. Threats were made and US military officials seriously suggested bombing the guilty Swedish plants. Fortunately, their suggestions were ignored but an angry Roosevelt administration hurled threats of blacklisting and seizure of Swedish holdings in the United States.

John Foster Dulles, brother of Allen Dulles, the OSS chief in Switzerland and later Eisenhower's Secretary of State, headed the legal team in the United States which was able to mitigate any substantive punishments. The Swedes agreed to extend large credits to Stalin, then a Roosevelt ally, and the threats gradually began to vanish. Several years after the war when Stalin's Soviet Union was viewed by the US as an enemy, pressure was again made on the Swedes to stop selling vital war material to Stalin.

As the Swedes had ignored repeated Allied orders to stop selling to the Germans, they also ignored US orders to stop the Soviet-Swedish trade.

After the war, the US believed that the Third Reich had shipped over $21 million in gold, most of which had been looted, to Sweden. The Swiss, according to the same report, received over $378 million during the same period.

The lower figure is not accurate and German secret records indicate that over $200 million were sent to Sweden. Some of this, 13 tons of gold, was returned to various European countries when it could be identified as having come from Belgium and the Netherlands, but the rest has officially remained unaccounted for.

Ascertaining the origin of bar gold is not difficult. Different state banks refine their gold holdings and add small but controlled amounts of various metals such as silver and platinum to the molten gold prior to its being poured into ingots and stamped with official markings. As Müller has indicated, gold which has been re-refined and has had the identifying additives removed or altered does not lend itself to easy identification.

The Wallenberg family owned enormous and profitable holdings in Sweden and continue to do so. Raoul Wallenberg, nephew of the head of the house, vanished in Hungary towards the end of the war. Many interesting and creative stories about his fate have been circulating since that time but as all of them originate from former Soviet sources, they cannot be taken with much seriousness. It is true that the post-*Glasnost* Russian government turned Wallenberg's passport and notebook over to his family but their accompanying story was vague and certainly not verifiable.

The former KGB was a veritable factory of disinformation and forgery. They have offered for sale the following "rare and historically valuable" files: Adolf Hitler (650 files with 70 thousand documents), Josef Goebbels (1140 files), Hjalmar Schacht (65 files), Otto Strasser (9 files), World War I German intelligence chief Walter Nicolai (90 files), IG Farben (6270 files), August Thyssen (12 files), and the Vienna branch of the Rothschild banking family (419 files).

Payment in US dollars is preferred and the ex-Soviets give their famous "blue smoke" guarantee of authenticity. When they see the blue smoke of some eager journalist's car driving towards the Moscow airport, the guarantee automatically expires.

The fate of young Wallenberg, seen at various times and places after the war in the Soviet Union by reliable witnesses, is as explainable as Müller's statement that he had Wallenberg shot by his one-time deputy, SS Colonel Willi Krichbaum, later an employee of the US CIA-operated Gehlen organization. In 1974, a man touted as a major defector from the KGB, Oleg Gordiefsky, went to work for British Intelligence and was whole-heartedly accepted as a truly valuable source. Gordiefsky joined forces with Christopher Andrew, an in-house historian for the British MI 5, and published a comment on Wallenberg to the effect that he, Gordiefsky, had seen the Wallenberg file in the secret KGB papers in Moscow. He claimed these files showed that the Soviets had executed Wallenberg in 1947. It was later discovered by US intelligence that Gordiefsky was a double-agent, and had never seen any Wallenberg file.

Mention was made of Vichy French gold which ended up in Spain. This was not transported in by Swiss diplomatic trucks like other huge shipments of gold, but was flown to Spain in 1944 in a German Ju-52 transport plane piloted by one of Müller's Gestapo agents.

After the Allied invasion in June 1944, German authorities in Berlin determined that bullion holdings of the French government which were still under their control should be flown to Berlin where they could be re-refined and shipped to Swiss, Swedish or Portuguese banks for safe keeping. The gold was taken from Paris bank vaults under heavy guard and loaded onto a waiting tri-motored transport. Also on the airfield were two Messerschmitt *BF 109* fighters, designated as escort aircraft to protect the gold-bearing transport until it landed in Berlin.

The pilot of the transport was a *Luftwaffe* officer, and also a member of the Gestapo. His destination was not Berlin, but Spain. To prevent any word of his defection reaching the authorities before he had crossed into neutral Spanish airspace and landed safely, the officer engaged in friendly conversation with the escort pilots. He asked to climb into the cockpits of their aircraft which were new models. He then stuck a screwdriver into the aircraft radios, disabling them completely.

The flight started at 1400 hours and after gaining altitude, headed east. A convenient and very extensive overcast permitted the transport pilot to turn in an unobserved half-circle while the unsuspecting escorts flew above him in the opaque cloud cover. When the Messerschmitt pilots emerged from the clouds near Luxemberg and discovered that they had been abandoned, they quite naturally attempted to radio this news to higher authority. Unable to do so, they circled for some time until their gas was low and finally landed in Germany. It was initially assumed that the transport had crashed or somehow been shot down by allied fighters. But the discovery that both radios had been crudely disabled raised the suspicion that the transport pilot had somehow made off with his cargo.

By the time this discovery was reported to Berlin and in particular Müller, the transport pilot was trying on civilian clothes he had packed in his suitcase and was, no doubt, filled with regrets at having to suffer the rest of the war somewhere on a Mediterranean beach, home to many enforced emigrants with comfortable bank balances.

Lord Acton once said that absolute power corrupts absolutely, but he should have added gold to his equation.

The primary interest of the American and British authorities in the immediate postwar years was to locate loot hidden by German institutions and individuals. Their actual purpose, of course, was not to restore it to its rightful owners but to become its rightful owners on a first come, first served basis. The Swiss and Swedish holdings were tempting targets but difficult to acquire since the countries involved had an equal interest in remaining the rightful owners. An unseemly squabble between British and US intelligence over who was entitled to find, exhume and possess the buried holding of Globocnik was frustrated by the lack of a proper map. When this was eventually located, neither of the two contenders were still looking and had other fish to fry.

In later years, yellow gold has been replaced by the white gold of the international drug cartels, and the astronomical sums generated by its sale has corrupted the highest government officials in every country where it is traded.

It has been said that the corruption of the best is the worst, but at this point in history, that qualification has no validity whatsoever.

Fine Art as a Commodity

During the course of the Second World War, the Germans systematically acquired all the fine art they could lay their hands on. France, Belgium, Holland, Poland, Soviet Russia and later, Italy, were stripped of paintings, sculptures, tapestries, silver, furniture, coins, rare arms and armor, wood carvings, prints and anything else of artistic or intrinsic value. The finest pieces were delivered to Hitler and were designed to be displayed in a huge museum complex located in his boyhood town of Linz in what had been Austrian territory. This project was called the *Sonderauftrag Linz* and was headed by Dr. Hermann Posse, formerly of the State Gallery at Dresden.

At the end of the war, there was a great descent by Allied art experts, and others less altruistically inclined, to locate the stolen art and, at least by the official commissions, to return it to the proper owners.

Much of this enormous treasure trove was recovered, but many precious items vanished. At least some of the missing pieces played a role in the Cold War.

Q The problem is, General, that some things are very difficult to merchandise, if you take my meaning.

M Clearly. But, they do represent assets, don't they?

Q Yes, they do, but one often needs to convert assets to cash and how can that be done with something that is easily recognized?

M I thought you were an art historian. Why ask me such a silly question? There are rich collectors that will buy anything just to have it and keep it locked up where only they can look at it—something behind a panel or in a hidden room somewhere.

Q But you just can't go around trying to sell such things openly.

M You might not be able to, but I certainly can.

Q And I am sure do.

M Perhaps, but I am a collector with pieces not on display, which you well know. Are you trying to put the knife into me just a little?

Q No, far from it. Just perhaps an inquiry about connections in the area.

M I thought you were making moral judgements again.

Q I try not to do that.

M Not a bad idea. Still, we have been helpful to each other, haven't we? I saw an article in the paper last night about a certain prominent Swiss citizen vanishing while on a hiking trip. Terrible tragedy for all concerned. They'll be dragging the lakes and peeking down into crevasses for weeks. Makes work for people so it must have a higher purpose. As I recall, I mentioned the name to you several weeks ago, didn't I?

Q I can't recall.

M I am probably in error. Still, there will be mourning in Moscow, believe me. One of their best sources went for a walk in the woods.

Q In this case, I think you are right. I have a question for you: If you knew who he was and what he was doing, why not have one of your people visit him?

M He didn't know I was here and he was not spying on me but you. Several Soviet creatures have vanished here over the years and I can't say I'm sorry about it.

Q What do you mean by "several"?

M Dozens. Several dozens perhaps. Old age, rich food, too much exercise, problems with their noses. That can be fatal. I can see from your expression that you wish to discuss other matters: Art.

Q Yes. Connections are always important. Selling off certain assets...

M Can be difficult, especially if you don't want them to be traced back to you in the end.

Q You have some lovely pieces, I must say...

M Certainly. I have developed an appreciation for fine art along the way, especially when I realized that it was portable and very saleable. It is an investment in my present and future, as it were. Banks are acceptable but art is better to look at. You were involved with the Linz business, weren't you? You must have seen some beautiful things then. There were enough of them around.

Q Too many.

M Did you keep any little mementos of your time in the service?

Q General, I really...

M No, of course not. You were on the side of the angels, of course. But such temptation for a man of taste without a great deal of money. Unlike you, I came from a family that was not rich. My father would have aspired to a Spitzweg at best...

Q Terrible stuff. We have a painter named Rockwell in the States who does generic art. Looks good on the cover of the "Post" but I wouldn't want to own one.

M Hitler was fond of that sort of thing. The quickest way to his heart was to give him a Spitzweg. They were forging them up all over the place in those days. No, I don't think I would be interested in such subjects.

Q I would think not.

M And when I come to visit your wonderful country, I intend to bring some of my better pieces with me. I think for company, more than anything else. I have the crates built for two pieces in particular. The coins I can carry in a suitcase.

Q I could guess which two you want.

M Do you agree with them?

Q Is the Bellini coming?

M No. I will leave the sacred here and take the profane with me.

Q The Signorelli? My choice would be that one first.

M Yes, we can agree on art at least...and some composers.

Q Why term it "profane"?

M The Bellini is a Madonna while the Signorelli deals with the pagan, Pan. A small joke. If I knew then what I know now, when I was in Rome, I would have driven up to Orvieto to look at the Signorelli frescos. That is something I regret not doing.

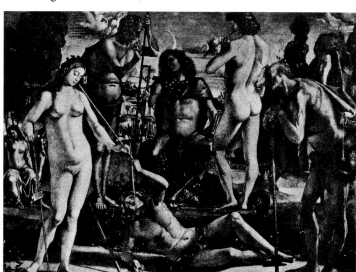

Luca Signorelli's "Pan," missing and once thought to have been destroyed in Berlin at the end of the war.

Giovanni Bellini's "Madonna and Child," which disappeared from the Kaiser Friedrich Museum in Berlin.

Raphael's "Portrait of a Gentleman": the "Czartoryski," once belonging to Hans Frank.

Q I have one on you there, General. I have seen them and they are stunning, but the Pan is far superior—his earliest work.

M There is a question about that but I would agree that it is certainly one of his earliest works. That's why it's hanging in my bedroom where I can see it just before I go to sleep and the first thing when I awake.

Q I envy you.

M Don't. I was just fortunate to have been in Berlin at the right time and have a friend who wanted a big favor from me. Marvellous payment, wasn't it? You know the other piece, of course.

Q The Raphael.

M Yes. Why not? It is a magnificent piece and the history is so complex. From the Czartoryski collection to Frank, then to Berlin, then back to Poland, then back to Germany at the end, and then into my hands. Too bad I couldn't bag **147**

the Leonardo as well. Now there was a stunning piece. My associate called her the "Lady with the Rat" but never mind. I had to make do with a Raphael. Still, for a poor Bavarian policeman, I have done quite well after all.

Q Bragging is so offensive…

M Especially when you wish you had bagged it. To get back to business now. I take it your people are looking for a safe outlet for certain art. You want the profits but not the mess or the danger in having it traced back to an American intelligence agency. You would have to dispatch all kinds of art dealers, their mistresses or boy friends, go-betweens and so forth. I can assist you if you wish but there will be a charge involved.

Q What sort of arrangements did you have in mind?

M Half at the time. No more, no less. I give you security and a guarantee of the best price. Does that sound acceptable? And perhaps we could do a bit of trading back and forth…

Q The Signorelli?

M No, and not the Raphael either. I could get you the Monbijou panels we talked about. I suddenly remembered where they might be now.

Q In Germany? They were last heard of in Königsberg…

M Berlin. Then in the Munich area and now here. I had thought about mounting them here but I think that was not a good idea. Besides, I don't have the furniture, and a room with the panels alone without the furniture would be flat somehow. There is a collector here in Switzerland who would buy the lot. I wish to keep three small examples for my own collection and your people get the balance in gold Swiss francs. I will get you the best price. I might even cut my half down to twenty-five percent if your people will let me have the Dürer you got from the Berghof collection. Don't shake your head…I know you have it put away. You couldn't sell it anyway, and I want it. Give me that, the three panels of my choice, and I guarantee millions in your pocket. Could anything be fairer?

Q Yes, you could be so grateful to us you could forget the Dürer.

M Gratitude is why I decided to give you this huge profit in gold in the first place. I know you are empowered to negotiate and I've given you a simple deal. If you agree, deliver the Dürer here and within 24 hours you will have your money in cash…in gold. You never even have to know the buyer.

Q I think we can work it out. Two Leonardo drawings are also available.

M Give me pictures. You know the procedure.

Q Perhaps you might be interested in them.

M Four framed Renoirs, a Monet and a decent Fragonard plus a small gold work by Cellini. Excellent craftsmanship but not attractive at all.

Q Leonardo is priceless after all! You want to trade for Renoir? Nonsense!

M The Cellini is well worth the drawings. I collect prints and perhaps I can comfort myself for having lost the Frank piece with some drawings. Think about it tonight and we can talk later.

Q On the panels, I am sure we will want to proceed at once.

M Having a problem with your annual budget, are you?

Q New agencies have trouble justifying the expenditure…

M You don't need to tell me about such things. We sometimes have similar problems. One of your superior's wife is a pianist of some note. I happen to have several original Chopin scores put away. Let me give them to you to present to him as a gift from my heart.

Q That certainly would help.

M And stop making eyes at the Czar's malachite box. I don't dislike you but that is too big a piece. A nice emerald ring presented by the Czar to a German Prince…actually a relative of his wife. She was German, you know…

Q Hessen.

M Prince Phillip of Hessen ended up in a concentration camp for giving information to the British. He won't miss the ring at all. A present to you.

Above: A tray of looted antique jewelry, a tray of snuff-boxes, and an ornamented silver casket, all found at the castle of Neuschwanstein in the mountains near Fussen, Bavaria.

Left: A member of the monuments, fine arts and archives section of the US Seventh Army examining the tray of antique jewelry.

Q In my experience, Bavarians are such gracious hosts.

M When I was in office, I would never have even considered doing what we are doing now. I acknowledge that towards the end of the war, I made it a point to secure my financial situation in the event that I managed to survive, and one thing simply led into another. From a poor, hardworking Bavarian police officer, I have more or less evolved into a dealer in fine art.

Q You certainly managed to sequester enough money. Why did you ever decide to involve yourself with art?

M Actually, because I began to like it. I have always been a careful person who likes to know exactly what I am doing and not make mistakes. So I began to study the market and to do that, one has to know something about the merchandise. I found that having actual pieces in my possession was far more rewarding than merely looking at pictures of them in a book. I enjoy my small collections and because I don't work as hard as I used to, I find it a way to occupy myself. I suppose working for your agency will reduce my time for collecting, but at this point in my life, not the interest.

Q You have access to quite a bit of valuable art that is not particularly famous. That is, unlike the "Lady with the Ermine", many smaller, though equally valuable pieces seem to have either passed through your hands or be in them. Even in bank vaults or wherever you have hidden them. I was requested to ask you if perhaps some smaller but valuable pieces might not be available to us for professional reasons.

M Do you expect these to be gifts or will there be some sort of exchange in return?

Q We have quite a bit that somehow fell through the holes and I don't think we want to be in the position where someone might find out about this. We could exchange some of the warmer pieces to you for items less problematical, if you follow me.

M I do. I know that there were vast numbers of smaller pieces in the Linz collection. Rupprecht was kind enough to ship me a few crates of these things, at least insofar as he had any control over them. You have seen some of my arms and armor in the hall and I can assure you that Rupprecht was one of the best in that field. On other pieces, he just used the inventories.

Q Like the coin collection.

M Yes. The Rothschilds can't possibly miss them and there is really no way they can be traced. In a few years, when I am ready, I will put them into auction just as I do with other pieces that are safe. I can take your 50,000 American dollars a year, triple that comfortably through the auction houses, and add the interest from my other investments, and I will make more money in a year than your President. It's too bad I couldn't get my hands on Globocnik's treasure but there are too many rivals in that field, aren't there?

Three paintings of great value—the one on the left is a Chardin, stolen from the famed Rothschild collection.

Also looted from the Rothschild collection during the German occupation of France—gold and hand-painted snuff-boxes.

Q It's a pity we can't, either. The British are frantically digging all around the Weissensee but haven't found a thing.

M I can sympathize with you. What sort of items would you be interested in?

Q Small pieces, preferably in gold. We did manage to get off with some of the *Reichsbank* gold and there was a terrible time smuggling it into the United States. I will tell you about that sometime. And it had to be melted down, refined, and have various metals added to change the composition so an analysis wouldn't reveal where it originated.

M I know about that game, believe me. I can tell you an interesting story about the Vichy gold and what happened to it. Flew it out to Spain in an Auntie Ju.* That was a fascinating story, but too long for this session. They had to rerefine it, just as you said. Franco got some of it; several SD people got some of it; and some came into the hands of a small company I have an interest in. Small items?

Q Yes. And another thing as well. Do you have any small pieces that we could present to various members of Congress? Unofficially, of course.

M Helps out with the appropriations, doesn't it?

Q Always.

M I have quite a few pieces that came up from Florence, some of which were supposed to go to Linz but somehow didn't. A very nice collection of small Della Robbia pieces. That would be perfect for you because many of these were made from molds and unless there are some special marks or perhaps catalog photographs, who can tell? They would be excellent for the religious people, but I think the Jews in your Congress would much prefer money. We can do something on that. I am surprised that your OSS people didn't get away with more when they were helping to return the pieces to their countries of origin.

Q Senior Army officers grabbed everything in sight. General Clay stole so much he had to get a special train to take it all to the docks. My God, that man is a regular pack rat. He stole doors, lighting fixtures, rugs, paintings, porcelain vases, sets of silver, tapestries and anything that he could get his hands on. A damned whole train full but most of the pieces were not considered art. Clay has no taste at all.

M My dear fellow, who does? Except for ourselves, that is. I have been watching you quiver when I show you something interesting. The set of pistols by Boutet made for Fouché, for example. He was Napoleon's Minister of Police and I have some affinity for him.

Q Did you read Zweig's biography of him?

M Yes. It was forbidden, you know, Zweig being a Jew and all, but I thoroughly enjoyed the book. A professional interest there.

Q Yes, and the pistols are magnificent.

M I have a hunting sword given to Napoleon that is a real masterpiece. He never hunted, of course, but the piece is a marvel of workmanship. And don't forget his breast star for the Legion of Honor. As a German, I have mixed feelings about Napoleon but as a collector, I can forgive much. A Swiss is interested in trading a very fine collection of Greek coins to my agent for a number of German 16-century wood carvings. One, I am sure, is a beautiful Madonna by Stoss which I want to keep, but perhaps the coins might be worthwhile. A very fine collection indeed.

---

*Junkers 52 transport airplane. The account of the fate of the Vichy gold appears in the previous chapter.

By all means draw up a list of the pieces you wish to dispose of and I will be very happy to see if we can work discreet exchanges. We should, by all means, keep your legislators happy and contented and by this contentment, eager to assist you. You should also keep discreet files on them just in case they have moral qualms at some point. I always did.

Historical Significance—Reflections of the Author

The looting of art objects by conquering armies did not begin in 1939 but the Germans were more organized and effective than Napoleon or the Allied troops who looted the Imperial Palace in Peking, China, after they suppressed the Boxer Rebellion in 1900. It was Hitler's aim to establish a huge museum complex in the provincial Austrian city of Linz where he had lived as a child. To this end, he set up the *Sonderauftrag Linz* where much of the art located by his agents in Europe was to be cataloged and eventually displayed in the projected museums. Hitler had rivals in this art collecting—Hermann Göring was the most prominent. But by and large, the Linz project garnered an enormous collection of the most valuable art in the world.

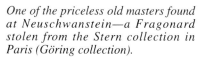
One of the priceless old masters found at Neuschwanstein—a Fragonard stolen from the Stern collection in Paris (Göring collection).

When the war ended, various Allied commissions, directed by the Americans, located most of this art and made attempts, mostly successful, to return it to the original owners. Many items, however, managed to disappear—some before the end of the war into the hands of Germans looking for portable treasures, and after the war into the hands of its liberators for precisely the same reason. Much of the *Reichsbank* bullion vanished into the purses of individuals

Art treasures found in Hamburg, believed to be von Ribbentrop's war acquisitions. The nude is an Ingres, the still-life a Manet.

as well as agencies. Many paintings, sculptures, rare books, manuscripts and other valuables have never surfaced in public since the war ended in 1945.

A careful analysis of Müller's holdings, as reported in his interviews, indicates that he was indeed in possession of extremely valuable art and was obviously engaged in buying and selling it.

The Signorelli mentioned is the "School of Pan," one of Signorelli's earlier paintings and is considered his masterpiece. It vanished in Berlin in 1945 when someone stole it from the holdings of the Kaiser Friederich Museum. The Bellini, a Madonna, also disappeared from the same holding at the same time. The Raphael mentioned belonged to the wealthy Polish Czartoryski family. It had been taken by the Germans, along with the famous Da Vinci picture titled "The Lady with the Ermine" and given to Hans Frank, the Governor of the former Polish territory. Frank brought the painting back to Germany since he had to evacuate his post as the Soviets advanced into Poland. The Raphael was taken from Frank by the Gestapo, and the Americans seized the Da Vinci and later returned it to the Poles. The Raphael painting, "Portrait of a Gentleman," is still listed as missing.

Of much greater historical interest are the so-called "Mon Bijou" panels mentioned by Müller as being available for sale. There is no record of any such "Mon Bijou" panels existing, but research indicates that in 1716, King Frederick William I of Prussia, father of Frederick the Great, presented the Russian Czar, Peter the Great, with a yacht, panels, and furniture made of amber from his Berlin palace of Mon Bijou in return for giant Russian soldiers for the Prussian King's military unit of tall men. These panels were installed in the Czar's palace near St. Petersburg, called the Amber Room and later removed by the Germans in 1941. The Russians took the amber furniture before the

Germans arrived. However, some of the panels remained and were later removed and returned to Germany. The panels have never been found and have become a bone of contention between the two countries.

A portion of the magnificent Amber Room as it appeared in 1930.

The Rothschild coins referred to consisted of a collection of over 2,000 rare gold coins taken from the Vienna branch of the Rothschild family and kept at the Hohenfurth monastery in Czechoslovakia for safe keeping. These coins were taken from the Linz collection in the last month of the war by Dr. von Hummel, Bormann's secretary, and Dr. Rupprecht, curator of Hitler's armor collection and an acquaintance of Müller. The collection was transported by car to Berchtesgaden and vanished from sight.

The value of the amber panels is impossible to determine, but the coin collection alone is worth over $4 million. The coins are easily converted to cash in the international numismatic market.

Both the Raphael and the Signorelli would be impossible to sell in public auction, but there are always wealthy collectors delighted to add such pieces to their private collections.

A large number of lesser-known items looted from the Linz collection at the end of the war, as well as items stolen by the armies of the victors from France, Italy and Germany, have without a doubt, passed through the hands of major international art auction houses and galleries. These agencies publish heavily illustrated catalogs and it might be instructive to read back issues and compare the art with the files of stolen property.

Excerpt on Raoul Wallenberg

Raoul Wallenberg, born August 4, 1912, was a member of a wealthy and influential Swedish banking family. In 1944, the Swedish Foreign Minister, Günther, sent Wallenberg to Budapest as a minor diplomat. Wallenberg vanished after the war, and his eventual fate has been a subject of speculation for half a century.

Q Your man Eichmann…actually he was your man, wasn't he?

M Yes, he worked for me. When I grew tired of the immigration problem in 1939, I eventually turned it over to Eichmann. During the war, his job was to find workers for SS projects and also evacuate Jews from areas we controlled. You haven't found him yet, have you? Who knows, he might be dead.

Q No, I don't think we have found him, but we really aren't interested in him. But when he was down in Hungary in 1944, I understand he had had some dealings with Raoul Wallenberg from the Swedish Legation there. Do you know about any of that?

M A very great deal. What do you want to know about that business?

Q There have been inquiries made by the Swedes about Wallenberg and I thought you might know something about him. There is a rumor that the Soviets have him somewhere.

M No, I am sure they do not have him, at least alive.

Q You think they killed him?

M No, I don't. Wallenberg was a small pawn in a very large game.

Q "Was?"

M Wallenberg is dead, just like Bormann.

Q Are you sure of this?

M I ought to be sure, under the circumstances. What do they say? "Knowledge is power." Isn't that right? I wonder why you are interested in an insignificant individual who disappeared in the mass destruction of a whole society. I said he is dead and he is still dead. What have you heard about this man?

Q The Soviets claim the Szalasi[1] people murdered him for interfering with the deportation of the Hungarian Jews.

M No, the Hungarians had nothing to do with Wallenberg's departure from this life. I speak to this with some authority because I had Wallenberg shot.

Q My God, don't say things like that. There will be terrible trouble…

M Not if you don't tell anyone, there won't.

Q Can you tell me what happened?

M Why not? I can make it very simple for you as you won't put it in a report, I am sure, or I can give you a little background if you want. I don't think you care…

Q About Wallenberg? Of course not, but I do care about you…

M How touching. I never knew…

Q Please, this is not the place for your unpleasant sense of humor. I care about your reputation I should say.

M Again I say, how touching of you. Do you want the story or are you going to give me flowers?

Q General…

M Well, the flowers can come later. Wallenberg was of the Swedish banking family. He was also a devoted communist. Don't interrupt. I said a devoted communist. He knew the Soviet Ambassador, Mrs. Kollontay. The Ambassador to Sweden. Quite a woman, that one. Intellectual woman and very quick. Wallenberg was seen as a good instrument and Kollontay went to Günther, the Swedish Foreign Minister, and persuaded him to send Wallenberg to Budapest to assist the Hungarian Jews there. Günther had no problem with this because of the family position.

But there are other matters here too, more important than a Swedish Jew in Budapest. In 1943, Stalin made certain overtures to us through Kollontay about a peace settlement. Hitler refused these out of hand but Himmler…Himmler was another matter. He was always looking towards his own future and he saw a strong connection with Sweden as valuable to him.

When Eichmann was transporting the Jews out of Hungary, at the repeated and strong request of their government, I might add, this Wallenberg set up his own private passport agency and was selling various passes and certificates to the Jews and anyone else who was willing to pay for them.

Q I understood he gave them out…

M Yes, for money. Eichmann called me and asked me what to do about this

[1] *Hungarian Premier, Ferenc Szalasi. He replaced Admiral Horthy in 1944 and headed an extremist right-wing political movement.*

person who was becoming a nuisance. The Hungarians were furious with him as well, because he was doing all manner of things that was hindering their expulsion of their Jews. I didn't care what the Hungarians thought about anyone but there were implications, especially when I learned that Wallenberg had extensive contacts with the Soviets at one time in his life.

This became a serious business so I went with it to Himmler who began to do his schoolmaster business with me. He obviously did not want to make a bad impression on the Swedes and counseled me to be discreet and inform Eichmann to leave young Wallenberg alone. By now, it was evident to anyone with any sense that the war was not going well for us and Himmler was playing many cards here and there, trying to keep himself out of trouble. He said to me then, "Müller, we must keep our eye on the future of Germany and our Order. It took us so long to build everything up and if we are not careful, it could all be gone in an instant. We must look to the future. Even a negotiated peace is not to be despised."

That I recall specifically because I made a note of it later that day. I told Eichmann to get me all the information he could on Wallenberg and send it to me by courier—which he did. I had some connections in the Hungarian police, and I made use of them to learn what I could and in the end, I put together a picture of an intellectual, rich young man with a bent for radical politics—just the sort of clay that a master sculptor like Mrs. Kollontay would love to get her hands on. We didn't need any more Soviet agents in Hungary at that time, especially ones who were using diplomatic immunity to sell fake papers to God knows who. I thought about it for a few days and then decided

Raoul Wallenberg.

that Himmler or not, I would take care of the business myself. I contacted one of my more reliable men and told him to discreetly dispatch Wallenberg and anyone connected with him. Also, I wanted any documents that could be found. And I stressed "discreet," believe me. I was later told that everything went well and Wallenberg was dead.

Q Was your source trustworthy?

M You know him, fairly well, I believe.

Q Who?

M Do you really want to know who shot him in the head and buried him under a dung heap in the Budapest suburbs?

Q I have to know this. I must know whom I'm dealing with after all.

M Our mutual friend, Willi.

Q My God. You mean Krichbaum?

M If Gehlen and your people love him, leave it be. Of course, if it ever comes out about Wallenberg, there will be trouble.

Q Sometimes I dread these meetings.

M Now, one minute you tell me how much you care for me, and the next you want a divorce. Such inconsistency. If you ask questions, you will get answers, even though you aren't happy with them...

Q Not with this business. I hope you have about run your course with problems for us.

M I am not making problems for you. Wallenberg was making problems for Germany, and I personally had him neutralized. Do you like that word? "Exterminated" sounds better? "Liquidated?"

Q You didn't bury the poor man under a dung pile did you?

M Ask Willi about that. I would be unhappy if he lied to me.

Q Can't we just let this drop now?

M Certainly. Will you be staying to dinner this evening? Or are you feeling ill?

Q No, just a little unnerved. Who, by the way, were the gangsters going into the back entrance when I drove up?

M Gangsters? I think all the gangsters are in Chicago. Who are you talking about?

Q People in dark coats with what looked like weapons in boxes. You are not up to anything unpleasant are you? A Saint Bartholomew's slaughter after dinner?

M Oh, now I know what you are talking about. You saw some musicians coming in with their instruments. I thought a little musical evening might be in order after the dinner. You do like music, don't you?

Q Yes, of course I do. They did look rather sinister.

M You've been too long in intelligence agencies.

Q What sort of program?

M Now, do I tell you about my menu in advance? Aren't you always surprised at what comes onto the table?

Q I have no complaints about that.

M Maybe you would like Russian folk music? African war dances? Perhaps a little Mozart or Bach? Some Negro jazz? Be a good man and wait and see. Now, you wanted to ask me about some really important matters, didn't you? Or are you still interested in dead intellectual Bolsheviks?

Q Yes. I mean no. I am not interested in such things. And for God's sake, when the Admiral's man comes next week, do not discuss such things with him. We understand your humor, but they don't.

M Such disappointments. By the way, that's a very nice tie you're wearing today. Where did you get it?

Q In London. Would you like one? I bought three at the time.

M How thoughtful of you, young man. I would rather have had the flowers but a nice tie will do very well. Shall we proceed?

Historical Significance—Reflections of the Author

Raoul Wallenberg has appeared as a minor character in the historical annals of the Second World War and is credited with saving the lives of thousands of Hungarian Jews as the Hungarian government and German SS sought their deportation in 1944. Wallenberg was credited with giving away reams of Swedish permits and documents, which stated that the bearer was a Swedish citizen exempt from deportation.

In 1940, Spanish and Portuguese consular officials in France provided similar documents to many Jews and permitted them to enter their countries en route to safer havens. In 1943, when Germany occupied Vichy France, Italian diplomats saved thousands of terrified French Jews the same way. And, a Japanese diplomat in the Baltic provided a similar humanitarian service. Unfortunately, American diplomats were under specific instructions by a senior State Department official, Breckenridge Long, not to give refugee Jews any kind of transit papers. When prominent American Jews brought this matter to the attention of President Roosevelt, he supported Long's policy.

It should be noted that the humanitarian acts performed by various diplomatic officials were not done with profit in mind. Wallenberg vanished at the end of the war, and there are several versions of his disappearance. One scenario is that the Hungarians murdered him for interfering in the deportation process and another version is that the Soviets seized him after the war and he died in a Soviet prison in 1947. The Russians gave some of his personal effects to his family during the advent of *Glasnost* in 1989. It is doubtful that

Müller would take credit for an act that had serious propaganda consequences But at the time of his interviews, the United States had other fish to fry besides the Wallenberg affair, and it is evident from the interviewer's remarks that the issue should be ignored.

The Russians now claim that they imprisoned Wallenberg and he died in their captivity. Why they should have arrested him in the first place has never been explained, but the convoluted thought processes in senior Soviet political and intelligence agencies defies rational analysis.

Müller was considered a die-hard nationalist who strongly opposed any negotiated peace with the US or the Soviet Union. He sabotaged such offers, all of which came from Stalin, at every opportunity and ruthlessly pursued any German who attempted to implement them. Because of his strong opposition to communism and the Soviet system, US disinformation that he went to work for Stalin after the war borders on the idiotic, in the same category as the notorious "single bullet" theory put forward during the investigation into the assassination of President Kennedy.

Very evident from this fragment is Müller's ruthlessness in his public actions as opposed to his urbane private face. Also evident is the attitude of his visitor towards Müller's actions.

The Admiral mentioned was Admiral Roscoe H. Hillenkoether, Director of the CIA from May of 1947 to October of 1950.

Müller himself was an accomplished classical pianist. His chief, Reinhard Heydrich, was a violinist of comparable achievement. When time permitted, the two participated in musical evenings with other musicians. An observation from the notes of his chief American questioner states: "On Saturday, I found General Müller in a creative mood. He entertained us with a rendition of the entire *Klavier* solo from Bach's Brandenburg Concerto No. 5, allegro movement. A *tour de force* after a fashion…" and in the same entry:… "the dinner was followed by a concert in which we heard, among other works, a superb rendition of the Telemann Viola Concerto in G which Müller says is his favorite work and which was, although very short in length, a beautiful example of its kind."

To Each According to His Need

In modern history, the use of civilians to attack invading or occupying armies began during the Franco-Prussian War in 1870. This was raised to a fine art by the communists during the course of their empire building and in 1948 was a subject of some concern to the United States whose intelligence agencies were considering using the same methods on the communists in Europe in the event of a Soviet attack. Vietnam, Afghanistan, and various eruptions in Central America were still in the future.

Q I do agree that your agency was not specifically involved in the partisan movement, at least as far as interdiction is concerned, nevertheless, you do have some knowledge of the workings of the apparatus, don't you?

M Of course, some knowledge. In France and Greece, I had some experience and less perhaps in Italy. The rest of Europe was relatively peaceful, but I don't consider the Balkans as a part of Europe after all.

Q In the event the Russians make a military move into Europe, we know they will make the most of their supporters and actual agents in these areas.

M Certainly they will. They have in all countries, including your own, cadres of personnel waiting orders from Moscow as to when and where to strike. Please note here that all orders to partisan bands come only from Moscow. Local commanders are given no latitude whatsoever. Stalin does not permit independent actions ever.

Q Do you have knowledge of these dormant groups?

M Very difficult until they start to raise their heads. In France, for example, we knew that there were a number of communist groups but until we attacked Stalin in 1941, we never had any trouble with them. Quite the opposite. The French communists were ordered to cooperate fully with us until then and they did. After June of 1941, they became our enemies and did their best to provoke us to take actions against the general French population. This failed because the average Frenchman had no interest in making trouble and merely wanted his peace and quiet. German occupation troops were under strict orders to behave properly to the civilian population and they did.

Q The French Resistance was quite powerful, wasn't it?

M Nonsense. Both our counterintelligence agencies and the French police had little trouble with them. There were, after all, only a few thousand such people, and they were relatively ineffective in the end. I have read accounts about huge battles in post-war books, but I can tell you that is all nonsense. The so-called resistance movements were divided between the de Gaulle people and the communists, and they spent most of the time denouncing each other to the Germans or the French.

Q You did damage them in the end. I read that 50,000 Frenchmen were executed for their roles in the Resistance....

M Such nonsense. No more than several hundred at best. I must have read a thousand reports both from my people and the SD, and I can assure you that the number executed was no more than 300. The number of dead on their side inflicted by each other was far in excess of this figure and after the war...

Q Oh yes, I know about that. Everyone denounced everyone else, and there was great slaughter after the Germans left.

M Like the Czechs, after all. Oh now they tell a great story about great resistance to us but believe me, they were docile and turned out weapons for the Germans until the last. When Heydrich was killed in 1942, it wasn't the Czech underground that did it but British assassins.

Q I recall Lidice...

M So do I. I had a hand in that action, believe me. It emerged from searches made by our security people, on many tips from the Czechs themselves let me say, that the agents had been hiding in Lidice. One of them had a relative in the town, and we found a hidden room in a barn with British weapons, uniforms, papers, explosives and radios. That was the end of that nest of spies, I can tell you. I was at a meeting with Himmler present when the punishment of the protectors of the killers was brought up. I must say that I repeatedly insisted that we must make an example of such creatures and shoot the lot of them. No women or children but everything else. Our informants inside the town said everyone seemed to know about this and we heard these stories from a half a dozen Czechs so there went Lidice, and I could frankly care less.

No, we had little trouble with the Czechs, and the French were too busy robbing and killing each other to be of much damage. We had complete control of the Dutch underground; the Danes were a pacifistic joke.

I think only the Poles had any real courage. I think that, as I have said before, the Poles are stupid barbarians, but they did continue to fight us. Of course, we continued to counter them. You recall the Warsaw rising in 1944? They did fight us but then, let me say, so did the Jews in Warsaw. I don't suppose they wanted to be done away with so, for the first time, the Jews actually fought

SS General Jürgen Stroop (center) during the Warsaw Uprising.

back. They put up quite a fight, too. Stroop, our SS commander, told me that they really surprised him. I suppose you know that the Polish police rushed in as soon at word of the rising in the ghetto reached them, and were eager to take the opportunity to slaughter as many Jews as they could. The Poles were not nice. You were telling me about their police butchering sick Jews at Auschwitz after we left the place in their care.

Of course, the Jews now hate us with a passion but I can tell you that they hate the Poles almost as much. I suppose now that they have their own country, they will start in putting Arabs in concentration camps. People are so predictable, aren't they? And let us not talk about the Jews anymore. You want to know about the communists and their organizations.

Q General, sometimes I find your attempts to avoid responsibility for the actions of your people quite unpleasant.

M Our actions? Do you read history? Let me mention something to you...give you a little story here. A European power is occupying, by military troops, a neighboring country. The citizens of this country, naturally, are unhappy about the occupation and express their desire to be free. The occupying power makes use of locally raised police to assist them in keeping order but eventually, the citizens rise up and try to overthrow their enemies. There are very severe military reprisals with unarmed civilians brutalized, imprisoned without trial and finally, shot dead in the streets. Partisans begin to attack the occupying power, a little unorganized in the beginning but, with outside aid from your country, make serious problems for their overlords.

So far, this sounds very much like what we have been talking about, doesn't it? And the occupying power increases its control and sends in an army of mercenaries who commit all manner of terrible atrocities against the civilians, such as raiding their homes, murdering the occupants from time to time, and looting and burning while drunk. The partisan warfare escalates, and terrible atrocities are committed on both sides until the occupation troops are suffering far greater losses than their enemies. Would you say that sounds like the situation in Russia after we invaded? The Balkans?

Q I would say that was fairly typical of the pattern of German aggression and brutality during the war. Yes, in Russia for certain, but from my own experience, in Italy as well.

M Perhaps you are right. I had in mind Ireland from 1916 to 1922.

Q Oh for God's sake...

M But it is true, you see. I knew many Irishmen, some of whom worked for the Army until we took over their intelligence units. Oh yes, I speak English as you know, and I have heard many such stories. The British don't publish White Papers about their behavior, but I think if you put your mind to it, you will find that I am quite correct. I usually am quite correct, am I not?

Q Not always.

M Always. I don't open my mouth until I am sure. Once I thought I was wrong, but I found out later I was in error. Look it up. Not the Germans, my dear friend, but your friends and allies.

Q Justification...

M I don't need to justify and you know it. I have had the opportunity of dealing with assassins and professional communists before. If I can use someone, or I can get information from them, all well and good but if not, off to the woods in a minute.

I can tell you that Hitler once said that terror could only be broken with counter-terror. He was right, and while I did not always agree with him on that issue, we were in perfect accord. If such business breaks out in Europe, you will yourself do just as I have said. You will start out by being astonished that the sheep have bitten you and will end up with a good deal of mutton on the table.

You plan to wait until Ivan has poured into Europe and then you will eradicate the traitors and partisans. Why not save all of us the trouble and we can do it now? The Russians believe in the scorched earth policy so why not be taught by them and move first? The world would be better off with a few hundred active partisan leaders under the ground in a literal sense. It is better to step on the poisonous snake the moment it is hatched from its egg than to let it mature to the point where its bite could be fatal to you. Smash it now, not later.

Of course, there are several points to consider here. In the first place, I seriously doubt if the Soviets will physically invade Europe. You have had my reasons on that before, and you will no doubt have them again in the future. If they do not invade, and I am sure that you will have ample warning of this invasion, then it might not be politically expedient to go about slitting the throats of such men as Malreaux.

On the other hand, we had a program called Night and Fog wherein we simply snatched up such individuals and made them permanently vanish. That has its advantages as well. Messy assassinations, on the other hand, serve as a very public and immediate warning of what is to come to others who might want to put their feet on the path of sedition and treason.

In our country and yours, there was an immense fifth column composed of trade unionists, university professors, students, pseudo-intellectuals and the like just waiting for the call from the Kremlin to do their dirty work. Even with the Soviet pact in place, I never for an instant forgot who our real enemies were, and not once during the time it was operative did I stop my work. I only kept it under cover, and of course, Hitler knew that this was to be a very short marriage indeed. Stalin, I believe, actually thought that we were fooled by his cooperation...did you know that they even gave us the names of some of their sympathizers in various countries as a token of their good will? Oh yes. And actual people as well. No doubt those whom they wanted us to liquidate because Stalin had become unhappy with them.

Anti-bandit warfare is really very simple if you understand the communist mentality. In an occupied country, or in your own country for that matter, there are always elements that are potential troublemakers. You cannot, as Mr. Wisner wants, simply send out armed units to arrest and execute all these people. Regardless of your views on Germany, we were basically a country of laws and such behavior, although entirely justified, would have caused great unrest among the others. They would wonder, I think, if they would be next, and such people can become very restive. Read how Joseph Fouchè brought down Robespierre. Here was a man of almost no power facing the virtual dictator of France, a man who had instituted the Terror and who was feared and obeyed by everyone. Fouchè used this Terror against its instigator by whispering to the delegates of the Assembly that their name was on one of Robespierre's death lists and frightened them into taking collective action against him, which they did and within a few hours, the monster was dead under the knife of his own guillotine. You would do well to read about Fouchè.

Q I have, and I know what you are talking about, but as you said earlier, mass arrests and executions are not possible, at least at the present time.

M Who knows what the future will bring? Your country, in spite of being a loudly touted democracy, is quite capable of such behavior if its past history is any indication. Your Attorney General began a *razzia* against radicals after the 1914 war, didn't he?

Q Palmer. Yes, of course Wilson was incapacitated with a stroke and Palmer could do what he wanted. Parenthetically, Hoover was one of his top aides in those days.

M You see, you can get Hoover and his men to do this, that is, if Hoover is anti-communist...

Q Which he is. Very much so.

M We have these conversations about what might happen. It is well for all of us to remember that what is now in the past was once in the future,

Q I learned that in university.

M I hardly claimed it as original. I doubt if there are very many original thoughts. We think we have a new idea only to find out that some Greek philosopher said the same thing in 200 BC. But what I said is true. We can worry about the future as much as we wish, but it is only when it becomes the past that we can understand it, and only after a hundred years have passed to let passions cool.

Q Our Civil War is a case in support of that point. It has been less than a hundred years since it was over and a rational, balanced view of it still hasn't come forward.

M And as both of us have an interest in fine art, consider that an artist living and working now lives and dies in complete obscurity. A hundred, or even two hundred, years later, his work brings huge sums in the marketplace, while some of the popular artists end up in the dustbin. Everything changes and certainty is illusion. Now we have had our philosophy lesson for the day and we can get back to discussing the matter at hand. And, I believe that was guerrilla warfare.

Aside from your campaigns against the British during your revolution, your country has no experience with this form of warfare. Nor did ours, and it is this inexperience that gives the partisan his edge. The British had experience of rebellion in their empire but in India, for example, they crushed such activity with a terrible ruthlessness that warned others to take care what they said and did. They decided to invade the Zulu territories, thinking they were up against a handful of spear-throwing blacks only to suffer a terrible military defeat at the hands of these same savages. One can imagine the fury in Whitehall and the terrible reprisals inflicted on the blacks later. This animal is dangerous: When attacked, it defends itself. But, we are not talking here about those who are invaded but about subversive rebellions from within, encouraged, ordered and supplied from without.

Now that Roosevelt is dead, the communists in your country have had their head cut off, but they will grow a new one. Maybe Wallace will become President yet. Who knows? And if that shows signs of happening, kill him quickly. Best to get some crazy leftist to do it. That's Stalin's way with political assassinations. Never use a leftist to do that sort of thing. Get someone from the right to do it, and move the accusing finger in another direction. You shouldn't have any trouble finding some idiot to stand up and point a gun at someone you wish to remove permanently. I personally prefer the heart attack or the automobile accident to the assassin because the accident or the health problem is never questioned. Something in the milk, some culture, and the man is dead of liver disease within two months. A post mortem discloses his liver has gone, and that is the end of the matter. Blame the microbes. And, this has the added advantage of not having a live assassin to question, and perhaps prompt, to say inconvenient things in public.

But running an assassination bureau is not what is wanted here, is it? I will have no problem on setting up an internal program to deal with the professional partisan, none whatsoever. And these you must treat differently from the intellectual idiots. The former should be quietly killed in a private way, and you can watch the others. If they get too dangerous, arrest them for tax problems or disgusting sexual behavior with farm animals. That effectively ruins their reputations and makes their audience turn away in disgust. Suppose it was revealed at the time that V.I. Lenin kept a sheep under his desk? People would laugh at him, and no one would pay the slightest attention to him. There are many ways to deal with such people, killing being the least desirable.

Q I think your true nature is starting to show, General.

M My true nature? Tell me what that is. At home or with my friends I am one thing, but in the office, in uniform and on duty, quite something else. I leave my uniform and cap at the front door, believe me.

Q At the front door of your office?

M No, of my home. And I should tell you that the Canaletto drawings came in today on approval, and I should like to have you look at them with me. It would be a pleasant change from the discussions here, don't you think?

Historical Significance—Reflections of the Author

It has been very accurately said that one man's freedom fighter is another's terrorist. As Müller points out, it all depends on one's point of view. In a historical context, both Germany, Soviet Russia, Great Britain and the United States have been occupying powers and all have suffered the ravages of guerrilla warfare: Germany in Europe and Russia, Britain in half of the world, the Soviets in their own country and eastern Europe, and the United States in Southeast Asia. All of these powers dealt with their dissidents in the same way: extensive use of force and terror. Concentration camps have been called "detention" or "relocation centers" but in the final analysis, they are prisons where the politically dangerous are caged, often tortured, and left to the ravages of disease, hunger and neglect.

The Regional Interrogation Centers of the CIA in Vietnam differed little from their counterparts of the Gestapo or the NKVD. The aims of these entities was to elicit information and destroy the will to resist in the occupied countries. Extensive exposure of these methods have done absolutely nothing at all to eradicate them—witness the barbarity of the Serbs against their neighbors in Bosnia and Croatia.

A low-key controversy has been bubbling for a number of years concerning the deaths of a large number of German prisoners of war in the months following the end of the Second World War. Revisionists claim that after the collapse of Germany, huge numbers of prisoners were left in exposed, outdoor camps with only meager rations—certainly not enough for all of them—and the death tolls were tremendously high. Apologists for the captors claim that while there were a few deaths, due to natural causes, a pattern of deliberate starvation and neglect did not occur.

Dwight Eisenhower, Supreme Allied Commander in Europe, has been singled out for blame in this matter. Although blame is difficult to place, it should be noted that Eisenhower despised the Germans, not just the defeated military but *all* Germans. Some apologists have credited Eisenhower's loathing of Germans to his discovery of the horrors in the concentration camp system. However, Müller's papers contain a thick dossier on Eisenhower that may offer a different reason for his attitudes and actions. According to what appears to be a thoroughly researched study, one of many kept on Allied leaders both political and military, the Eisenhower family was Jewish and emigrated to the United States in the 19th century from the Saxon city of Pirna. If this is true, it would explain Eisenhower's hatred of Germans. It would also explain why Müller retired from US government service in 1952, albeit as a Brigadier General of reserve, just prior to Eisenhower's inauguration as President. It is doubtful if the new President was ever informed of the actual identity of one of the senior intelligence advisors in the previous administration.

The State of the Union

For the most part, the interviews with Heinrich Müller were conducted by James Kronthal, CIC station chief in Bern, Switzerland. Towards the end of the lengthy transcript, Kronthal was joined by a senior member of the CIA, flown over from Washington at the request of Admiral Hillenkoetter, then the director of that agency. The second interviewer is only identified by his military rank throughout the transcript.

Here, the newcomer is identified as "Q-2," and Kronthal as "Q-1."

Q-1 We have all been introduced and I believe my associate has a number of points he would like to clarify with you. If you don't mind…?

M Not at all. I trust your accommodations are satisfactory, Colonel, and should you have any requests, please give them to me at any time. By all means, let us go on.

Q-2 Thank you, sir. As to accommodations, I am more than satisfied and perhaps I can stretch this out so as to enjoy them better. Now…(pause) here I have a number of points of information that I have been requested to present to you. In the first place, my associate here has, as I understand it, discussed the financial aspects of this matter with you?

Q-1 Yes, we covered that earlier.

M Quite acceptable to me, with my conditions, of course.

Q-2 Conditions?

Q-1 I mentioned this to you. About his agents.

Q-2 Oh yes, of course, we covered that. Washington has no problem with that business so if we have this out of the way…?

M Then go on, please?

Q-2 Let me give you a picture of the problems we have had over the last ten or fifteen years with internal espionage and then you can give me any suggestions that you might have. This may take some time. Are you planning to take notes? I can always repeat myself if you want me to do so.

M No, no, I have a good memory and I don't need to take notes. Please proceed.

Q-2 Very Well. The basic problem lies with the late President Roosevelt and his attitude towards international communism. Roosevelt was a very astute domestic politician, as you might know, and found that the American communists were very powerful in the labor movement and in other areas so he openly courted their support in his elections. He came into office at the height of the Depression and had very little experience with economics so he began to seek advice from the more radical of the economists—the far left wing as it were. When these persons saw that Roosevelt knew nothing about the economy and was not opposed to their attitudes, they began to draw more and more of their kind into the new agencies Roosevelt set up to administer his various policies.

At the same time, we had very radical Jewish elements coming into the government in social welfare programs and of course they too brought in their friends, relatives and political cronies so that even before the war broke out, the bureaucracy was either controlled or directed by the very far left.

Now this left can be broken down into several levels. One level, the management level, was run by political activists—either communists or radical socialists which is a difference without much of a distinction. They convinced Roosevelt of the rightness of their various agenda, and in most cases, he willingly went along with them. The second level consisted of muddleheaded intellectuals who ran around interfering with what they saw as the repressive landlord class in every way that they could. Combining the two groups, we had a parasitic growth on the body politic that you simply could not believe.

M Oh, I can easily believe it. Look at Spain in the Middle Ages.

Q-2 A point well taken. The Marranos ran Spain.

M Until the institution of the Holy Office, that is.

Q-2 Again, well taken. Cleansing the stables, as it were, was vital for the growth of Spain as a Spanish and Catholic country.

M More expulsions and burnings.

Q-2 We don't plan on going that far. I would say a few thousand voluntary departures would not do America any harm.

M We do understand each other in this.

Q-2 As the war came, Stalin activated many of these intellectual communists and sent in many of his own agents. He wanted to be sure of Roosevelt's support and also to find out what American intelligence knew. Roosevelt put Donovan in as head of the OSS and told him specifically that he believed that only communists could effectively deal with the partisans in Eastern Europe. In fact, the President instructed Donovan to allow as many active communists as possible into the OSS.

General William "Wild Bill" Donovan, head of the Office of Strategic Services (OSS).

M I well know about this from my own experience. I am in complete agreement with your analysis. The ones we captured and executed when we could, were without any doubt, agents of Moscow.

Q-2 Not the United States. They served Moscow first.

M It was my experience that both the communists and the Jews served either Moscow or their co-religionists and had no loyalty to their country.

Q-2 Their country of welcome, as they say.

M Exactly so.

Q-2 Now, the intelligence agencies, which included the military branches, knew what was happening but we discovered that any attempt to expose or punish Soviet spies would be grounds for immediate dismissal from the service. When we found their spies operating inside the atom bomb project, we were told that Roosevelt personally forbade us to touch any of these people. We were also strictly forbidden to listen in on their radio contact with Moscow, but of course we paid no attention to the President, because that is an area that he had no control over.

I recall that one time the Army made a recording of Mrs. Roosevelt having a lesbian affair with her secretary in a hotel room. They were looking for Joe Lash, a communist agent who was friendly with the Roosevelt creature and hoped to get some information on his activities. When the President heard about this, he was in a fury for weeks and punished everyone he possibly could. The recordings still exist and having heard them, I could suggest that Eleanor ought to hire a drama coach.

M I think that if anyone in Germany had made a recording of Eva Braun, I would have been given orders to shorten them by a head immediately. Democracies are so forgiving.

Q-2 That is the point exactly. Here we were, knowing that Soviet agents were running loose all over Washington, going in and out of the Pentagon, rummaging through all our most secret papers and aware that any attempt to stop them would result in instant punishment from on high. I can tell you that all you could hear in Washington the day Roosevelt died was the popping of champagne corks in officers' messes. We didn't know about Truman, of course, but we thanked God that lunatic communist, Wallace, wasn't next in line. Depending on how the new President felt, there was serious talk in the higher headquarters about conducting a purge in Washington and I mean the kind of purge Hitler carried out in 1934. Shooting about 200 high-level New Deal people would have been a real pleasure.

M Oh, I can certainly identify with that attitude. Only the one who tended to the communists and Soviet agents was myself and I was somewhat more subtle but many more than 200 went behind the wire or under the knife, believe me. And I slept very well at night because of it. I have great fondness for dogs but rabid ones have to be shot on sight to protect everyone else. Still, I trust you are not planning any bloodlettings in Washington.

Q-2 No, please don't be concerned about that. It's too late now, anyway.

M In my experience, one does not need to send out the military and shoot people in the streets. I was always more concerned for public order than that. If it were necessary to remove a traitor who might be well placed, I used the heart attack, the road accident and the suicide. The heart attack was the best. I kept a doctor on the staff who complained to me that he was getting a sore thumb from all the injections he gave people. But much less mess and no need to cover these things up. Car accidents were always unpleasant and suicides not always easy to arrange, so I settled on the heart attack. After all, think of how difficult it would be to lure a seventy-year old cripple up into the mountains and shove him over a cliff. There are bound to be witnesses and inconvenient relatives who wonder what Uncle Hans was doing trying to climb up the Watzmann in a wheelchair. On the other hand, if Uncle Hans was found dead in his bed from a heart attack, who would suspect?

The doctor, by the way, was French. He had fled from his country because too many wealthy persons had heart attacks while under his care and questions were eventually asked of their suddenly rich relatives. I found him useful and I might add, a very good cook. He used to whip up excellent salads and light lunches for us in Berlin and I can still remember his lamb with garlic.

Q-2 Sounds like our kind of person. I don't suppose…

M Oh, I am certain he could bring his medical and his culinary talents into your headquarters without any problems.

Q-2 We can talk about this later. Does it always work? And are there any traces? **173**

M First answer is "yes," and the second is "no". Here, you are dealing with a professional, after all!

Q-2 I assume you mean your doctor?

M I mean myself. Do you think I would have some spastic butcher around that injected dog urine into people's hearts?

Q-1 General, please…

M My friend has such a sense of propriety. Please go on.

Q-2 It's all right. I find the General refreshingly frank. Now, we have conducted some minor operations against agents in place; true, but your man sounds delightful. Let me progress here. Truman very cautiously began to shut these people down as soon as he could but his problem was that as a Democrat, he could not attack the circle around Roosevelt without losing the support of his party. And even mass heart attacks couldn't begin to touch the problem. I will say that actual agents died rather fast, but how could we shoot the Secretary of Commerce or Labor? You can't do things like that.

M Well, perhaps a burglar could bag one of them, but you can't wipe out the former Cabinet, I agree.

Q-2 And, for example, one of the top men in the FBI was one of their people. How can you get at him? If we told Hoover, God knows what he would have done.

M A night of long knives, I agree, is counter-productive except that it not only removes traitors without the bother and expense of trials, but puts the fear of God into the rest. Of course, they just go to ground and then you have to either dig them out of their holes or find some other means of getting rid of them.

Q-2 We could gas them, couldn't we General?

M Such an unkindness, Colonel. I detect a certain reference here about the Jews?

Q-2 Well, most of the spies are Jewish.

M That wasn't my experience. Jews were activists in Germany and certainly ran the NKVD for Stalin, but most of our traitors were intellectual Germans. I told your friend here that I do not wish to get involved in any further persecution of the Jews.

Q-2 I was only speaking in humor to you.

M And besides the bureaucracy and the President's highest level helpers, where else have the agents gathered?

Q-2 Some in the military, very many in universities and far more in the motion picture industry. Oh, and of course, in the labor unions. You see, we have to first neutralize them, which we have done by removing most of them from access to sensitive material and by supporting anti-communist labor leaders and encouraging them to drive out all of the New Deal communists. In those areas we have been very successful. The universities and the motion picture industry are more difficult to deal with.

M If you could bring some of this out in the open, say by official publicity, you might be able to stir up the public enough to allow you to conduct employment purges.

Q-2 Yes, that's our aim now. If we can obtain solid information from you and couple it with our own material, we can attack these swine and get rid of them.

M Don't attack them yourself. No, no, get someone or some other group not connected with the government to go after them. Then you can reap the benefits of the exposure without taking the blame for the results. A lamb of God could deliver sermons against these pests, and of course, with information provided to him. What about Father Coughlin?

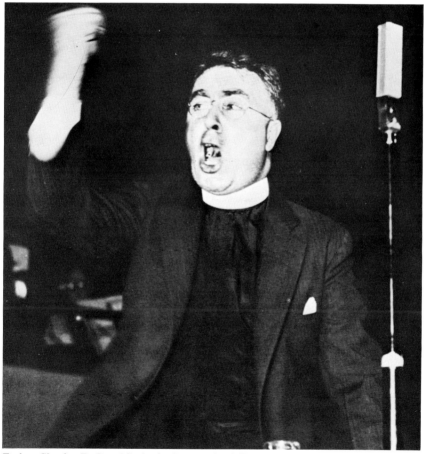

Father Charles E. Coughlin had a huge radio following and broadcast every Sunday from the Shrine of the Little Flower in Royal Oak, Michigan. He was an avid anti-communist and anti-Roosevelt, calling the President a "great betrayer." He also attacked "the Jewish bankers," labor unions and industrial capitalists. Coughlin and his political views were finally silenced on radio by mid-1940, after intense pressure from many quarters.

Q-2 Roosevelt made a deal with the Pope and he was shut down. I believe we can use someone in Congress to do this. Tydings comes to mind but there are others.

M Yes, give them the information and let them use it. Then, you can always stand back as a neutral party and weigh in at just the right time.

Q-1 I told you this man is a jewel, didn't I?

M Shame on you praising me to my face. You will give me such a big head that I can't wear my hat anymore. I have bribed this man with fine wines and good cigars to say nice things about me.

Q-2 No, I quite believe him. Since neither of us want to take the blame for the cleansing of the stables, we well need to work out a long-range and effective program to implement this without danger to anyone who matters.

M Such a sensible man, Colonel. How far will the President go to implement any of this and will he support attacks on Roosevelt's people?

Q-2 Oh yes, he will go along with all of this provided—and I do stress that word, "provided"—that none of these attacks can be traced to him in any way.

M Could we blame Hoover for them?

Q-2 No, I don't think we could do that. Truman would have to fire him if it came out and Hoover has been blackmailing Washington bigwigs for years. The first hint that Truman was going to fire him and Hoover would be running around to half the Senate with stories about terrible revelations. The Senate would sit on Truman and Hoover would stay.

M I assume Hoover keeps a safe full of nasty secrets. I know I did. Find those and remove them and then you can blame Hoover.

Q-2 Let it be from others and they can take the blame in the end.

M Always be kind to yourself and the rest will follow. Get a Savanarola and sit back and enjoy a good cigar.

Q-2 It would be better from inside Washington. A religious fellow might believe his own crap after a time. I think we have one or two we can use. Now then, we will need to compare notes extensively. You have names, I understand. I have seen some of your names.

M Do they surprise you?

Q-2 No, they do not. I'm surprised not to see Mrs. Roosevelt on some of them. Of course, she is crazy and I doubt if even Stalin would be interested in her. Besides, now that Franklin the First is dead and rotting in his grave, she has no power at all. Let her go around and give lectures all she wants. When she was romancing women, I'm surprised she didn't bring home a Pickaninny.

M Please?

Q-2 A nigger.

M Oh yes, from the Niger River in Africa.

Q-2 You weren't cursed with them, were you?

M Oh, during the French occupation of the Ruhr, they brought in the blacks just to torment us and there were a number of tan babies left behind.

Q-2 Saddle-colored boys, we call them.

M That's an interesting description. Very few in Germany, but the French seem to like them.

Q-2 The French like anything strange. They like to eat snails. Let us get back to the issues at hand. If we combine our knowledge, we should be able to have more than enough evidence to root out these damned weeds once and for all.

M Remember that if you don't get the roots, the weeds will grow back. Nits make lice.

Q-2 Make it so hot for them that they'll either run to Moscow or Jerusalem and leave the rest of us to get on with our lives.

M I don't mean to be negative, Colonel, but these ideologues have had, how long? Twelve years? That long to dig in. They are no doubt in the educational system for life and if they don't control the newspapers yet, they will soon enough. You will have chopped off the weeds, as you like to say, at the ground, but with the roots still in the ground there will be more growth later. My recommendation would be to lock up as many as you can, deport the rest and keep a permanent vigil on the garden to prevent more trouble. To do this would be to have a system like the Gestapo permanently in place and permanently active. I doubt if your public opinion would approve of this for too long. In Germany we controlled the press. Goebbels ran it with an iron hand and we never had any trouble from that quarter. You have to decide whether or not to establish a permanent watchdog to keep the pigs out of your garden, and I would suggest that you do so as quickly as possible. Those enemies of the state—the traitors and international types whom you cannot destroy by one means or the other—must be so afraid to engage in anti-government activity or spy for the enemies that they will sit at home and teach curses to the parrot.

Q-2 "Eternal vigilance is the price of liberty."

M Exactly. If you think that some kind of a swift housecleaning will be enough, you think in error. You must watch and watch some more and as long as Stalin sits in Moscow, he will try to infiltrate your country and destroy it from the inside. These are your enemies, not your friends, and if they win, they will destroy you faster than you can imagine. Look what happened in Russia after the Revolution. Root them out, destroy them and their friends or you will live to regret it. Try these ideas out through the medium of some deniable source— a minister or a senator, as you say. See what kind of a reaction you get. If the public really wants to be rid of them, you have permission from them to proceed. You have a democratic government, in the end, and you must fit your actions to suit this system. Democracy has its advantages, I suppose, but I **177**

personally find it a very difficult process to deal with. Here, in Switzerland, is the only real democracy in the world. You in America have a republic, not a democracy. There is a real difference there. However, I am a professional and as such, I will follow my instructions to the letter. I thought it fair to give you my views.

Q-2 Appreciated. I was born into this system, the republic or democratic state, and you were born and raised under other systems. I think, in the end, that we can sum this up by using the term "professional." Our agency is professional as was your's but this is not the forum for political philosophies, is it?

M No. Leave that to the academics and the people who make propaganda films. And, by the way, the makers of films and printers of newspapers deserve special attention. This is where Stalin has great interest as did Lenin. The people receive some of their education from the schools but a great deal from the films and the press. In America, where is the press now?

Q-2 Anti-Roosevelt, but the film industry is very left wing. I remember the "Grapes of Wrath" film, which is pure communism. Have you seen it?

M No. I read the book and your Steinbeck is a very good writer but also very much the left wing ideologue. Artists tend to be this way, I have found. Filled with a boundless love for the lower classes and a desire to aid them on their path to what the creative ones think is a new paradise, but what in reality is the grave we all go to. I hate to see time wasted and that's what all that idealistic nonsense consists of.

Q-2 Henry Wallace and his friend Rex Tugwell are prime examples of the jackass brigade. And you can add Macleish to that as well. The poet of the people.

M The Soviets have Ehrenburg. We could probably put both of them in the zoo with the lions and see if the lions would lie down with the lambs or eat them. But I think we move from the important specific to the interesting general. I will draw up some suggestions for you concerning integrating our respective areas of knowledge and then we can try to work out an operational plan. I should tell you that I am not that well acquainted with specifics in your country, but one can learn. Why, in the last several months, I have been improving my English and, as our mutual friend here can testify, I have been reading many American history books. We can have an exam if you like.

Q-2 Oh, not now. We have already been having one, haven't we?

M Of course we have.

(At this point, there is a break in the transcript which subsequently resumes with a dialog between Müller and the original interviewer.)

M I ought to offer my apologies to you for what has happened here.

Q Please explain, if you will.

M This is, after all, my house, and I find the attitude of your associate unacceptable. I have no control over him, of course, but as a matter of correctness, I feel I ought to make my own views clear to you. I am making reference to some of your Colonel's remarks. To make them to me, in private, is one business, but to do so in front of you is in bad taste certainly.

Q I don't think he had any animosity towards me at all.

M That makes the matter even worse. He sits here and makes strong anti-Semitic remarks in the presence of someone whom he must know the background of and does so without thinking? We have been accused of being the worst anti-Semites in the world, but it now seems that the Americans are worse. If a high level American official talks in that way, does he represent the thinking in America?

Q Unfortunately, yes. When I said that he meant nothing personal, I meant that he was not attacking me. The establishment, especially the military officer class, all think the same way.

M Such a lack of tact after all! Do you have any blacks in positions like yours?

Q My position? No, none at all.

M But certainly Jews?

Q Yes, a number.

M And senior officials have such an attitude that they speak in this manner in front of them? And I note that your superior would love to conduct *pogroms* in America. Do you believe this?

Q To answer your question, I think they would like to do this, but as he pointed out, they can't.

M But, they would if they could. Here, and for my record here, we have a country that is still expanding and has no knowledge of how to do things without assistance. They want to rid America of all communists, no doubt the Jews and certainly the blacks. That is an impossible task in any of the categories. To do this would bring anarchy in the country. Most of the citizens would balk at such behavior and then the military would have to become even more oppressive. I have seen these things in person and I am amazed that anyone thinks that merely by having some idiot get up in the church or in your Senate and preach against the communists, a great desire will arise in the people to destroy all communists. And believe me, if they start public attacks on communists, this will also include Jews as well. Given the structure of your system, which I have studied very carefully, believe me, all of this is wishful thinking on the part of bigots. Now, understand that I do not like communists, recognize how dangerous they can be because they owe their total allegiance to Soviet Russia. But, even in my position in Germany, I could not simply round up all the known and suspected communists and put them into camps. We could and did, get the spies and traitors and even the most active and aggressive communist supporters, but the others we had to watch until they made mistakes. Also, let me point out, the Gestapo simply did not go around dragging German Jews out of their homes and shoving them into camps. Many, many German Jews lived unmolested in Germany during the war and survived.

There were anti-Jewish laws in Germany during that time that precluded Jews from engaging in business or cohabiting with Germans—that is quite true. And our offices received constant complaints from Germans about violations of these laws. We, in the Gestapo, had to investigate all of these allegations and let me tell you that if we found the charges baseless and coming from jealousy or whatever motive, we threw the false complainers into jail and left the accused alone. If we couldn't have mass arrests and executions of suspected communists in Germany, how in God's name can you expect to do this in the United States, and given your own background, how can you work for such people?

Q Let me put a question to you, then. If you find their attitudes impractical or objectionable, why are you willing to work for them?

M My question came first.

Q They aren't all that way you know. And I have an important position in a new and significant agency.

M You will never rise very high in your agency, given their attitudes, and will only be a token presence. Get out of it and do something else and I mean this in a friendly way, believe me. My answer? This country is comfortable and I do well here. I speak English after my way but they speak German here and that is one point. However, there is potential danger to me and you can realize that as well as I. Your government will have every incentive to supply me the most thorough protection if I go there—something I cannot get here. Also, $1 million and $50,000 salary a year is an inducement.

I found many of the Third Reich leaders obnoxious and distasteful but I worked for the state just the same and did very well for myself. I am not a Jew and during the earlier time I had to sit around and listen to hours of anti-Semitic rantings which I never bothered to pay attention to. If my new employers like to do the same thing, I am used to it and I won't pay any attention to that either. Your friend spoke of professionalism, but he is not professional at all, nor very well educated either.

It is possible to remove communist agents from their posts, that much is certain. Going after intellectual Marxists or sympathetic writers is another business. You might like to do it but in practice, it is impossible and has ugly implications. I have no problem giving advice and technical assistance to your people, none at all. I agree that the upper levels of your government are full of communist agents, not intellectual Marxists, who ought to be rooted out as quickly as possible.

I am positive that Stalin hates America, sees it as his main enemy now that Hitler is gone and will do everything he can to destroy you. He would be afraid to attack you after he has seen what you are capable of, but he will concentrate on infiltrating your establishments with his agents or with persons who are in sympathy with his system. I have warned you in the past that this will be Stalin's approach. Your military and their supporters can say all they want about Soviet tanks in Washington, but that will not be the way Stalin will beat you. Infiltration, sabotage and propaganda are his weapons, not tanks and soldiers. There I can do some good, but since I could never hold the sort of position I had in Germany, all I can do is to advise people who are bigger ideologues than the communists and who are subject to changes in government that would leave them exposed and powerless. I cannot become involved because of who I am and I would dislike not having the ability to execute my plans but have to depend on a rabble of others to distort them as they see fit. I do not foresee a lengthy or profitable relationship but it will certainly advance my position in the world and I take what I can get.

As to you, and I am speaking now in all friendliness, I suggest you can find a position in the art world where you will be happy amongst people like yourself, or perhaps you could go into some business like the banking or exchange world or perhaps even teach. You could do all of those things, but you will not do yourself justice where you are not wanted. Am I offending you?

Q No. I appreciate your concern and I recognize that you mean well, but I am trapped in my work.

M Are you planning to discuss this with your Colonel friend?

Q Oh no, of course not. They want you and for a time they will use you. My advice to you is to get as much as you can on them and then retire in safety in the United States. They will never betray your presence because if they do, there will be real trouble with everyone else. Now that's my advice to you. Am I offending you now?

M What? By stating the obvious? I think not. Keep in touch with me and if you need any assistance, let me know. Now your friend, the Jewbaiter, will be coming back and we can all look serious and prepared for work. And I note you looking at my stenographer. I shouldn't worry about her. She knows enough to bury all of us so we must be nice to her and when you leave here for the last time, be sure to give her a bouquet of flowers.

(The transcript of this conversation runs to over 150 pages. The following excerpt is of interest because it concerns the projected post-war use of refugees from Eastern Europe and the Balkans in clandestine intelligence operations.)

Q-2 Most especially interested in our use of the eastern European manpower in possible insurrections against the Soviets. How much do you have about them?

M Not a great deal. I had little to do with the Eastern People, as we used to call them. Of course I had the use of captured agents but these were almost always White Russians or German refugees sent back into Germany.

Q-2 I had in mind the Latvians and the other Baltic types and the Ukranians and Yugoslavians, especially.

M I should suggest that you not involve yourself with those people—any of them.

Q-2 Reasons?

M I found most of them, especially the Yugoslavians, not to be trusted. The Balts and the Ukranians had a bad record for killing anyone they did not like, including babies. During the eastern campaign, we used many of these people as auxiliaries and one can say that many of them were first-class soldiers. I am not thinking here of soldiers. I am thinking of the police and political types like the Ustacha or the Baltic police, not to mention the Ukrainian police people. We had a terrible time with these during the war, because if we did not supervise them carefully and give them German officers and non-commissioned officers to control them, their actions were barbaric. They did kill Jews because they thought we wanted them to, but they also slaughtered peasants, small merchants, and on and on. They left a trail of blood and death behind them that made one think one was back in the dark ages.

Q-2 We see them as just the ones to start revolution inside Russia. Can't you see them that way?

M I'm sure they have sold themselves to you that way but my experience, and admittedly it is not first-hand, is that most of those people are not reliable. Now, if you take these refugees into your control, think how much trouble you might have if it turns out that your chairman of this or that free peoples of Serbia or the Banat turns out to have set fire to barns full of screaming peasants or to have beat to death hundreds of unarmed Jews in Pinsk. Eh? Then what would you do? I don't think your generals would like that very much. And given the number, how can you screen out the monsters from the innocent?

Q-2 Do we need to screen them? Doesn't anti-communism matter?

M I assume many are anti-communist, but most are stupid and vicious peasants, local fascists, lunatics, rapists, and so on. I don't think you want to have any large numbers of these men in your agency. I would not use them myself.

Q-2 With proper training...

M With proper training you can teach a dog to beg, but it is still a dog after all.

Q-2 The concept of a guerrilla army was successful for us during the war against you, both in Russia and the Balkans. Not in France because the French are all cowards...

M I would take exception to that. The French are not cowards. Most of them didn't want the war and didn't want to get involved in guerrilla activities. I assume you were with the OSS from your comments earlier. Am I correct?

Q-2 You could say that.

M I have. You use the title of "colonel." Were you a military man then?

Q-2 That isn't important, is it?

M We are talking here about military-style operations, aren't we?

Q-2 Clandestine operations are not the same.

M If you don't run these along military lines, you have nothing but murderous rabble that will turn on you as soon as someone else. That's why I asked you about your military background. A legitimate question I am sure you will permit.

Q-2 Actually, I was in the navy.

M Well, I was a pilot in the 1914 war and did not fight on the ground, but as I said, guerrilla activity needs to be done by soldiers, not rabble. Better to train your own troops—Americans—and not bother with these others. And believe me, internal security inside Russia is so secure that there will be no internal revolution unless the central government—and by that I mean Stalin and his secret police—collapses and that is not certain. Stalin is not young and can die, just like the rest of us, but we do not know when, where, or how. Are you planning to drop these armed refugees into Red Square, by any chance?

Q-2 Now General, please let us make these decisions. We are only interested in your knowledge of potential operators.

M There is a difference between a trained agent and an armed peasant, if you mark me.

Q-2 I think that if the balloon went up, say in the Soviet Union or elsewhere, the people would rise up to a man and then our clandestine army could be of the most vital importance in overthrowing the Reds.

M Colonel, or whatever, let me tell you that someone has been selling themselves to you. I would seriously doubt if there will be any more revolutions inside the Soviet empire, unless and until, Moscow looses its iron grip. If you wish to set up such groups in your country, be careful not to arm them because you would live, or probably not live, to regret it. Using the more intelligent ones as agents on a limited basis is much more sensible and we all are sensible men, aren't we sir?

Q-2 There are policies we are now formulating that we have already mentioned and this policy is very important to me and to our program. I hope you can understand that.

M I certainly can, but when I say that you can do other things than train Slavs to wave your flag in Belgrade streets. In the first place, most would defect to Stalin, who would naturally kill them at once. Your battle against Stalin should be an economic one, not a military one. Russia will never be a full industrial power like you are. There you might beat him but not with gangs of Slavic bandits in the woods. There are still Ukranians fighting the Soviets in the woods to this day, but to what end? You should read Clausewitz, not Karl May. **183**

Q-2 May? Clausewitz, I know.

M May wrote adventure books about your West. Cowboys and Red Indians. Very popular with little children, and some not so young, in Germany in the last century.

Q-2 That's beside the point. This is not a romantic venture but a real war against the communists.

M Sir, I conducted a real war against the communists all my adult life and with great success. Now, I am an advisor, and I am advising you, that's all.

Q-2 I understand this, but let me ask you to keep these views to yourself, if you would. There is too much riding on our programs for you to throw cold water on it.

M Of course, but of what use am I if I merely rubber-stamp all of your ideas? I mean, in private here? Surely, you don't want me to kiss your backside, do you?

Q-2 That isn't it at all. We can work all this out later. I think we understand each other, don't we?

M I think so. Like my friend here, are you an academic?

Q-2 I attended the university and also law school.

M Ah, an attorney! Well Hitler had some views on attorneys which we do not need to discuss here. No, I have no intentions of causing trouble for you, but I can support my views with facts, if you want them.

Q-2 Well, perhaps sometime later, but now I think we should get back to any lists you have on collaborators we might look for.

M Certainly, Colonel, and Europe is full of them. Bring cigarettes and you will find many collaborators. Since there is no patriotism, money helps and America is a rich country.

Historical Significance—Reflections of the Author

The obvious anger and frustration expressed by Admiral Hillenkoetter's representative may seem appalling but taken in context with the times, not exceptional. There is no question whatsoever that during the Roosevelt administration, many radical leftists joined his New Deal and their ill-conceived and abrasive activities infuriated many Americans. In a democracy, such behavior can usually be curbed if it becomes too prevalent. However, during the Roosevelt era, the President was battling the Great Depression, which suddenly flared up again in 1938, and his skillful presentation of right-wing dictatorships in Germany, Italy and Japan were viewed as potential threats to America. These two factors, economic and ideological, helped keep Roosevelt in office. Although, after his own dictatorial attempt to control the Supreme Court failed in Congress in 1936, his popularity in the polls was steadily shrinking.

After Roosevelt actively aided and abetted the United States' entry in the war, his tenure in the White House was secure until the war was over. Those historians who praise Roosevelt as a great man, claim that he, indeed, schemed to involve America in global war but did so because Germany and Japan were planning to invade the continental United States. However, post-war searches of captured German and Japanese state archives have not produced a shred of evidence in support of this invasion theory.

Throughout his entire life, Roosevelt was dominated by his mother who was possessed of exceptionally strong personal prejudices. She ran her only child like a Swiss railroad. On her annual European trips, Mrs. Roosevelt preferred to mingle with correct British society and found her hotel stays in Germany abhorrent. Mrs. Roosevelt was anti-Semitic and her deep hatred of Germans was instilled in her son from an early age. She constantly referred to black Americans as "niggers," and so her prejudice became his prejudice, also.

The flowering of leftist views in Washington left many Americans furious but because of the President's general popularity, America was powerless to vote him out of office. This continuing frustration produced a flood of savage anti-Roosevelt commentary and a heightened detestation of the shrill importunings of the extreme left governmental appointees.

When Roosevelt died suddenly in 1945, his successor Harry Truman was viewed as an unknown entity. Truman, who was no fan of Stalin or his ideology, acted cautiously to remove the New Deal activists from power. This earned Truman unpopularity with some factions of the media and especially the American motion picture industry, which was a strong supporter of left-wing causes.

President Truman speaks at a Jefferson Day dinner in the capitol, 1948.

The conversation between Müller and his CIA interviewers took place just before the Presidential elections of 1948. The mainstream American media, still very much anti-Roosevelt, was loudly predicting Truman's defeat at the hands of the colorless Thomas Dewey.

There was the belief in conservative circles of the US government that Dewey would be a better man than Truman, and that he would give the order for a general cleansing of the Rooseveltian stables. Truman, as a Democrat, may have been anti-communist, but he was still compelled to seek the support of his party. Of course, he had to walk with great care, lest he lose his political support from the party machinery.

Senator Joseph McCarthy of Wisconsin has been described as a madman on the socio-political scene, and depicted as a power-mad politician who accused innocent Americans of communist beliefs or activities. In fact, McCarthy was kept well-informed of facts either known to official Washington or uncovered by various investigative agencies. Much of his information came from senior Catholic church sources in Washington who, in turn, received their information from anonymous, but accurate, official sources. Given that Müller was well-connected with the church, a review of his post-war notes indicates that much of his information possessed prior to the end of the war or acquired after it, fell into McCarthy's hands and was used, or misused, by him.

Prior to the Army-McCarthy hearings, Senator McCarthy (right) is shown with Senator Stuart Symington.

McCarthy's statement inaugurating his attacks on American communists, in which he stated that more than 80 known communists worked in the US Department of State, was entirely accurate. McCarthy either did not know, or neglected to mention, that they were identified communists who had been removed from the OSS by Truman in 1945, and were awaiting a graceful departure from government service.

Although Truman and his successor, Dwight Eisenhower, have been depicted by biographers and historians as appalled and disgusted by the activities of McCarthy, neither man made the slightest effort to silence him even though there was certainly sufficient material to accomplish this. McCarthy, who drank heavily, eventually lost his sources, became incoherent and brought the wrath of the Senate down upon him.

Some ideological historians and journalists have portrayed McCarthy as the sole and discredited voice of anti-communism in America. Such a portrayal, however, is a gross error. Müller's transcript clearly shows that strong anti-communist attitudes were well entrenched in the United States and if McCarthy had not attacked the ultra left, then someone else would have pursued the communists—perhaps with more explosive results.

Müller's attitude towards both Kronthal, his initial interviewer, and his superior from Washington is indicative of his own feelings and not an indication of his actions.

Kronthal was a homosexual who had been arrested by the German police in Berlin before the war, and released by the intervention of Hermann Göring for whom he had been brokering confiscated Jewish works of art. Müller was well aware of Kronthal's homosexuality and throughout the entire transcript makes subtle remarks about it. This sarcasm is entirely in keeping with Müller's personality. Müller liked Kronthal, who was well-educated and intelligent, and this also shows up in the transcript. Kronthal should have listened to Müller's advice and left the CIA, but he did not.

When Müller left Swiss territory in November of 1948 and flew into Berlin to collect his files prior to flying to American territory, he sent a package and a note to Kronthal in Bern:

"This to my friend who considers himself well-born.

I am now away from Switzerland and my pleasant house and will end up in a tropical garden with permanent weather. I hope this will be an improvement and perhaps I will enjoy coconuts in the future. This is just a short letter to indicate my appreciation of your conduct with me and, I might also say, of your company.

I am afraid that I was sometimes a little sharp with you but you understand that that is how I am. There is nothing personal meant at all. If I had not liked you, you would not have been a guest in my house. I am afraid that my subsequent contacts with your countrymen will not be as pleasant and I do not have a particularly good opinion of either their knowledge or character.

I am sending this along with the Czar's cigarette box that you so often admired with the hope that you will enjoy it and have a longer and happier life than its former owner.

Perhaps we may meet again and can continue our chess games but if we do not, please keep as pleasant thoughts of me as you can.

With highest attentions,

Müller"

Soviet intelligence also discovered Kronthal's homosexuality and attempted to force him into working for them. He committed suicide on April Fool's Day, 1953. Kronthal did not have, as Müller had wished, better fortune than the previous owner of the malachite and gold cigarette box. Like the last Czar, Kronthal, too, was a victim of the communists.

The records will reflect that the individual identified in the transcript only as "Q-2" was, in fact, Frank Wisner who became Chief of Clandestine Operations of the Central Intelligence Agency shortly after that agency was formed.

Frank Wisner, shown here in uniform as a US Navy Lt. Cmdr. He was later a senior official of the CIA. Wisner's son is currently the US Ambassador to India.

Wisner, a former Lt. Commander of the United States Navy, had been an attorney and during the war was a member of the OSS. He had been a station chief in Bucharest, Romania, during the war. A dedicated anti-communist, Wisner convinced the National Security Council (NSC), in 1948 that the United States should institute a covert operations program against the Soviet forces in Eastern Europe based on the activities of the Vlasov Army during their cooperation with the Germans during the Second World War. Former Soviet General Vlasov had founded and commanded a large body of ex-Soviet soldiers who had joined the Germans after the invasion of the Soviet Union in 1941.

Wisner was a firm believer in the tremendous espionage potential to be found in the membership of former German allies in the fight against the Soviet partisan movement in Eastern Europe during the war. He also believed in their value as disseminators of anti-communist propaganda and an eventual cadre of agents who could carry out sabotage and assassinations in the Soviet satellites.

On June 10, 1948, the State, Army, Navy, Air Force Coordinating Committee (SANACC) under the Joint Chiefs of Staff, approved the execution of "Operation Bloodstone." This operation used Eastern Bloc anti-communists to carry out clandestine activities, sabotage and assassinations.

This was officially approved by President Harry Truman in June of 1948 by National Security Council Resolution 10/2. The wording of this resolution addressed "propaganda, economic warfare, preventative direct action including sabotage, anti-sabotage, demolitions and evacuation measures" as well as "subversion against hostile states including assistance to underground resistance movements and guerrillas."

This program, placed under the command of Wisner, was specifically sponsored by CIA Director, Rear Admiral Roscoe Hillenkoetter.

A section entitled Office for Policy Coordination (OPC), was set up under the control of Wisner to implement these official policies.

To better organize his clandestine units, Wisner had access to the Central Registry of War Crimes and Security Suspects (CROWCASS). This agency was initially created to locate Germans who might be tried for their actions during the war. Eventually, this agency became a roster which Wisner and his agents used to build a cadre for their guerrilla units.

In 1951 and 1952, Wisner began large-scale programs designed to bring thousands of eastern European refugees into the US either as a reward for services rendered or to train for his programs of clandestine warfare against the Soviets. The exact number recruited by Wisner is still classified, but records will indicate that the recruits numbered in the tens of thousands.

Wisner's activities led directly to the abortive Hungarian rising in November of 1956—a rising that was not supported by President Eisenhower's administration. The bloody suppression of the revolt which left 12,000 Hungarians and 3,000 Soviet military personnel dead.

This failure marked the eventual breakdown of Frank Wisner. He became extremely and irrationally abusive, drank too much and had a complete collapse in August 1958 when he had to be removed forcibly from his office under restraint. Later, after making a partial recovery, Wisner was sent as putative station chief of the CIA to London. But he was quickly recalled after he repeatedly made irrational outbursts to his British hosts—making him *persona non grata* in London.

Frank Wisner shot himself in the head with a shotgun on October 29, 1965. **189**

Conservative estimates reveal that Wisner's policy of sabotage and assassination was responsible for 30,000 deaths, excluding the Hungarian bloodbath.

As well as being a savage anti-communist, Wisner was also anti-Semitic, something he shared with many of the eastern European organizations he so assiduously courted during the course of his career.

Among the organizations Wisner valued were:

- The Russian People's Army (*Russkaya Osvoboditelnaya Narodnaya Armiya*) or RONA. Formed in liberated Soviet territory in January of 1942, in the town of Lokot, this militia was run by a former chemical engineer, Bronislav V. Kaminski. In September of 1943, RONA had 10,000 men, 36 field gun batteries and 24 tanks under their control. This group fought hard against Soviet partisan forces. In August of 1944, RONA detached a regiment of 1,700 men, under the command of Lt. Colonel Vrolov, to fight the Polish insurgents in Warsaw. They were, however, recalled after several weeks at the urgent request of the German military commander because of their savage, undisciplined behavior.

- The Croatian Ustascha, a political movement formed by Dr. Ante Pavelic, who subsequently became head of the Croatian state under German control. The militia arm of this organization brutaly fought against Serb communist partisans. The most feared of these militias was the "Black Legion" under Colonel Francetic.

- Members of various Ukranian, Balkan and Baltic police units who had spearheaded the brutal anti-partisan warfare in the east had a collective reputation for great ferocity in fighting the Soviets. Although anti-communism was put forward by Wisner as the attractiveness of these groups, in fact their general behavior throughout the anti-partisan campaigns was one of great brutality and not always directed at Soviet para-military units, but also against civilians in general and Jews in particular. Their anti-Semitic behavior was condoned because of their universal detestation of Soviet communists.

It is easy in retrospect to condemn Frank Wisner for his use of these groups, but his doing so does not make him a supporter of Third Reich racial attitudes. A mantra often chanted by the left is that an anti-communist is, therefore, an anti-Russian, and automatically pro-fascist and anti-Semitic.

Like Heinrich Müller, Frank Wisner (whom Müller found obnoxious) was a statist. Both of them believed that the security of the state was the supreme law. Müller, who was not anti-Semitic but far more professional than Wisner, clearly identified probable difficulties with the use of the refugees—an identification immediately rejected by Wisner.

At the same time Harry Truman authorized the National Security Council Resolution 10/2 in June of 1948, he also instituted a special intelligence and foreign policy oversight committee to assist him. Truman had been excluded from Roosevelt's inner circle and entered the Presidency without knowledge of such matters as the atomic bomb program. Aside from service as an artillery officer in the First World War, Truman did not have knowledge of military matters, especially in the highest levels.

This oversight committee was chaired by General Walter Bedell Smith, who had been Eisenhower's Chief of Staff. Smith was a ruthless professional officer who had served under George Marshall and Eisenhower and was later made head of the CIA. The oversight committee was directly under the control of the President, above the Joint Chiefs of Staff, and was never an official body although its actions often set national foreign and military policy.

When Heinrich Müller was interviewed by the CIA in 1948, higher authority in Washington realized what a prize they had—the former Gestapo chief—and transferred Müller to Truman's special oversight committee.

The main reason for this transfer was security. If foreign governments discovered that Müller was in American employ, the resulting uproar could prove disastrous. In the postwar years, both British and German authorities strongly suspected that Müller did not die in Berlin and might well be working for the Americans. American official records contain many references to these suspicions, but these documents are not available to researchers because of high-level security classifications.

The phrase "plausible deniability" did not come into official use until the Reagan presidency, but it can be easily applied to the existence of Heinrich Müller. The man who initially acted as liaison with Müller was James Jesus Angleton, a senior intelligence official of the CIA who was as ruthless as Smith, but far more intelligent.

Truman was aware of the actions of his oversight committee and, although knowing of the Müller connection, would have been able to deny any knowledge of it.

Given Müller's intelligence, abilities and extraordinary ambition, it should come as no surprise to learn from an intelligence resource, that eventually Müller resumed his former role as a major intelligence player. Future publications on this subject will cover the postwar activities of the Chief of the Gestapo in greater detail.

The General, the Company, and the Road to Damascus

The agency which initially interviewed Heinrich Müller in 1948 was the newly-formed CIA. The CIA, or the Company as it was known in the intelligence community, won a bidding war against British intelligence for Müller's services only to lose him to the US Army's military intelligence after a furious interdepartmental campaign.

Heinrich Müller was not the only German general officer involved in the intelligence game who worked for the CIA. Another general was Reinhard Gehlen, former head of the German Army's *Fremde Heer Ost* or Foreign Armies East.

M I think the problem with Krichbaum is that he's working for the wrong man.

Q Why do you think Gehlen is the wrong man?

M I did not have Gehlen in mind when I said that. Willi works for me, as you know, and no man can serve two masters. Or, do you read the Bible? Never mind. I should like to bring Willi with me to America but I think he's more valuable to me where he is. Still, here we have an interesting situation. You work for the CIA, of course. And so, also does Willi. He works for Gehlen who works for you. But Willi also works for me and keeps me current with what Gehlen is up to. But Gehlen reports to you just like Willi reports to me. It reminds me of a French bedroom farce with people running in and out of rooms in their underwear.

Q We want Willi right where he is for the time being, so you can't take him away.

M And why do you want him where he is?

Q You know that. He's Gelen's chief recruiter; that's why he stays.

M Of course. But Willi hires people I suggest or approve. In other words, your people are my people—or were. You play chess. Not as well as I do, but adequately. Never bring your Queen out too soon, young man.

Q That's cryptic, I must say.

M Actually, it isn't. But we can now discuss the Stockholm courier network unless you want to torment yourself about one of the souls in your breast attacking the other. Did you know that when someone quoted to Bismarck that they had two souls struggling in their breast, Bismarck laughed and said, "Two souls? Why I have a whole Parliament raging in there!" But a simple person like myself can't grasp these abstractions. We had best turn our attention to the Swedes now.

Historical Significance—Reflections of the Author

In 1944, Admiral Nicholas Horthy, Regent of Hungary, secretly negotiated with the Soviets to surrender and prevent a Soviet invasion of Hungary, a country which is difficult to defend from a geographical point of view. German intelligence caught wind of this and in a quick coup, removed Horthy and replaced him with Ferenc Szalasi, head of the pro-Nazi and violently anti-Semitic Arrow Cross Party. Szalasi formally requested Himmler, through his senior officer in Budapest, to remove the Jews from Hungary. Ever eager for more free labor, Himmler readily agreed and informed Heinrich Müller, whose Gestapo oversaw such transports, that as many of the Hungarian Jews as possible were to be deported as slave labor to Auschwitz.

*Ferenc Szalasi was arrested by US forces in Austria
and is shown as he arrives in Budapest for trial.*

Müller, in turn, passed this unpalatable mission on to his chief deputy and friend, *SS-Oberführer* (Senior Colonel) Willi Krichbaum. Krichbaum then went to Budapest along with Adolf Eichmann, the Gestapo official directly in charge of the human shipments which eventually totaled over 350,000 Jews. Most of these Jews did not survive the war.

Müller, Krichbaum and Eichmann survived the war and went their separate ways. Müller and Krichbaum found new careers with the victors. Eichmann escaped to South America where he was later kidnapped. After a trial, he was found guilty and executed by the State of Israel.

On May 22, 1945, a German *Wehrmacht* General, Reinhard Gehlen, the former head of the German Army High Command's Foreign Armies East, surrendered along with his key staff members to the United States military at Fischhausen in southern Germany.

Gehlen's unit was responsible for gathering and analyzing military intelligence on the Soviet Union,. His staff accomplished this by interrogating prisoners in army POW camps—captured Soviet military personnel and, in their headquarters—Soviet defectors. They also studied battlefield intelligence from captured Soviet documents, maps and code books. Further material was obtained by signals intelligence which listened to Soviet non-coded, low-level combat unit radio traffic. These methods of gathering combat intelligence are standard procedures still used by all armies.

During the war, Gehlen did not have intelligence agents in the Soviet Union. The General was not accustomed to gathering and analyzing Soviet political data. Unlike Müller, whose radio playback section had direct contact with very high-level Soviet intelligence agents inside Russia, Gehlen dealt strictly with combat intelligence.

Reinhard Gehlen was born in 1902 in Erfurt, Germany, the son of a publisher in Breslau. In 1920, he joined the *Reichswehr,* rising slowly through the ranks as an artillery officer. In 1933 he was sent to the General Staff college, and in 1935, Gehlen became a captain, the lowest rank in the General Staff.

Except for a brief period in 1938 when he was posted to the 18th Artillery Regiment as a battery commander, Gehlen spent his entire career in the German Army as a General Staff officer. On April 1, 1942, Lt. Colonel Gehlen of the General Staff was appointed head of Foreign Armies East in the High Command of the Army (OKH), a position he held until April 9, 1945 when he was fired by Hitler.

Like Müller, Gehlen had microfilmed all his files before the end of the war and he offered them, plus himself and his staff, to US Army intelligence. The offer was accepted. On August 26, 1945, Gehlen and four of his closest assistants were flown to Washington for substantive talks with US authorities. Gehlen was the subject of an inter-agency struggle when Allen Dulles of the OSS, once their station chief in Switzerland during the war, and General William Donovan, commander of the agency, attempted to secure Gehlen and his files for themselves. Dulles eventually won and his assistant Frank Wisner was appointed to oversee the former head of Foreign Armies East.

The Gehlen team was based at Fort Hunt, near Washington. Gehlen began his new career by preparing a series of reports which were well received. In July of 1946, Gehlen returned to Germany, and set up shop at Pullach, a former housing project for elite Nazi officials such as Martin Bormann. Gehlen was instructed to build an intelligence agency capable of conducting the highest

Reinhard Gehlen, here a colonel.

level surveillance of the Soviets. His microfilmed files were sold to US intelligence for $5 million. Considering that these files only contained material on Soviet military units that had long been disbanded or were no longer combat ready, Gehlen was very well paid for very cold coffee.

Since Gehlen had no experience with internal Soviet intelligence or with their foreign intelligence, he was hard-pressed to use his former army staff officers to supply the US with relevant material. In 1946, Gehlen hired Willi Krichbaum, formerly the deputy chief of the Gestapo, as his senior agent recruiter. While Gehlen had no experience with Soviet spies, the Gestapo certainly did, and Krichbaum immediately sought out to hire many of his old associates.

At the same time, Krichbaum contacted his former chief, Heinrich Müller, who was now a resident in Switzerland, and a respected and wealthy citizen. Müller was, by no means, inactive in his enforced retirement and was in contact with Krichbaum almost from the beginning of his exile. Lengthy handwritten reports from Krichbaum to Müller spanning nearly three years exist and, while Müller's correspondence to Krichbaum is not in his files, the Krichbaum correspondence indicates without a doubt, that "Gestapo" Müller was supplying his former deputy with reams of information on prospective employees for the new Gehlen organization, as well as a flood of concise directives on the structure necessary to implement the needs of the US intelligence.

In 1946, Gehlen began the construction of his new agency, while the Soviet military machine in the East Zone of Germany was in the process of down sizing. The Second World War had proven to be a terrible economic disaster to Stalin. His troops were in the process of dismantling German factories which were still intact, ripping up the railroad system, and sending their spoils back to Russia.

The American armed forces were also being sharply reduced, since the war in the Pacific had ended in 1945. Military units were disbanded and their soldiers returned to civilian life as quickly as possible. On the economic front, businesses that had enjoyed lucrative government military contracts found themselves with empty assembly lines and tens of thousands of laid off workers.

It has been said that there never was a good war nor a bad peace. While the latter was certainly beneficial to the Soviets and permitted them to rebuild their economy, it certainly was not beneficial for either the rapidly-shrinking military or business communities in the United States.

This situation permitted the development of the Gehlen organization and secured its position as a vital American political resource. The US had virtually no military intelligence knowledge of the Soviet Union. But the Germans, who had fought against them for four years, had. Gehlen and his military staff only had knowledge of wartime Soviet military units which were either reduced to cadre or entirely disbanded. However, this was of no interest to the senior officials of US intelligence. Gehlen was to become a brilliant intelligence specialist with an incredible grasp of Soviet abilities and intentions. This preeminence was almost entirely fictional. It was designed to elevate Gehlen in the eyes of American politicians including President Truman and members of Congress, and to lend well-orchestrated weight to the former General's interpretation of his employer's needs.

In 1948, Stalin sent troops into Czechoslovakia after a minority but efficient communist coup which overthrew the Western-oriented government. This act, in February of 1948, combined with the blockade of West Berlin, then occupied by the British, French and Americans in June of the same year, gave a group of senior American military leaders a heaven-sent opportunity to identify a new and dangerous military enemy—an enemy which could and would attack Western Europe and the United States in the immediate future.

To facilitate the acceptance of this theory, Gehlen was requested to produce intelligence material that would bolster it in as authoritative a manner as possible. This Gehlen did and to set the parameters of this report, Gehlen, General Stephen Chamberlain, Chief of Intelligence of the US Army General Staff, and General Lucius D. Clay, US commander in occupied Germany met in Berlin in February of 1948, immediately after the Czech occupation but before the blockade.

After this meeting, Gehlen drew up a lengthy and detailed intelligence report which categorically stated that 175 fully-equipped Soviet divisions, many armored, were poised to attack. General Clay forwarded this alarming example of creative writing to Washington and followed up with frantic messages indicating his fear that the Soviets were about to launch an all-out land war on

the United States.

Although the sequence of events might indicate that Clay was involved in an attempt to mislead US leaders, in actuality, he was misled by Chamberlain and Gehlen. They managed to thoroughly frighten General Clay and used him as a conduit to Washington. He was not the last to fall victim to the machinations of the war party.

General Lucius D. Clay.

The Gehlen papers were deliberately leaked to Congress and the President. This resulted in the Cold War between the Soviet Union and the United States. This was not a historical first by any means. Elements in England at the beginning of the 20th century, alarmed at the growing economic threat of a united Germany, commenced a long public campaign designed to frighten the British public and their leaders into adopting a bellicose re-armament program based on a fictional German military threat.

Gehlen and his organization were considered vital to US interests. As long as the General was able to feed the re-armament frenzy in Washington with supportive, inflammatory secret reports, then his success was assured.

The only drawback to this deadly farce was that the General did not have knowledge of current Soviet situations in the military or political fields. He could only bluff his way for a short time. To enhance his military staffs, Gehlen developed the use of former SS *Sicherheitsdienst* (SD) and Gestapo people, brought to him by Krichbaum, his chief recruiter.

At the same time, a joint British-American project called "Operation Applepie" was launched with the sole purpose of locating and employing as many of the former Gestapo and SD types now being employed by Gehlen. **197**

Imitation is the sincerest form of flattery, after all. During the course of this hunt, the prize was considered to be former *SS-Gruppenführer* Heinrich Müller, then in Switzerland. Contact with the former Gestapo Chief was through Krichbaum, acting on Müller's specific instructions.

In the resulting bidding war, the Americans easily defeated the British, and the British public was spared the possible discovery of Müller appearing, under a new name, on their New Year's Honors List instead of being made a Brigadier General of Reserve in the United States Army under a new name.

The recently uncovered files on "Applepie" are of such interest that they will be the subject of a further in-depth publication. Other document series of equal importance will include the so-called Robinson papers and a series of reports on the British use of certain former Gestapo and SD personnel in Damascus, Syria by John Marriott of the Security Intelligence Middle East (SIME). Robinson (or Robinsohn as he was known to the Gestapo officials) was a high-level Soviet agent captured in France as a result of the *Rote Kapelle* investigations. Robinson's files came into Müller's possession and reveal an extensive Soviet spy ring in Great Britain. Such highly interesting and valuable historical records should also encompass the more significant intercepts made of Soviet messages by the Gestapo from Ottawa, Canada to Moscow throughout the war. These parallel the so-called Venona intercepts which have been fully translated and are extraordinarily lengthy.

In 1948, control of the Gehlen organization was assumed by the new CIA and put under the direction of Colonel James Critchfield, formerly an armored unit commander and now a CIA section chief.

General Walter Bedell Smith, Eisenhower's Chief of Staff.

Allen Welch Dulles former Swiss station chief of the OSS.

At this point, Gehlen had a number of powerful sponsors in the US military and intelligence communities. These included General Walter Bedell Smith, former Chief of Staff to General Eisenhower and later head of the CIA; General William Donovan, former head of the OSS; Allen Welch Dulles, former Swiss station chief of the OSS and later head of the CIA; Rear Admiral Roscoe Hillenkoetter, first head of the CIA; General Edwin Sibert of US Army military intelligence and Generals Chamberlain and Clay.

American military intelligence officers were well aware that the Soviet Army threat was hollow and that the Soviets' act of dismantling the eastern German railroad system was strong proof that an attack was not in the offing, but they were strongly discouraged by their superiors from expressing their views.

In 1954, General Arthur Trudeau, chief of US military intelligence, received a copy of a lengthy report prepared by retired Lt. Colonel Hermann Baun of Gehlen's staff. Baun, who had originally been assigned to the German High Command (OKW) as an *Abwehr* specialist on Russia, eventually ended up working for Gehlen's Foreign Armies East which was under the control of the Army High Command (OKH). Baun was an extremely competent, professional General Staff officer who, by 1953, had taken a dim view, indeed, of the creatures foisted on him by Gehlen. Baun detested Gehlen who had forced him out of his post-war intelligence position with the West. Baun's annoyance was revealed in a lengthy complaint of Gehlen's Nazi staff members which set forth, in detail, their names and backgrounds.

General Trudeau was so annoyed with this report that in October of 1954, he took West German Chancellor Konrad Adenauer aside as Adenauer was making an official visit to Washington, Trudeau passed much of this information to the horrified Adenauer, who had spent time in a concentration camp during the war. Adenauer, in turn, raised this issue with American authorities

West German Chancellor Konrad Adenauer.

and the matter was leaked to the press. Allen Dulles, a strong Gehlen backer and now head of the CIA, used his own connections and those of his brother, John, Eisenhower's Secretary of State, to effectively silence Trudeau by transferring him to the remote Far East.

Trudeau's warning to Adenauer did not have a lasting effect and on April 1, 1956, former General Reinhard Gehlen was appointed as head of the new West German Federal Intelligence Service, the *Bundesnachrichtendiesnt* or BND. In this case, as in so many other similar ones, virtue is certainly not its own reward.

Who, then, were the Gehlen organization people Colonel Baun took exception to working with?

The first person on the list was former *SS-Oberführer* or Senior Colonel, Willi Krichbaum whom we have met before. Krichbaum was an associate of Müller[1] and later the Deputy Chief of the Gestapo. Krichbaum was in charge of the deportation of the Hungarian Jews in 1944—a deportation that took nearly 300,000 lives. According to Müller's files, Krichbaum is also the man who shot Raoul Wallenberg. The *Geheime Feld Polizei* or the Secret Field Police which Krichbaum had commanded[2] was responsible for all manner of atrocities, including the killing of Soviet prisoners of war.[3] Although Russia was not a member of the Geneva Convention, Germany was a signator and this Convention forbade the execution of prisoners of war. Krichbaum, of whom Müller once said, *"war mit Blut verschmiert"* (was smeared with blood) was not only Gehlen's chief recruiter, mostly of former Gestapo and SD people, but also informed Müller of the inner workings of the Gehlen organization which was considered a highly secret American intelligence resource. Krichbaum continued to work for Gehlen, according to an interview with Colonel Critchfield, until at least 1956 when the West German government took over control of the group.

The second name on the list was *SS-Standartenführer* or Colonel Walter Rauff who had a most interesting career. In 1942, Walter Rauff was chief of the SD units attached to the AOK Afrika, Rommels' *Afrikakorps*. In 1943, after the collapse of the DAK, Rauff worked in Italy as the chief of the SD in Milan. In this capacity, Rauff was involved with SS General Karl Wolff's negotiations to surrender the German troops in Italy in 1945. This was a pet project of Allen Dulles and was called "Operation Sunrise." During the course of the negotiations, Dulles became very friendly with Rauff. Consequently, as the new Gehlen organization was formed, Dulles was instrumental in acquiring Rauff for an advisory position with them.

In 1941, Rauff had been involved with the SD anti-partisan activities in the captured areas of the Soviet Union. Rauff conceived, constructed and personally supervised the use of gas vans. These vans had the exhaust pipes vented

---

[1] *Had extensive World war I combat experience, was a Freikorps activist, was an anti-communist, and an early Party member.*

[2] *From the beginning of the war.*

[3] *Krichbaum was still carried on the rolls of the RSHA as a SS-Oberführer and Colonel of Police. He was never an army officer.*

```
K r i c h b a u m , Willi
Alter: 46 Jahre                    Beruf: Oberst der Polizei
Eintritt in die ##: 7.1o.33        ##-Nr. 107 039
Letzte Beförderung: 2o.4.39        P.-Nr.: 5 820 987
Dienststellung: Chef der Geheimen Feldpolizei
gedient: ja
erreichter Dienstgrad: Unteroffizier - Hauptmann d.Sch.
Fronteinsatz: ja
Auszeichnungen: EK I u. II u.A.
verwundet: ja
verheiratet: ja        Alter der Ehefrau: 31 Jahre    Kinder: 1
Konfession: ggl.

K. wurde am 5.4.1940 zum Oberregierungsrat und Kriminalrat
und am 21.5.41 zum Oberst der Polizei ernannt. Seit Beginn des
Krieges ist ##-Staf.Krichbaum als Chef der Geheimen Feldpolizei
beim OKW eingesetzt.
```

National Archives document indicating that Krichbaum was Chief of the Secret Field Police since the beginning of the war. Right: Willi Krichbaum.

SS-Standartenführer Walter Rauff as he surrenders his garrison to US forces in Milan, Italy, on April 30, 1945.

201

inside the rear compartments which were then filled with Jews who died of carbon monoxide poisoning. While it spared some SD men from the guilt associated with murdering large numbers of civilians, it did have certain negative aspects—the collection of bodies in the back of the van. When the rear door was opened to remove the dead, the stench proved to be a serious occupational hazard. An ingenious man, Rauff had a special fitting constructed that helped alleviate this unfortunate problem. A lengthy file on Rauff's gas vans is stored at the National Archives.

At the end of the war, Rauff was imprisoned in Italy. He later emerged in Germany, happily working for the Gehlen group. Unfortunately for him, his presence became known to the wrong people, and he found it necessary to move to Syria where he continued to represent Gehlen's interests. As the stress of discovery there became too much for Gehlen to bear, it was decided that Rauff should move to Chile. His friend and later protector, Allen Dulles, ordered that he be given new identity papers and funds for travel and relocation. While in Chile, the loyal Rauff continued to provide intelligence reports to Gehlen and his other protectors.

Another senior Gehlen aide was former *SS-Oberführer* Dr. Franz Six. Six was an intellectual academic, Professor of Political Science at Königsberg University. Six joined the SS on April 20, 1935 and became a member of the SD. In 1941, Six was in command of an Einsatzgruppe and was directly responsible for the murder of the Jews in the Russian city of Smolensk. Following this military triumph, Six was made the head of Section VII of the RSHA. In 1943 he was sent to the Foreign Ministry where he was in charge of the Cultural Division. In 1946, Dr. Six was an early member of the Gehlen organization but was eventually tracked down and his supporters were unable to prevent his standing trial in April of 1948 for his actions. He received a sentence of 25 years. However, US authorities interceded on his behalf and on September 30, 1952, Six was released and at once returned to his duties with Gehlen.

Dr. Franz Six.

Alois Brunner.

SS-Sturmbannführer (Major) Alois Brunner was a Gestapo official who worked directly under Adolf Eichmann in the deportation department. Ambitious and energetic, Brunner was an instigator of the notorious *razzia* carried out in France in 1942 against the Jews of Paris. So outraged was his putative chief, Müller, that Brunner was transferred to Sofia in Bulgaria. He was sentenced to death by a French court, *in absentia* because Brunner had gone to Damascus, Syria, as Gehlen's resident agent. He used a number of names including "Georg Fischer" and "Waldo Munk." Brunner was later made a part of a CIA-directed program to train the security forces of Abdel Nasser and Israeli agents attempted to blow him up with a letter bomb but failed. In addition to the French death sentence, Brunner was also on the wanted list of the CIC.

Probably the worst offender of all was *SS-Gruppenführer* Odlio Globocnik, once the *Gauleiter* of Vienna until fired by Hitler for theft and pillage. Globocnik went on to run the Lublin camps in Poland where he stole millions more and was responsible for the gassing of large numbers of Jews and Poles. His stolen millions saved him from prosecution. After working for a time for the British, he eventually ended up as an American resource, also in Damascus. The name of the program that sent him there was called "Argos."

Like its Biblical counterpart, the 20th century road to Damascus was traveled by converts to the new religion of the West.

There were many more individuals connected with the Gestapo or SD who openly worked for Gehlen including *SS-Standartenführer* Frederich Panziger, another old friend of Müller's who had married into his family. Panziger was not responsible for wartime atrocities but was a key player in the break-up of the *Rote Kapelle,* a Russian spy ring considered to be of great value to Gehlen.

If retired Lt. Colonel Hermann Baun had thought to damage his nemesis Gehlen, he was in error. His lengthy and detailed report only made Gehlen more popular with the US intelligence agency that ran him and, through them, with the US-controlled puppet government of West Germany—a government that did exactly what it was told and clicked its heels together while doing it.

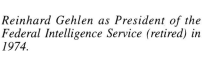

Reinhard Gehlen as President of the Federal Intelligence Service (retired) in 1974.

What did the CIA and those in the more elevated US positions of command know about the flawed membership of their prize German possession? Was the quickly suppressed Baun report the only indicator that had surfaced between 1948 and 1956? If there was any substantive material on this subject, it certainly would never be made available to anyone and would, undoubtedly, be sequestered in some remote place in Arizona or perhaps even somewhere on the grounds of an academic institution closer to hand.

The author's correspondence and conversations with Colonel James Critchfield, once the CIA overseer of the Gehlen organization during its tenure as an American agency, has shed considerable light on the subject.

Critchfield initially acknowledged awareness of the use by the CIA-run Gehlen agency of a number of the individuals encountered earlier in this chapter. However, the Colonel, now living in comfortable retirement in Williamsburg, Virginia, stated that aside from Dr. Six, he had no knowledge of any of the allegations of war crimes against his former employees, which he termed "outrageous." He stated finally that Krichbaum, whom he had earlier claimed to have played a "very important role in our history" was certainly not a member of the SS, not Müller's Deputy Chief of the Gestapo, not involved with the deportation and deaths of the Hungarian Jews, and could never have shot Raoul Wallenberg. The question of the Wallenberg killing comes solely from Müller's statements and no corroboration of it can be found though it is unlikely that Müller would admit on the record that he had ordered such a potentially damaging act unless he actually had. The membership of Krichbaum in the SS, his rank, and his position inside the Gestapo organization is absolutely beyond doubt. All of Willi Krichbaum's official history, as that of the others included in this study is presently available for public inspection in the US National Archives records in Washington.

Also beyond doubt is the participation of a significant number of unsavory individuals in the CIA-controlled Gehlen organization and no question whatsoever as to the atrocities they committed while members of the SD and Gestapo.

From 1945 on, the US had control of the Berlin Document Center, which was the repository for all SS, Gestapo and SD personnel files. US investigators were *required* to check the backgrounds of *all* potential German employees against their records. In addition, CROWCASS (Central Registry of War Crimes and Security Suspects) files contained the names of suspected or wanted war criminals. The CROWCASS information was widely circulated to American agencies, including the CIA, which were in a position to hire or come into contact with such people. These files, which contained a great deal of potentially damaging information on German nationals, were turned over to Gehlen in 1948, no doubt to assist his recruitment drives.

When pressed, Colonel Critchfield acknowledged the existence of the background and personal history files and dossiers but averred that the investigation of his employees had been a matter for the Central Registry of the
CIC. When asked if he had ever been advised by this agency that many of his

senior functionaries were on the wanted lists, Critchfield gave no response.

Intelligence agencies have a tendency to place former military personnel in positions of responsibility precisely because they are trained to obey, without questioning, orders from superiors.

Reinhard Gehlen is not the actual focus of this study. The actual focus is the use by American intelligence agencies of persons who had no particular substantive intelligence value and whose employment by them was then and is now, indefensible. The knowing employment of the CIA of Krichbaum, Dr. Franz Six, and many others whose names can be found in the Baun report and the fact that this specifically led US intelligence to depend heavily on these badly flawed individuals is the issue.

By their dependence on these people, the US agencies permitted ideological Germans with a strong and pervasive detestation of the Soviet Union and an overriding urge to seek revenge for their defeat by this country to promote, often with great success, their own agendas which in most cases were self-serving and certainly not in the best interests of the American public.

In 1996, the San Jose, California, *Mercury-News* published material alleging that elements of the CIA knowingly permitted and encouraged the sale of narcotics by Latino drug dealers to essentially black, inner city residents. The strong implication contained in this report is that the wave of dangerous, disruptive and fatal drug sales and use in the black communities stemmed, in large part, from CIA instigation, and an attempt on their part to finance the Contras of Nicaragua who were then engaged in guerrilla warfare with the Marxist Sandinistas. The CIA has long and often been accused of utilizing monies from the transportation and sale of illegal drugs, in the main heroin and cocaine, to fund many of its operations for which they were unable to obtain official Congressional monetary support.

In the case of the *Mercury-News* coverage, the resultant uproar from the outraged black communities brought responses from the CIA that were both predictable and instructional.

The *Washington Post* and the *Los Angeles Times,* long known as friendly resources for official Washington, rushed into print with rebukes of both the San Jose newspaper's stories, editors and its reporter—a theme eagerly seized upon by other such media outlets. There is an old adage that "Once a newspaperman, always a whore." This is an erroneous and insulting statement. Whores perform their acts solely for money and nothing else. A slut, on the other hand, conducts her sexual rampages merely because it feels good. In the interest of accuracy and in defense of the character of whores, it might be better said that with few exceptions, the media are sluts ready to work for free for the US intelligence community.

John Deutsch, embattled Director of the CIA, made a public relations trip to Los Angeles where he spoke at an open meeting of the black community. He was booed and insulted by them, disbelieving his pious denials and promises of a "thorough investigation" into the allegations.

A predictable Congressional hearing into the issue was regaled by testimony from former Contra leaders who denied any of the published allegations. Again, their testimony was greeted with vocal outbursts from the audience who claimed that the business was being officially covered up, not unlike the previous hearings on the massacre at Waco, which were full of official sound and fury, signifying nothing.

The statements contained in this chapter concerning the known use by the US intelligence community of identified war criminals are based solidly on fact and record. This will certainly not prevent those in government service, both official and unofficial, from following a parallel course to the countering of the *Mercury-News* coverage.

For some years it has been said that a controversial issue does not gain credibility in the eyes of the public until it has been officially denied in Washington. To this official denial must be added confirming attacks by the media, the official public relations outlet for the government. No one believes them either.

Listing of Communist Groups in the United States

The following list was attached to a lengthy file in Müller's papers and was an official US government document:

American League for Peace and Democracy
268 Fourth Avenue
New York City
   Dr. Harry F. Ward, chairman
   R.M. Lovett
   Earl Browder (head of the CPUSA)
   Clarence Hathaway

Amalgamated Clothing Workers (CIO)
15 Union Square
New York City
   Sidney Hillman, president
   Jacob F. Potofsky

American Association for Social Security
41 Union Square
New York City
   Abraham Epstein, secretary
   Bishop F.J. McConnell

American Civil Liberties Union
31 Union Square
New York City
   Dr. H.F. Ward
   Roger N. Baldwin,
   Arthur Garfield Hays
   Robert W. Dunn

American Federation of Teachers, Local No. 5
114 East Sixteenth Street
New York City
 C.J. Hendly, president
 Rev. Jerome Davis, national president
 Dr. Bernhard Stern

American Committee for Protection of Foreign Born
100 Fifth Ave.
New York City
 Rev. Herman F. Reissig, chairman
 Charles Recht
 Carol Weiss King

American Friends of the Chinese People
168 West Twenty-third Street
New York City
 M.S. Stewart, chairman
 M. Forsyth
 Prof. R.M. Lovett
 George S. Counts

American Friends of the Soviet Union
461 Fourth Avenue
New York City
 Corliss Lamont
 A.A. Heller, treasurer

American Student Union
112 East Nineteenth Street
New York City
 Joseph P. Lash, secretary
 Celeste Strack (units in 300 US colleges)

American Youth Congress
55 West Forty-second Street
New York City
 (Organized by the Young Communist League)
 W. Hinckley, chairman
 Joseph P. Lash

Young Communist League
464 Sixth Avenue
New York City
 Carl Ross

Celeste Strack
Angelo Herndon

Communist Worker's School
31 East Twelfth Street
New York City
   A. Markoff, director
   J.R. Brodsky
   Dr. H. Selsan
   L. Boudin
   H. Sacer
   Irving Schwab

Co-operative League of the United States of America
167 West Twelfth Street
New York City (Moscow affiliate)
   Dr. J.P. Warbuse, president

Communist Party, United States of America
35 East Twelfth Street
New York City
   W.Z. Foster, chairman
   Earl Browder, general secretary
   H. Benjamin
   W. Weiner
   J.W. Ford
   A.W. Berry
   A. Markoff

Congress of Industrial Organizations, New York State Council
1133 Broadway
New York City
   John L. Lewis, national president
   New York State, A.S. Haywood, president

China Aid Council
268 Fourth Avenue
New York City
   M. Forsyth
   J. Waterman Wise
   Rabbi S.S. Wise
   M. Stewart,
   Joseph P. Lash
   J.P. Davis
   O. Lattimore

Communist Worker's Bookshop
50 East Thirteenth Street
New York City

Daily Worker
50 East Thirteenth Street
New York City
  Clarence Hathaway, Editor

Federated Press
30 Irving Place
New York City
  Frank L. Palmer, president

Federation of Architects, Engineers, Chemists and Technicians (CIO)
  L.A. Berne, president
  M.E. Scherer, vice president

Descendants of the American Revolution (born)
126 East Nineteenth Street
New York City
  M. Hatfield, national chairman
  Arthur Garfield Hays, attorney

Garland Fund (American Fund for Public Service)
2 West Thirteenth Street
New York City
  R. Baldwin
  Morris L. Ernst

International Labor Defense (Moscow affiliate)
112 East Nineteenth Street
New York City
  Vito Marcantonio, president
  J. Brodsky

International Ladies Garment Workers Union
2 West Sixteenth Street
New York City
  David Dubinsky, president

International Publishers
381 Fourth Avenue
New York City
A. Trachtenberg

Jewish Daily Freiheit
50 East Thirteenth Street
  M.J. Olgin, editor

Jewish People's Committee versus Fascism and Anti-Semitism
1133 Broadway
New York City
  W. Weiner, president

Labor Research Association
80 Fifth Avenue
New York City
  R.W. Dunn, director (Garland Fund-aided)

International Workers Order
80 Fifth Avenue
New York City
  W. Weiner, president
  J. Brodsky, attorney

League for Mutual Aid
104 Fifth Avenue
New York City
  A. Schulkind, executive secretary
  J. Davis,
  J. Baker

League of American Writers
381 Fourth Avenue
New York City
  D.C. Stewart, President
  F. Fulsome, executive secretary
  M. Gold
  G. Hicks

League of Women Shoppers
220 Fifth Avenue
New York City
  E. Preston (Mrs. R.N. Baldwin)
  M. Forsyth

Methodist Federation for Social Service
150 Fifth Avenue
New York City
  Bishop F.J. McConnell

National Committee for People's Rights
150 Fifth Avenue
New York City
    R.. Kent, chairman
    M. Gold

National Lawyers Guild
31 Union Square
New York City

National Maritime Union (CIO)
126 Eleventh Avenue
New York City
    J. Curran, president

National Mooney-Billings Committee
112 East Nineteenth Street
New York City
    Rabbi S.S. Wise

National Negro Congress
35 East Twelfth Street
New York City
    A.P. Randolph, president
    J.W. Ford
    A. Herndon
    J.P. Davis

National Urban League
1133 Broadway
New York City
    Rev. L. Hollingsworth Wood
    W.C. Poletti

National Women's Trade Union League
247 Lexington Avenue
New York City
    R. Schneiderman
    A. Nestor
    M. Schwartz

Negro Youth Congress
35 East Twelfth Street
New York City
    W.F. Richardson, chairman

E.E. Strong, secretary

New School for Social Research
66 West Twelfth Street
New York City
  A. Johnson, president
  B. Bass, attorney
  Heywood Broun

North American Committee to Aid Spanish Democracy
381 Fourth Avenue
New York City
  Bishop F.J. McConnell

Peoples Press
1133 Broadway
New York City
  Corliss Lamont, owner
  J. Waterman Wise
  R.S. Childs

Progressive Women's Council
80 East Eleventh Street
New York City
  C. Shavelson, president
  Rose Nelson, secretary
  R. Chaikin

Rand School of Social Science (socialist)
7 East Fifteenth Street
New York City
  D. Alexander
  Norman Thomas

Social Economic Foundation, Inc.
  Corliss Lamont
  A.A. Heller
  C. Recht
  M. Van Kleek, directors

Social Work Today (magazine)
112 East Nineteenth Street
New York City
  B. Goldman
  S.M. Issacs
  L. Merrill
  M. Van Kleek

Scottsboro Defense Committee
112 East Nineteenth Street
New York City
 Rev. A.K. Chalmers, director

Socialist Party, United States of America
11 West Seventeenth Street
New York City
 Norman Thomas
 J. Altman

Southern Tenant Farmers Union (CIO)
112 East Nineteenth Street/50 East Twelfth Street
New York City
 H. Kester

Transport Workers Union (CIO)
80 East Eleventh Street
New York City
 M. Quill, president
 A. Hogan
 T. Santo

United Christian Council for Democracy
150 Fifth Avenue
New York City
 W.F. Cochran, president
 R. Niebuhr

United Office and Professional Workers of America (CIO)
30 East Twentieth Street
New York City
 J. Merrill, president

Workers Library Publishers, Inc.
39 East Twelfth Street
New York City
(Specialists in CPUSA propaganda)

Workers Defense League
112 East Nineteenth Street
New York City
 J. Davis
 R. Morss Lovett
M. Shapiro

Norman Thomas

Workers Alliance, New York State Section
781 Broadway
New York City
  S. Weisman, president
  D. Lasser

Women's International League for Peace and Freedom
150 Fifth Avenue
New York City

Young Pioneers
80 Fifth Avenue
New York City
(Branch of CPUSA)

Bookniga Corporation
245 Fifth Avenue
New York City

This list, as the second list, was an official list, but it was issued on August 1, 1939 and drawn from FBI investigations and other investigative agencies. The second list was prepared in 1948 and amended through 1953. Communist-controlled groups noted in the pre-war list and post-war catalog are marked with an asterick.

In the interim, a number of labor organizations had purged their ranks of communists and some of the more blatant pro-communist groups disbanded or were shut down by government action.

Although Roosevelt flatly forbade interception of Soviet message transmissions between the United States and Russia, the intelligence agencies involved in these interceptions continually disobeyed him. Membership in these various associations, councils, committees and Soviet-supported groups did not prove that a member was an active communist or a spy. Thousands of individuals of a strong liberal bent joined many of these organizations without being communists or even supporting communist aims. The proliferation of these groups clearly shows how Moscow set a myriad of attractive traps for the unsuspecting or the mildly sympathetic. From this large pool of candidates, Moscow often selected future spies. Many of these individuals were instructed to withdraw from incriminating associations, go underground, become members of conservative groups and even criticize former members.

Post-1948 List of Communist Identified Organizations
Abraham Lincoln Brigade
Abraham Lincoln School, Chicago, Illinois
Action Committee to Free Spain Now

Alabama People's Educational Association
American Association for Reconstruction in Yugoslavia, Inc.
American Branch of the Federation of Greek Maritime Unions
American Committee for Protection of Foreign Born *
American Committee for Spanish Freedom
American Committee for the Settlement of Jews in Birobidjan, Inc.
American Committee for Yugoslav Relief, Inc.
American Committee to Survey Labor Conditions in Europe
American Committee for a Democratic Greece
American Council on Soviet Relations
American Jewish Labor Council
American League Against War and Fascism
American League for Peace and Democracy
American Peace Crusade
American Peace Mobilization
American Poles for Peace
American Polish Labor Council
American Polish League
American Rescue Ship Mission
American Russian Institute (aka American Russian Institute for Relations
    with the Soviet Union)
American Russian Institute, Philadelphia
American Russian Institute of San Francisco
American Russian Institute of Southern California, Los Angeles
American Slav Congress
American Women for Peace
American Youth Congress *
American Youth for Democracy
Armenian Progressive League of America
Benjamin Davis Freedom Committee
Boston School for Marxist Studies, Boston, Massachusetts
Bridges-Robertson-Schmidt Defense Committee
Bulgarian American People's League of the United States of America
California Emergency Defense Committee
California Labor School, Inc., 321 Divisadero Street, San Francisco, California
Carpatho-Russian People's Society
Cervantes Fraternal Society
China Welfare Appeal, Inc.
Chopin Cultural Center
Citizens Committee for Harry Bridges
Citizens Committee of the Upper West Side (New York City)
Citizens Committee to Free Earl Browder
Citizens Emergency Defense Committee
Citizens Protective League

Civil Liberties Sponsoring Committee of Pittsburgh

Civil Rights Congress (and its affiliated organizations, including
  Civil Rights Congress for Texas)
Veterans Against Discrimination of Civil Rights Congress of New York
Comite Coordinador Pro Republica Espanola
Comite Pro Derechos Civiles
Committee for a Democratic Far Eastern Policy
Committee for Constitutional and Political Freedom
Committee for Peace and Brotherhood Festival in Philadelphia
Committee for the Defense of the Pittsburgh Six
Committee for the Negro in the Arts
Committee for the Protection of the Bill of Rights
Committee for World Youth Friendship and Cultural Exchange
Committee to Abolish Discrimination in Maryland
Committee to Defend the Rights and Freedom of Pittsburgh's
  Political Prisoners
Committee to Uphold the Bill of Rights
Commonwealth College, Mena, Arkansas
Communist Party, USA (its subdivisions, subsidiaries and affiliates)
Communist Political Association (its subdivisions, subsidiaries and affiliates,
including:
  Alabama People's Educational Association
  Florida Press and Educational League
  Oklahoma League for Political Education
  People's Educational and Press Association of Texas
  Virginia League for People's Education)
Congress Against Discrimination
Congress of American Revolutionary Writers
Congress of American Women
Congress of the Unemployed
Connecticut Committee to Aid Victims of the Smith Act
Connecticut State Youth Conference
Council for Jobs, Relief and Housing
Council for Pan-American Democracy
Council of Greek Americans
Council on African Affairs
Daily Worker Press Club
Dennis Defense Committee
Detroit Youth Assembly
East Bay Peace Committee
Emergency Committee to Save Spanish Refugees
Everybody's Committee to Outlaw War
Families of the Baltimore Smith Act Victims
Families of the Smith Act Victims
Finnish-American Mutual Aid Society
Frederick Douglas Educational Center

Freedom Stage, Inc.
Friends of the Soviet Union
George Washington Carver School, New York City
Harlem Trade Union Council
Hawaii Civil Liberties Committee
Hellenic-American Brotherhood
Hollywood Writers Mobilization for Democracy
Hungarian-American Council for Democracy
Hungarian Brotherhood
Idaho Pension Union
Independent Party, Seattle, Washington
Industrial Workers of the World
International Labor Defense *
International Workers Order (its subdivisions, subsidiaries and affiliates) *
Jewish Culture Society
Jewish People's Committee
Jewish People's Fraternal Order
Joint Anti-Fascist Refugee Committee
Joseph Weydemeyer School of Social Science, St. Louis, Missouri
Labor Council for Negro Rights
Labor Research Association, Inc. *
Labor Youth League
League for Common Sense
League of American Writers *
Macedonian-American People's League
Maritime Labor Committee to Defend Al Lannon
Massachusetts Committee for the Bill of Rights
Massachusetts Minute Women for Peace
Maurice Braverman Defense Committee
Michigan Civil Rights Federation
Michigan Council for Peace
Michigan School of Social Sciences
National Association of Mexican Americans
National Committee for Freedom of the Press
National Committee for the Defense of Political Prisoners
National Committee to Win Amnesty for Smith Act Victims
National Committee to Win the Peace
National Conference on American Policy in China and the Far East
National Council of American-Soviet Friendship
National Federation for Constitutional Liberties
National Labor Conference for Peace
National Negro Congress *
National Negro Labor Council
Nature Friends of America

Negro Labor Victory Committee

New Committee for Publications
North American Committee to Aid Spanish Democracy *
North American Spanish Aid Committee
North Philadelphia Forum
Ohio School of Social Sciences
Oklahoma Committee to Defend Political Prisoners
Pacific Northwest Labor School, Seattle, Washington
Palo Alto Peace Club, Palo Alto, California
Peace Information Center
Peace Movement of Ethiopia
People's Drama, Inc.
People's Educational Association (Los Angeles Educational Center)
People's Institute of Applied Religion
People's Programs (Seattle, Washington)
People's Radio Foundation, Inc.
Philadelphia Labor Committee for Negro Rights
Philadelphia School of Social Science and Art
Photo League
Pittsburgh Art Club
Political Prisoners' Welfare Committee
Polonia Society of the IWO
Proletarian Party of America
Protestant War Veterans of the United States, Inc.
Provisional Committee of Citizens for Peace, Southwest Area
Provisional Committee on Latin American Affairs
Quad City Committee for Peace
Queensborough Tenants League
Revolutionary Workers League
Romanian-American Fraternal Society
Russian American Society, Inc.
Samuel Adams School, Boston, Massachusetts
Santa Barbara Peace Forum, Santa Barbara, California
Schappes Defense Committee
Schneiderman-Darcy Defense Committee
School of Jewish Studies
Seattle Labor School, Seattle, Washington
Serbian-American Fraternal Society
Serbian Vidovidan Council
Slavic Council of Southern California
Slovak Workers Society
Slovenian-American National Council
Socialist Workers Party, including American Committee for European
    Workers' Relief
Southern Negro Youth Congress
Syracuse Women for Peace

Tom Paine School of Westchester, New York
Trade Union Committee for Peace
Trade Unionists for Peace
Tri-State Negro Trade Union Council
Ukranian-American Fraternal Union
Union of New York Veterans
United American Spanish Aid Committee
United Committee of Jewish Societies and Landsmanschaft
United Committee of South Slavic Americans
United Defense Council of Southern California
United Harlem Tenants and Consumers Organization
United May Day Committee
United Negro and Allied Veterans of America
United World Federalists
Veterans of the Abraham Lincoln Brigade
Virginia League for People's Education
Voice of Freedom Committee
Walt Whitman School of Social Science, Newark, New Jersey
Washington Bookshop Association
Washington Committee for Democratic Action
Washington Committee to Defend the Bill of Rights
Washington Commonwealth Federation
Washington Pension Union
Wisconsin Conference on Social Legislation
Workers Alliance
Yiddisher Kultur Farband
Young Communist League *
Yugoslav-American Cooperative Home, Inc.
Yugoslav Seamen's Club, Inc.

The incredible proliferation of Marxist groups was only matched by their choice of misleading titles. The great majority of these entities sprang up after Roosevelt's election in 1933 and were extremely active during the Second World War. After Roosevelt's death in 1945, there was a general whithering of these groups. With the advent of the Cold War their fortunate demise was certain.

Heinrich Müller, who understood the nature of communism better than most, once commented that communism had to be viewed as a religion and not as a political movement if one wished to fully comprehend its attraction to certain people.

If Rome were to vanish in some natural disaster, Catholics of the world would not become Baptist. Rather, they would merely relocate the center of their church to another area. When the Soviet Union disintegrated, Marxists in foreign countries did not become conservatives but instead attempted to move the center of their church to a safer area.

That the United States might well become the next Marxist nest has become evident in the intense activity of hardcore liberals attempting to gain control of their country to replicate their own Rome.

Following a pattern that became evident during and after the heyday of the New Deal, these Marxist devotees have quickly moved into the fields of education, the media, the diverse ethnic movements, and the bureaucracy of the nation with an intensity that is frightening. Müller's comments regarding the failed intellectual's frenzy to control others in order to promote his own faith is certainly analogous to post-Moscow's frenetic search for a new nesting place.

Hence, the triumph of evil is far more certain in the absence of vigilance.

The Browning Version: An Examination of Sources

In his book, *The Path to Genocide*[1] published in 1992, Dr. Christopher Browning states; "In the summer of 1941, probably in July, Hitler indicated his approval for the preparation of a plan for the mass murder of all European Jews under Nazi control, though just how and when this was communicated to Himmler and Heydrich cannot be established."

The probability of such an approval has been elevated to fact in a subsequent study by Dr. Browning, *The Euphoria of Victory and the Final Solution: Summer-Fall 1941*.[2] "When Hitler gave his "victory" speech in mid-July, instigating the immediate implementation of the Final Solution on Soviet territory…" is the specific quote. Since this speech and its implications are of considerable historical importance considering the total lack of such a specific order in official German documents, a careful search was made of Hitler's speeches during the summer months of 1941.

From the opening of the campaign against the Soviet Union on June 21, 1941 until October 1941, Hitler made no speeches, and the speech he did make on October 3 at the *Sportspalast* in Berlin at the opening of the Winter Aid campaign contained only references to the German military successes in the East and made no mention of any "final solution."[3] In response to a query by the author as to the date of this victory speech, Dr. Browning replied in a letter dated November 23, 1994 that the speech in question was taken from Nuremberg Document 221-L. He explained further that the reference he made to a speech was not really a speech but a monologue to a limited audience.[4]

---

[1] *"The Path to Genocide"*, Cambridge, 1992 p. 25.

[2] *"The Euphoria of Victory and the Final Solution: Summer-Fall 1941"* German Studies Review, October, 1994, pps 473-481.

[3] *VB Nr. 278 of 5. October 1941; Domarus, "HITLER-Reden und Proklamationen 1932-1943," Vol.II, Munich, 1965, pps. 1758-1767.*

[4] *Letter from Dr. Christopher Browning to author, 23 November 1994.*

A search of the German language records of the International Military Tribunal located Document 221-L in Vol. 38, pp. 86-94. Dr. Browning was incorrect. The "speech" was in reality a documentary record taken by *Reichsleiter* Martin Bormann, Hitler's secretary, at a closed meeting held in Hitler's headquarters on July 16, 1941.

It was neither a speech nor a monologue but a precis of a high-level conference concerning, primarily, the administration of newly-acquired territory in Russia. This precis speaks for itself, certainly without an interpretation. In the following translation of the precis, the reader may judge as to the specifics of what Dr. Browning has termed the "implementation of the Final Solution."

Dr. Browning's article focuses on the decision for a Final Solution, which he defines as the Germans' "attempt to murder every last Jew in Europe." He claims that there were two possible plans of action for carrying out the extermination of Jews. The first plan was created in mid-July of 1941 and was specifically designed towards the "total mass murder of Soviet Jewry." Dr. Browning states: "In mid-July, convinced that the military campaign was nearly over and victory was at hand, an elated Hitler gave the signal to carry out an accelerated pacification and racial 'cleansing' of the newly acquired territories in European Russia." He states further: "When Hitler gave his 'victory' speech in mid-July, instigating the immediate implementation of the Final Solution on Soviet territory…"

A reading of Dr. Browning's source, Nuremberg document 221-L, however, does not bear out his thesis. The conference concerns itself entirely with the administration of the newly-acquired territories. The only subjects that even remotely approach Dr. Browning's specific claims refer to the combating of the recently-instituted Soviet partisan movement, the establishment of a security system in the territories and the evacuation of Soviets from the Crimea to colonize the area with Germans.

There is not one word in the text of this conference that refers to Jews or any theoretical plan for their mass extermination in former Soviet territory or elsewhere. The only possible connection is the discussion concerning the ruthless combating of partisans, which were led by political commissars and high-level communist party functionaries, contained such phrases as "shooting" and "rooting out." Because the leadership of the partisans, the commissars and party leaders was almost exclusively Jewish, a tenuous conclusion could be argued that by destroying the partisan movement, Hitler was calling for the destruction of Jews in the eastern territories.

As to the participants in this conference addressing any kind of a "Final Solution," there is not one word contained in the notes of the conference alluding to the extermination of the Jews.

Convoluted, inverted logic seem to be the hallmark of *fin de siècle* historical writers, demi-journalists and ideologues when they deal with the subject of the persecution of Jews in Europe and Russia between 1933 and 1945.

Both Dr. Browning's article and the following article by Richard Breitman, "Plans for the Final Solution in Early 1941," in the same journal, contain a number of phrases which strongly indicate that those who write on the subject are reduced to suppositions, theories and, in the majority of cases, fictive renderings or strained couplings of unrelated facts.

In Dr. Browning's article, the following phrases tend to support this latter thesis, "Were Hitler's decisions of implementation long preceded by 'basic' decisions and 'secret plans'? Here the historian is necessarily on much more speculative grounds...My reasoning in this regard is admittedly speculative, as is that of other historians who wrestle with the issue." Dr. Browning offers "scenarios" which might be acceptable for a playwright or a short story writer, but fall totally short of any usefulness to a person attempting to work with historical fact. The word "seems" appears a number of times: ..."Himmler *seems* to have known" and "...Hitler...*seems* to have incited similar planning for the murder of European Jewry in mid-July."

Richard Breitman's article in the same edition of *German Studies Review* is presented in a similar vein as that of Dr. Browning.[5]

Here are found such quotations as "Deciphering Hitler's exact intentions at a given time, however, is both tricky and subjective, given his habit of concealment and his disinclination to give explicit, written orders. There is a constant pattern of veiling measures against Jews (and other victimized groups) with euphemisms." Breitman mentions various meetings of top Third Reich leaders with such comments as "There is no record of who else (besides Hitler) was present or exactly what was discussed...The content of these meetings of the key authorities on the Final Solution went unrecorded—or at least no notes of them have survived." Breitmann speaks of "ambiguous language, euphemisms, and camouflage" and begins his penultimate paragraph with "To my knowledge, neither Heydrich or Himmler referred directly to the date of plans for the Final Solution or of Hitler's authorization of it in a form that has reached posterity."

In short, both Browning and Breitman support the theory that no written proof exists concerning the Final Solution.

Franciszek Piper discusses this theory when he writes on the number of victims of anti-semitism during the period of the Third Reich. Piper speaks of the reliance of researchers on "discrepant and imprecise data from testimonies and depositions of witnesses, former prisoners, and Nazi functionaries and on court decisions and fragmentary and incomplete records of camp registries, archives and other institutions."[6]

The former Soviet Archives contain the complete file of the German concentration camp system seized by Soviet troops at Oranienburg camp in 1945. These are not fragmentary records but complete and from these, it is apparent that the death tolls in all the camps from their beginnings to the end of the war was approximately 400,000.[7]

[5] *"Plans for the Final Solution in Early 1941,"* German Studies Review, October, 1994, pps 483-493.

[6] *"Anatomy of the Auschwitz Death Camp"* ed. Gutman and Berenbaum, Indiana University Press, 1994, p. 62.

Any researcher who has attempted to discover factual material concerning this subject will attest to the enormous proliferation of published material which started during the war and is still in progress, and whose thrust is far more commercial and self-serving than historical. Since historians traditionally pilfer from one another without footnoting the source, it is a laborious task to attempt to locate specific original period sources for intentions, orders and statistics.

Tracking backwards is a time-consuming and completely unrewarding experience. Finally, one comes to the realization that has apparently struck Messers Browning, Breitman and others: There are no specifics.

Lack of documentation on the Final Solution has led to another explanation: Code words were used to denote mass murder. "Deportation" was the code for transport to Auschwitz and mass gassings. "Forced labor," "emigration," "resettlement," "uprooting," and "expulsion" were also code words for transport to Auschwitz. The fact that nowhere in the vast archives of captured German documents can original documents be located that specifically address any state-ordered deportation and murder of Jewish civilians (as opposed to Jewish partisans) could either indicate that researchers are incredibly stupid or that no such documents ever existed because there was no such official program.

There is no question that Jews, both in Germany and, in fact, throughout Europe, were deported by official order. Most of these Jews were sent to the Auschwitz camp and many died while imprisoned and forced to work as laborers. But, to date there has never been one authenic document produced by any researcher or historian that establishes the existence of an official governmental policy of mass murder of Jews as a racial entity.

When a reputable historical journal publishes an article by an equally reputable academic writer who states that a public document contains specific orders by Hitler for the extermination of Jews and that document, in fact, contains absolutely nothing to support the author's thesis, then the question arises as to how many other treatments of this subject have been similarly distorted?

The recurring theme seems to be that since everyone *knows* that these enormous massacres are commonly believed to have occurred, then there has to be confirming, official documentation in support of their theories. Since no such documentation exists, historians determined to support their thesis can say, as they repeatedly do, that documentation *should* exist and since it *should* exist, the next step is to see that it does. Therefore, creativity eventually takes

---

[7]*An article on former Soviet archival material appeared in the New York Times of March 3, 1991 and addresses the total figure of 400,000 dead in the camps "under the Third Reich". It specifically refers to the 70,000 dead in Auschwitz from 1942 to 1945.*

The actual figures found on Soviet archival microfilms show a slightly higher figure for Auschwitz, viz 73,000. A response to these totals, astonishing in their nature, is that no allowance has been made for "secret lists" which, since they are secret, cannot be found.

the place of objectivity to the terminal detriment of both the historian's reputation and the validity of his theory.

Translation of 221-L
Führer Headquarters, 16. July 1941
Bo/Fu (Bormann/*Führer*)
Secret State Matters (Top Secret/non-military)
Documentary record
On orders of the *Führer*, a conference was held today at 1500 hours with *Reichsleiter* Rosenberg, *Reichsminister* Lammers, *Feldmarschall* Keitel, the *Reichsmarschall* (Göring) and myself (*Reichsleiter* Bormann).

The conference began at 1500 hours and continued, with a coffee break, until about 2000 hours.

The *Führer* began by stressing that he wished, first of all, to address certain basic concerns. Various measures were now necessary and as proof of this, for example, a statement in an impudent Vichy newspaper that the war against the Soviet Union is a European war, conducted for all of Europe.

Obviously, the Vichy paper wishes to say, by this hint, that the beneficiaries of this war should not be the Germans alone but that all of the European states should profit as well.

Essentially, we have not publicized our aims before the world; this is not necessary, but the main thing is that we ourselves know what we want. By no means should we make our way more difficult by making unnecessary statements. Such statements are unnecessary because where we have the power we do all we can and where we do not have the power, we can do nothing anyway.

The motivations of our actions before the world must also have a tactical point of view. We must act here exactly as we did in the cases of Norway, Denmark, Holland and Belgium. In these cases we also said nothing about our intentions and it is sensible to continue this.

We repeat, again, that we are constrained to occupy an area to bring order and security; in the interests of the occupants we must establish control in the interest of tranquility, support, commerce, etc., etc., It is, consequently, not perceived that by this means we establish the way for more definitive control! All necessary measures—shooting, resettlement etc.,— we can and should do.

We do not wish, however, to prematurely and unnecessarily turn the population into enemies. We shall act, therefore, as if we are exercising a mandate only. We must recognize at the same time that we will never leave these territories.

We should deal with this accordingly:
1. Do nothing to push ultimate control but keep such preparations in hand;
2. We proclaim that we come as liberators.

In specific:
The Crimea must be evacuated by all foreigners and settled by Germans. In the same manner, the former old Austrian territory of Galicia will become a

territory of the Reich. Presently, our relations with Rumania are good but one does not know what these will be in the future. We must consider this and formulate our borders accordingly. We should not have to be dependent upon the goodwill of others; we must plan our relations with Rumania in accordance with this principle.

Basically we have the task of apportioning this giant cake to suit our needs, so that we are able to:

first, to control it,
second, to govern it, and
third, to profit from it.

The Russians have now given an order to conduct partisan warfare behind our front lines. This partisan warfare also gives us the opportunity of rooting out all those who are in opposition to us.

Fundamental principles:

The creation of a military power west of the Urals should never again be possible, even if we have to engage in warfare for a hundred years. All successors of the *Führer* should know : The security of the nation depends on there being no foreign military presence west of the Urals. Germany must protect this area from all future eventualities. Our iron principle must be and must remain:

It must not be permitted for anyone but Germans to bear arms here !

This is especially important concerning the question of utilizing the armed assistance of the peoples of occupied territories. This is wrong! This policy can turn against us in the end. Only Germans can bear arms—not Slavs, not Czechs, not the Cossacks or Ukranians!

We should be no means adopt a vacillating policy such as we saw in Alsace before 1918. The mark of the English is that they constantly pursue *one* line and *one* goal! In this regard we should learn from the English.

Accordingly, we should at no time be dependent upon the personalities of individuals: The British suppression of the Indian princes, etc., is an example: The soldier must always secure the regime!

From the newly acquired Eastern territories, we must create a Garden of Eden; this is essential for us; against this, colonies play a subordinate role.

Likewise, if we divide up an area we must always act as the defender of the law and of the inhabitants. Accordingly, the present choice of words is to speak not about a new territory of the *Reich* but a necessary task imposed by the war.

Specifically:

In the Baltic, the area up to the Duna will have to be administered in coordination with Field Marshal Keitel.

Reichsleiter Rosenberg stresses that, in his opinion, treatment of the population should vary from district to district. In the Ukraine, we should commence with a cultural consideration. There we must encourage the cultural awareness of the Ukranians, must establish a university in Kiev and other similar things.

The *Reichsmarschall* points out that we must first think about securing our own food supply and everything else can come later.

(Pertinent question: Is there still a cultural stratum in the Ukraine or are higher class Ukranians found only in emigrants from Russia?)

Rosenberg continues that there are independent movements in the Ukraine which deserve encouragement.

The *Reichsmarschall* requests from the *Führer* information about which areas have been promised to other states.

The *Führer* responds that Antonescu desires Bessarabia and Odessa with an extension leading northwestwards from Odessa.

Upon objections from the *Reichsmarschall* and Rosenberg, the *Führer* responds that the new borders envisioned by Antonescu contained little outside of the old Rumanian territories.

The *Führer* states, further, that insofar as the Hungarians, the Turks and the Slovaks are concerned, nothing has been promised.

The *Führer* submitted for consideration whether one should add the old Austrian part of Galicia to the General Gouvernement; after objections were expressed, the *Führer* decided that this area will not be incorporated into the General Gouvernement but still placed under *Reichsminister* Frank (Lemberg).

The *Reichsmarschall* believes it proper to incorporate various parts of the Baltic territories, for example, the forests of Bialystok, into East Prussia.

The *Führer* stresses that the entire Baltic territory must be incorporated into the *Reich* as a district.

Likewise, the Crimea with an extensive hinterland (area north of the Crimea) should become a district of the *Reich;* the hinterland should be as large as possible.

Rosenberg expressed his objections because of the Ukrainians living in that area.

(Pertinent question: It has occurred to me a number of times that Rosenberg is partial to the Ukrainians; thusly, he wishes to aggrandize the former Ukraine to a considerable degree.)

The *Führer* stressed, in addition, that the Volga Colony must become a *Reich* territory and also the district around Baku; the latter will have to become a German concession (Military colony).

The Finns want East Karelia but the Kola Peninsula will be taken over by the Germans because of the nickel mines there.

The annexation of Finland as a confederated state must be prepared for with all care. The Finns have requested the area around Leningrad; the *Führer* will level Leningrad to the ground and then give it to the Finns.

Then follows a lengthy discussion about the suitability of *Gauleiter* Lohse whom Rosenberg has proposed as Governor of the Baltic area. Rosenberg emphasizes that as he has already spoken with Lohse, it would be very embarrassing if Lohse was not appointed; for the western part of the Baltic area, Kube would be appointed under Lohse; for the Ukraine, Rosenberg has planned on Sauckel.

The *Reichsmarschall* stressed the most important aspect for the present was exclusively: Securing of food supplies and, as far as necessary, of trade; securing transportation.

The *Reichsmarschall* emphasized that Koch should be given the Baltic area because he is well acquainted with it, or one should give Koch the Ukraine because he is the personality with the strongest initiative and the best preparatory training.

The *Führer* questioned if Kube could be made *Reichskommissar* for the Moscow area; Rosenberg and the *Reichsmarschall* feel that Kube was too old.

Rosenberg explained that after repeated interviews, he has apprehensions that Koch would very quickly ignore his instructions; in general, Koch had so indicated himself.

The *Reichsmarschall* pointed out that Rosenberg should not exert constant control, rather, these people must be very independent.

For the Caucasus area, Rosenberg put forward his chief of staff, Schickendanz. He stated that Schickendanz would fulfill his task well, something the *Reichsmarschall* doubted.

Rosenberg then stated that Lutze had proposed that he appoint several SA leaders, namely Scheppmann for Kiev, -Manthey-Dr. Bennecke-Litzmann- for Estonia, and *Bürgermeister* Dr. Drexler for Latvia.

The *Führer* expressed no objections to the employment of SA leaders.

Rosenberg then explained he had received a letter from Ribbentrop requesting participation by the Foreign Office; he requested the *Führer* to determine that the internal formation of the newly acquired areas are not the concern of the Foreign Office. The *Führer* is in agreement with this. For the present, it will suffice for the Foreign Office to appoint a liaison officer to *Reichsleiter* Rosenberg.

The *Führer* pointed out that the most important area for the next three years was doubtlessly the Ukraine. Therefore, it would be best to put Koch there; if Sauckel were to be used, it would be better to appoint him to the Baltic area.

Rosenberg explained further that he wished to appoint Schmeer, Selzer and Manderbach as Commissioners in the Moscow area.

The *Führer* wishes that Holz be used as well and that the administration of the Crimea be taken over by *Gauleiter* Frauenfeld.

Rosenberg explains he intended also to use *Hauptmann* von Petersdorff; general consternation, general rejection. The *Führer* and the *Reichsmarschall* declare that von Petersdorff was, without doubt, mentally ill.

Rosenberg explains further that *Oberbürgermeister* Stroelin of Stuttgart has been suggested to him as an appointee. There were no objections to this.

Since both the *Reichsmarschall* and Rosenberg both agree that Kube is too old for the Moscow district, Kasche will take over this district.

(Note for Pg. Klopfer: Please request immediately from Dr. Meyer the documents on the proposed organizations and on the proposed appointments.)

The *Reichsmarschall* emphasizes he wishes to give the Kola Peninsula to *Gauleiter* Terboven for exploitation. The *Führer* is in agreement with this.

The *Führer* emphasizes that Lohse, provided he feels equal to this task, should take over the Baltic area; Kasche, Moscow; Koch, the Ukraine;

Frauenfeld, the Crimea; Terboven, Kola; and Schickendanz, the Caucasus.
Rosenberg then brought up security for the administration.

The *Führer* said to the *Reichsmarschall* and the *Feldmarschall* that he has always stressed that the Police Regiments should be equipped with tanks; for the operations of the Police in the new Eastern Territories with a corresponding number of tanks, a Police Regiment can accomplish a good deal. In balance, declared the *Führer,* the security is naturally very thin. The *Reichsmarschall* will set up all of his training airfields in the new areas, and if necessary, even the Ju52s can drop bombs on any rebellions. This huge area must naturally be pacified as quickly as possible, and the best way to accomplish this is to "shoot anyone who only looks sideways."

Feldmarschall Keitel declared that the inhabitants must be responsible for their actions because it was naturally not possible to provide guards for each shed and each railroad station. The inhabitants should be aware that those who did not perform their duties were liable to be shot and that they would be held accountable for each assault.

Following a question by *Reichsleiter* Rosenberg, the *Führer* responded, newspapers—also, for example, in the Ukraine—must be reestablished to serve as sources of information for the inhabitants.

After the recess, the *Führer* declared that we must understand that today's Europe is nothing but a geographical term; in reality, Asia extended up to our former borders. *Reichsleiter* Rosenberg then described the organizational structure he intended to establish; he did not intend to appoint a permanent deputy for the *Reichskommissar,* but rather, call upon the services of the most efficient of the General Commissars to deputize for the *Reichskommissar.*

Under the *Reichskommissar* Rosenberg will form four departments:
first, for general administration,
second, for politics,
third, for economics,
fourth, for engineering and construction
(side comments: The *Führer* declares that activity on the part of churches, under no circumstances, is to come under question. Papen had sent him, via the Foreign Office, a long memorandum stating that now was the right moment to re-establish the churches; this, under no circumstances, will be considered.)

The *Reichsmarschall* will second to Rosenberg's office, *Ministerial Direktors* Schlatterer and Riecke.

Reichsleiter Rosenberg requested appropriate housing; he made a request for the Commercial Mission of the Soviet Union in the Lietzenburger Street; the Foreign Office had expressed the opinion, however, that the building was extraterritorial. The *Führer* replied that this was nonsense; *Reichsminister* Dr. Lammers was instructed to inform the Foreign Office that the building was, without further discussion, to be given to Rosenberg.

Rosenberg then proposed to second a liaison officer to the *Führer;* his adjutant Koeppen was to be appointed; the *Führer* agrees and adds that

Koeppen would fulfill a parallel role to that of Hewel.

Reichsminister Dr. Lammers now awaits from him the proposed draft (see Annex!)

A longer discussion took place about the areas of competence of the RFSS. Obviously, the participants also have the areas of competence of the *Reichsmarschall* in mind.

The *Führer*, the *Reichsmarschall* etc., reiterate that Himmler was to have no greater areas of competence than he had in Germany but his jurisdiction here was absolutely necessary.

The *Führer* reiterated that in practice, such disputes would quickly subside; he recalled the excellent cooperation between the Army and Air Force at the front.

In conclusion, it is decided to call the Baltic Areas *Ostland.*

Annex (missing)

The History and Organization of the Gestapo

The *Geheime Staats Polizei*, or the Secret State Police, grew out of the Prussian Political Police, which had been formed by Hermann Göring after he became Prime Minister of the state of Prussia in 1933. The new agency was created by Göring on April 26, 1933. He remained as head of the *Gestapo* but turned the day-to-day running of the agency to *Oberregierungsrat* Diels, who had been head of the Observation of Communism in the Reich Ministry of the Interior.

A. Southard

Rudolf Diels.

In 1934, Himmler persuaded Göring to appoint him to Diels' post. The *Gestapo* was not an official German agency until nearly three years after its inception. A series of decrees on February 28, 1933, March 8, 1934 and May 2, 1935 set forth the establishment of protective custody for political dissenters and the final decree of 1935 stated that the *Gestapo* was not subject to judicial control. On September 20. 1936, a state decree authorized the *Gestapo-Amt* in Prussia to assume all the duties of similar police units throughout the country. On October 1, 1936 the agency was henceforth to be known as the *Geheime Staatspolizei* (or Secret State Police) and was now a national rather than a regional organization and although it was a State agency, it came under Himmler's control.

The primary function of the *Gestapo* was originally of a counterintelligence nature, and in the main, detected and prosecuted crimes of a political nature. The following list indicates the German laws that were enforced by the *Gestapo*.

Landesverrat gem. 88-93 RStGB (Reichs-Strafgesetzbuch)	Treason according to articles 88-93 of the Reich Penal Code.
Hochverrat gem. 80-87 RStGB	High Treason according to articles 80-87 of the Reich Penal Code.
Weitere im RStGB enthaltene Tatbestände wie Öffentliche Beschimpfung des Staats	Other offenses specified in the Reich Penal Code, such as public libel and slander of the Government.
Öffentliche Beschimpfung der Partei und ihrer Gliederungen	Public libel and slander of the NSDAP and its organizations.
Aufruhr	Rioting or incitement to riot.
Verletzung der Wehrpflicht und der Wehrkraft	Avoidance of the Conscription Law and offences against the national military potential.
Unterlassung der rechtzeitigen Anzeige von Verbrechen des Hochverrats, des Landesverrats, usw	Failure to make an immediate report of any knowledge of high treason and other treasonable acts.
Feindliche Handlungen gegen befreundete Staaten	Hostile acts against friendly governments.
Verbrechen und Vergehen in Beziehung auf die Ausübung staatsbürgerlicher Rechte u.a.	Crimes and offenses against the exercise of citizens' rights and privileges.
Zuwiderhandlungen gegen das Gesetz gegen heimtükische Angriffe auf Staat und Partei und zum Schutz der Partei- uniformen vom 20. Dez. 1934	Offenses against the decree of Dec. 20, 1934 dealing with treacherous attacks on the Government and Party and Protection of Party uniforms.
Zuwiderhandlung gegen das Gesetz zum Schutz von Bezeichnungen der NSDAP vom 7. Apr 1937	Offenses against the Decree of April 7, 1937 for the Protection of Party Designations.
Zuwiderhandlungen gegen das Gesetz zum Schutze der nationalen Symbole vom 19. Mai 1933	Offenses against the Decree of May 19, 1933 for the Protection of National Symbols.

Zuwiderhandlungen gegen das Gesetz zur Abwehr politischer Gewalttaten vom 4. Apr 1933	Offenses against the Decree of April 4, 1933 for the Prevention of Political Terrorism or Acts of Violence.
Zuwiderhandlungen gegen das Gesetz gegen Verrat der deutschen Volkswirtschaft vom 12. Juni 1933	Offenses against the Decree of of June 12, 1933 against Treason towards the German Economic System.
Zuwiderhandlungen gegen das Gesetz der Verordnung des Reichspräsidenten zum Schutz von Volk und Staat vom 28. Februar 1933 getroffene Massnahmen	Offenses against any of the Statutes or Ordinances based on the Presidential Decree of February 28, 1933 for the Protection of Nation and Government.
Zuwiderhandlungen gegen das Gesetz über die Einziehung kommunistischen Vermögens vom 26. Mai 1933	Offenses against the Decree of May 26, 1933 covering the Expropriation of Communist Property.
Zuwiderhandlungen gegen das Gesetz zur Gewährleistung des Rechtsfriedens vom 13. Okt 1933	Offenses against the Decree of October 13, 1933 for the Protection of the Judicial Administration.
Zuwiderhandlungen gegen das Gesetz gegen die Neubildung von Parteien vom 14. Juli 1933	Contraventions of the Decree of July 14, 1933 against the Formation of new Political Parties and Factions.
Zuwiderhandlungen gegen das Gesetz gegen Wirtschaftssabotage vom 1. Dez 1936	Offenses against the Decree of of December 1, 1936 against Economic Sabotage.
Zuwiderhandlungen gegen das Gesetz über die Devisenbewirtschaftung Deviesengesetz) vom 12. Dez 1938	Offenses against the Statutes of December 12, 1938 dealing with the Administration of Foreign Exchange (Foreign exchange Regulations and Restrictions).
Zuwiderhandlungen gegen:	Offences against:
(a) die Verordnung über den Warenverkehr vom 18. August 1939	(a) the Ordinance of August 18, 1939 for the Control of Goods and Trade;
(b) die Verordnung über die Wirtschaftsverwaltung vom 18. August 1939	(b) the Ordinance of August 27,1939 establishing the German Economic Administration;

(c) die Verordnung zur vorläufigen Sicherstellung des lebenswichtigen Bedarfs des deutschen Volkes vom 27. August 1934	(c) the Ordinance of August 27, 1939 covering provisionally defined Priorities to provide for the Essential Needs of the German People (Food, Consumer Goods, Fuel, etc.);
(d) die zu den 3 vorerwähnten Verordnungen ergangenen Durchführungs- und-Ergänzungsverordnungen	(d) any other ordinances which were issued as directives and supplements to the three preceding ordinances.
Zuwiderhandlungen gegen die Verordnung über ausserordinliche Rundfunkmassnahmen vom 1. Sept. 1939	Offenses against the Ordinances of September 1, 1939 covering extra-ordinary measures relating to Wireless Transmitting and Receiving.
Zuwiderhandlungen gegen die Grenzzonenverordnung vom 2. Sept 1939	Offenses against the Ordinances of September 2, 1939 for the Protection of the German Border Regions and Internal Customs Zones.
Zuwiderhandlungen gegen die Verordnung über die Behandlung von Ausländern vom 5. Sept 1939	Offenses against the Ordinance of September 5, 1939 dealing with the Treatment of Foreigners (POWs, Non-German workers, etc.).
Zuwiderhandlung gegen die Verordnung gegen Volksschädlinge vom 5. Sept 1939	Offenses against the Ordinances of September 5, 1939 against the Enemies of the People (Antisocial Elements, as defined by German Decrees).
Zuwiderhandlung gegen die Verordnung zur Ergänzung der Strafvorschriften zum Schutz der Wehrkraft des deutschen Volkes vom 25. Nov 1939	Offenses against the Ordinance of November 25, 1939 supplementing the Penal Regulations for the Protection of Germany's war effort.
Zuwiderhandlungen gegen die Polizeiverordnung zum Schutze der nationalen Symbole und Lieder vom 5. Jan 1940	Offenses against the Police Ordinance of January 5, 1940 for the Protection of National Symbols and Songs.

On September 27, 1939, Heinrich Himmler, head of the SS, combined all of the State security forces together under the heading of the *Reichssicherheitshauptamt* (*RSHA*) or National Security Main Office. This new office was comprised of the *Sicherheitspolizei*, which consisted of the *Kripo* or Criminal Police and the *Gestapo* or Secret State Police and the *Sicherheitsdienst* (*SD*) of the SS. Internal references to this department were to the *Reichssicherheitsdienst*. For correspondence with outside agencies it was termed

Chef der Sicherheitspolizen und des SD. In specific cases, the terms *Reichsführer-SS und Chef der Deutschen Polizei* or *Reichsminister der Innern* (National Minister of the Interior). Sections IV and V were permitted to use the titles *Geheimes Staatspolizei* and *Reichskriminalpolizeiamt,* respectively. Depending on the subject addressed and the occasion, the controlling agency could be called the *RSHA, Chef SIPO und SD, RFSSSuChDtPol, RMdI* or *Geheimes Staatspolizeiamt.*

The organization of the *RSHA* in 1944 was as follows:

Amt I
Personal   Under *SS-Gruppenführer* Erwin Schulz
(Personnel)

Amt II
Organisation, Verwaltung und   Under *SS-Standartenführer* Rudolf
Recht (Organization,   Siegert
Administration and Law)

Amt III
Deutsche Lebengebeite   Under *SS-Brigadeführer* Otto
(Spheres of German Life)   Ohlendorf

Amt IV
Gegnerforschung und   (Also known as the *Geheime Staatspolizei*)
Gegnerbekämpfung   Under *SS-Gruppenführer* Heinrich Müller
(Investigation and combatting
of Opposition)

Amt V
Verbrechenbekämpfung   Under *SS-Standartenführer* Friedrich
(Combatting of Crime)   Panziger

Amt VI
Ausland   Under *SS-Brigadeführer* Walter
(Foreign Countries)   Schellenberg

Amt VII
Weltanschauliche Erforschung   Under *Oberführer* Dr. Franz Six
und Auswertung
(Ideological Research and its
Exploitation)

Militärisches Amt
(Military Intelligence)   Under Schellenberg

The *Gestapo* went through numerous alterations as it expanded, and in 1944 it controlled almost all of the intelligence and counterintelligence operations in the *Reich.*

When the Army's *Abwehr* was broken up in 1943, Müller obtained domestic counterintelligence, and by 1944, he had control over almost all other intelligence functions, both inside and outside of Germany.

The final organization, in early 1945, of the *Gestapo* was:

RSHA Amt IV - Gegner-Erforschung und Bekämpfung
Gruppe IVA

IV A 1
Opposition

IV A 1 a

Kommunismus, Marxismus und Neben-organisationen (Nationalkommittee "Freies Deutschland") in Deutschland, den besetzten Gebeiten und auch im Ausland	Communism, Marxism and affiliated organizations (National Committee "Free Germany") in Germany, occupied territories and foreign countries.
Rundfunk-Verbrechen	Violations of broadcasting regulations.
Illegale kommunistische und marxistische Propaganda	Illegal communist and marxist propaganda.
Feindpropaganda—durch Flugblätter und Auslansendungen—und deren Verbreitung	Enemy propaganda—through leaflets and foreign broadcasts—and its dissemination.
Bandenunwesen in Deutschland, der Untersteiermark und Oberkrain	Guerrilla activity in Germany and annexed portions of northern Yugoslavia.
Deutsche und verbündete Kriegsgefangene in Sowjetrussicher Gefangenschaft	German and allied prisoners of war in Soviet captivity.

IV A 1 b

Reaktion	Reactionary movements.
Opposition	Opposition.
Liberalismus	Liberalism.
Legitimusmus	Monarchism.
Pazifismus	Pacifism.
Heimtückeangelegenheiten	Treacherous spreading of rumors, etc.
Zersetzung der Wehrmacht und Miesmacherei	Undermining of the morale of the Armed Forces, grumbling.
Defaitismus	Defeatism.
Unzufriedene Wehrmachtsangehörige in Deutschland, auch in Kriegsgefang-schaft und deren Angehörige	Discontented members of the Armed Forces in Germany, also those in enemy captivity and their next of kin.

IV A 2
Sabotage

IV A 2 a
Sabotageabwehr und -Bekämpfung	Prevention and combating of sabotage.
Politische Attentate	Political assassinations.
Politische Pass- und Ausweisfälschungen	Forgery of passports and identity papers for political purposes.
Terrorism	Terrorism.
Syndikalisten	Syndicalists.

IV A 2 b
Fallschirmagenten	Parachute agents.
Funkspiele	Radio play back.

IV A 3
Abwehr (Counter Intelligence)

IV A 3 a
Gesellschaftsspionage	Combating of espionage in society.
Fahrlässiger Landesverrat	Treason through negligence, careless talk, etc.
Spionage	Combating of political espionage.

IV A 3 b
Wirtschaftsangelegenheiten in Deutschland, den besetzten Gebieten, im Verkehr mit dem Ausland und umgekehrt (siehe auch unter Amt III-RSHA)	Economic matters in Germany and the occupied territories, trade with foreign countries (see also Amt III of the RSHA).
Wirtschaftsspionage	Combatting of espionage.
Surveillance in der Schweiz	Surveillance activities in Switzerland.
Devisenvergehen	Violations of foreign exchange laws.

IVA 3 c
Grenzangelegenheiten, kleiner Grenzverkehr und Grenzzwischenfälle	Frontier Control, local border traffic and frontier incidents.

IV A 3 d
Abwehr über Nachrichtenverkehr	Signals and Communications counterintelligence (monitoring, censorship, etc.).
Verstösse gegen den Nachrichtenverkehr	Illegal Communications traffic.

IV A 4
Weltanschauliche Gegner (Ideological Opponents).

IV A 4 a
Katholizismus und Protestantismus, Catholicism and Protestantism,
Sekten, sonstige Kirchen, Freimaurer sects, other religious agencies,
in Deutschland und den besetzten Freemasons, in Germany and in
Gebeiten the occupied territories.

IV A 4 b
Juden, Emigranten, Volks- und Staats Jews, émigrés, Enemy and
feindliche Vermögensangelegenheiten, Opposition Property, removal of
Aberkennung der Reichsangehörigkeit, Reich citizenship at home, in the
im Inland, den besetzen Gebeiten occupied territories and abroad.
und Ausland

IV A 5
Sonderfälle (Special Cases)

IV A 5 a
Schutzdienst Protective Service (for leading
Party and Governmental
personalities).

Sonderaufgaben Special duties.
Asoziales Verhalten gegen Evakuierten Anti-social attitudes towards
evacuees.

Deutsche Arbeitsbummelanten German work-dodgers.
Gemeinschaftswidriges Verhalten Anti-social behavior.

IV A 5 b
Parteiangelegenheiten und Presse Party matters and the press.

IV A 6
Karteien und Fahndung (Card Indexes & Wanted Persons)

IV A 6 a
Kartei und Personalakten Card Index, Personal Files
Auskunft Information.

IV A 6 b
Schutzhaft Protective Custody.

IV A 6 c
Ausländische Arbeiter und Fremdländische Foreign workers and prisoners
Kriegsgefangene of war.

Fluchtabsichten und Fluchten ausländischer Arbeiter in Deutschland und den besetzten Gebeit (siehe auch Amt V- RSHA)	Escapes and attempted escapes by foreign workers in Germany and the occupied territories (see Amt V-RSHA).
Unerlaubte Briefvermittlung	Illegal transmission of mail to and from foreign workers.
Arbeitsverweigerung der Ausländer	Refusal to work by foreigners.

Gruppe IV B
Abwehrangelegenheiten — (Military Counter Intelligence)

IV B 1 — Western Europe, English-speaking countries, Scandinavia.

IV B 1 a
Frankreich, Belgien — France, Belgium.

IV B 1 b
Holland, England, Nordamerika, Kanada — Holland, England, North America, Canada.

IV B 1 c
Dänemark, Norwegen, Schweden, Finnland — Denmark, Norway, Sweden, Finland.

IV B 2 — Eastern Europe.

IV B 2 a
Ostgebeite, sowie Sowjet Union — Eastern territories & Soviet Union.
Weissruthenische, ukranische Emigration, Vertrauenstellen — White Ruthenian and Ukranian emigration, confidential agents.

IV B 2 b
General Gouvernment — General Government (Poland).

IV B 2 c
Protektorat, Slovakei — Protectorate, Slovakia.

IV B 3 — Southern and Southeastern Europe, Africa and South America.

IV B 3 a
Balkan mit Ungarn und Rumänien, BulgarienTürkei, Ferner Osten — Balkans, including Hungary and Romania, Bulgaria, Turkey, Far East.

IV B 3 b
Schweiz, Italien, Spanien, Portugal,   Switzerland, Italy, Spain, Portu-
Afrika, Südamerika   gal, Africa, South America.

IV B 4
Passangelegenheiten   (Passport Matters)

IV B 4 a
Passwesen   Passports.

IV B 4 b
Ausweisen, Kennkarten   Identity papers and cards,
Ausländerpolizei   Registration and Control of
    Foreigners.

IV B 4 c
Zentrale Sichtvermerkstelle   Central Office for Issue of Visas.

The *Gestapo* was divided into *Stapo-Leitstellen* or Regional Offices. These units were generally established in a Military District or *Wehrkreis* or in the administrative center of a *Reichsgau*. In general, the head of a Regional Office held the rank of *Oberregierung- und Kriminalrat* which was the equivalent of a Lt. Colonel.

There also existed *Stapo-Stellen* or *Gestapo* Office. These units were not under the control of the *Leitstellen* but were independent of them. Both levels were self-contained and operated as independent units. The head of a *Gestapo* Office was usually a *Regierungs- und Kriminalrat* which was the equivalent of a Major.

All of these *Gestapo* units were under the control of the *Befehlshaber der Sipo und des SD* or Commander of the Security Police and the Security Service.

STAPO-LEITSTELLEN
(Regional Headquarters of the *Gestapo*)

Berlin
  Area:
    Gross-Berlin and *Provinz*
      Mark Brandenburg
    Reg. Bez. (Regierungsbezirk) i.e., Administrative District
      Potsdam and Frankfurt (Oder)
  In direct control of:
    Gross-Berlin *(Reichshauptstadt Berlin)*
  Address:
    C 2, Grunerstr. 12
    Tel: 510023
  Chief:
    SS-Oberführer Bock

Under:
B.d.S. (Befehlshaber der Sicherheitspolizei) Berlin
Supervising:
St.(Stellen) Potsdam
St. Frankfurt/Oder
Branch Offices:
Grepo (Grenzpolizei) Berlin-Tempelhof Airfield

Breslau
Area:
Provinz Niedersachsen (*Reg. Bez.* Breslau, Liegnitz)
In direct control of:
Reg. Bez. Breslau and *Reg. Bez.* Liegnitz
Address:
Museumstr. 2-4
Tel: 22211
Chief:
SS-Obersturmbannführer Dr. Scharpwinkel
Under:
B.d.S. Breslau
Branch Offices:
AuDSt. (Aussendienststelle) Glatz, Glogau, Görlitz,
Gross-Wartenberg, Guhrau, Hirschberg, Liegnitz
Militsch, Waldenburg
Stapo Sagan
Arbeitserziehungslager Rattwitz (Kreis Ohlau)

Brünn
Area:
Mähren
In direct control of:
Area Mähren
Address:
Eichhornerstr. 70
Tel: 19988
Chief:
SS-Oberführer Dr. Rennau
Under:
B.d.S. Prag
Branch Offices:
AuDSt. Iglau, Kremser, Mährisch Ostrau,
Mährisch Weisskirchen, Olmütz, Prerau,
Prossnitz, Ungarisch-Hradisch, Westin
Greko (Grenzpolizeikommisariat) Zlin
Grepo (Grenzpolizei) Bila, Bilnitz, Blumenbach,
Göding, Landshut, Oberlitz, Welka/Strassnitz
Arbeitserziehungslager Gross-Kunzendorf, Witkowitz

Danzig

Area:
Reichsgau Danzig-Westpreussen (*Reg. Bez.* Danzig, Bromberg and Marienwerder)

In direct control of:
Reg. Bez. Danzig, *Landkreise* Marienberg, Marienwerder, Rosenberg , Stuhm

Address:
Neugarten 27
Tel. 2105/56

Chief:
SS-Oberführer Venediger

Under:
B.d.S. Danzig

Supervising:
St.(Stelle) Bromberg

Branch Offices:
AuDSt. Elbing, Dirschau, Konitz, Marienwerder, *Greko* Gotenhafen controlling:
Grepo Gotenhafen-Hafen, Helaheide, Danzig Hafen

Dresden

Area:
Land Sachsen

In direct control of:
Reg. Bez. Dresden-Bautzen

Address:
A 24, Bismarckstr. 16/18
Tel: 44021

Chief:
SS-Sturmbannführer Willy Müller

Under:
B.d.S. Dresden

Supervising:
St. Chemnitz, Leipzig

Branch offices:
AuDSt Bautzen

Düsseldorf

Area:
Rheinprovinz (*Reg. Bez.* Düsseldorf, Aachen, Koblenz, Köln, Trier)

In direct control of:
Reg. Bez. Düsseldorf

Address:
Ratingen, Mühlheimerstr. 47
Tel: 2521/22

Chief:
  SS-Obersturmbannführer Nosske
Under:
  B.d.S. Düsseldorf
Supervising:
  St.-Köln
  St.-Koblenz
Branch offices:
  AuDSt. Duisburg, Essen, Hamborn, Krefeld,
    Mülheim/Ruhr, München-Gladbach/Rehydt,
    Oberhausen, Remscheid, Solingen, Velbert,
    Wuppertal
  Greko Emmerich controlling:
  Grepo Emmerich-Bahnhof, Elten-Babberich,
    Emmerich-Hafen, Lobith
  Greko Kaldenkirchen/Rheinland controlling:
  Grepo Kaldenkirchen/Bahnhof, Kaldenkirchen-
    Schwanenhaus
  Greko Kleve controlling
  Grepo Geldern, Goch, Kranenburg-Bahnhof,
    Wyler-Wylerberg

Hamburg
Area:
  Hamburg, *Reg. Bez.* Lüneburg and Schleswig
In direct control of:
  Hansenstadt Hamburg and *Reg. Bez.* Lüneburg
Address:
  Dammtorstr. 25
  Tel: 341000, 341612
Chief:
  SS-Oberführer Blomberg
Under:
  B.d.S. Hamburg
Supervising:
  St. Kiel (for Reg. Bez. Schleswig)
Branch offices:
  AuDSt Celle, Fallingbostel, Hamburg-Bergedorf,
    Hamburg-Harburg, Lüneburg, Soltau, Stadt des
    KdF-Wagen/ Fallersleben
  Greko Hamburg

Hannover
Area:
  Reg. Bez. Hannover, Hildesheim, Osnabrück
In direct control of:
  Reg. Bez. Hannover

Address:
Ruchmkorffstr. 20
Tel: 60031 and 60269

Chief:
SS-Obersturmbannführer Rentsch

Under:
B.d.S. Braunschweig

Branch offices:
AuDSt. Göttingen, Hildesheim, Neinburg, Nordhorn

Karlsruhe

Area:
Land Baden

In direct control of:
Land Baden

Address:
Reichstr. 24
Tel: 8582/85

Chief:
SS-Obersturmbannführer Gmeiner

Under:
B.d.S. Stuttgart.

Branch offices:
AuDSt Baden-Baden, Freiburg/Breisgau,
    Heidelberg, Mannheim, Offenburg
Greko Konstanz, controlling:
Grepo Konstanz-Kreuzlingertor
Greko Lörrach- controlling:
Grepo Lörrach-Stettin/Strasse and
    Lörrach-Stettin-Bahnhof, Grenzacherhorn,
    Weil am Rhein-Bahnhof
Greko Singen/Hohentweil controlling:
Grepo Singen-Bahnhof, Gottmadingen-Bahnhof
Greko Waldshut controlling:
Grepo Waldshut-Brücke, Erzingen
Greko Kehl /Rhein, Müllheim/Baden
Stapo Ettlingen, Mosbach, Pforzheim, Rastatt, Villingen

Kattowitz

Area:
Reg. Bez. Kattowitz, Oppeln, Troppau

In direct control of:
Reg. Bez. Kattowitz

Address:
Bernhardstr. 49 (Strasse der SA)
Tel: 32923/27

Chief:
  SS-Obersturmbannführer Dr. Thümmler
Under:
  B.d.S. Breslau
Supervising:
  St. Oppeln
  St. Troppen
Branch offices:
  AuDSt. Auschwitz, Beuthen, Bielitz, Gleiwitz,
    Rybnik, Sosnowitz
  Greko Teschen
  Grepo Mosty

Königsberg
Area:
  Provinz Ostpreussen
In direct control of:
  Reg. Bez. Königsberg, Reg. Bez. Allenstein
Address:
  Lindenstr. 7-15
  Tel: 64331/36
Chief:
  SS-Obersturmbannführer Freytag
Under:
  B.d.S. Königsberg
Supervising:
  St. Tilsit
  St. Zichenau-Schröttersburg
Branch offices:
  AuDSt. Allenstein, Braunsberf/Ostpr., Lötzen,
    Neidenburg, Ortelsburg (also *Greko*),
    Rastenburg
  Greko Lyck, Ortelsburg (also *AuDSt*), Pillau
  Grepo Devau-Flughafen, Gehlenburg
  Stapo Johannisburg/Ostpr.

Magdeburg
Area:
  Provinzen Magdeburg, Halle-Merseburg, *Land* Anhalt
In direct control of:
  Provinz Magdeburg, *Land* Anhalt
Address:
  Klosterkirchhof 1
  Tel: 33745/48
Chief:
  SS-Obersturmbannführer Mohr

Under:
    B.d.S. Braunschweig
Supervising:
    St. Halle/Saale
Branch office:
    AuDSt Dessau

München
Area:
    Reg. Bez. Oberbayern, Schwaben
In direct control of:
    Reg. Bez. Oberbayern, *Reg. Bez.* Schwaben
Address:
    Dietlandenstr. 32-43
    Tel: 28341/45
Chief:
    SS-Obersturmbannführer Schaefer
Under:
    B.d.S. München
Branch office:
    AuDSt Augsburg
    Grepo München-Riem (Airport)

Münster/Westf.
Area:
    Reg. Bez. Münster, Minden, Arnsberg
    Länder Lippe und Schaumberg-Lippe
In direct control of:
    Reg. Bez. Münster, Osnabrück, Minden
    Länder Lippe und Schaumberg Lippe
Address:
    Gutenbergstr. 17
    Tel: 41854/56
Chief:
    SS-Obersturmbannführer Landgraf
Under:
    B.d.S. Düsseldorf
Supervising:
    St. Dortmund
Branch offices:
    AuDSt. Bielefeld, Bottrop, Buer, Gelsenkirchen,
       Gladbeck, Meppen, Osnabrück, Paderborn,
       Recklingshausen
    Greko Gronau/Westf. controlling:
    Grepo Glanerbrücke, Gronau-Bahnhof
    Greko Bentheim controlling:

Grepo Bahnhof Bentheim, Nordhausen-Frensdorferhaar, Springbiel
Greko Borken/Westf. controlling:
Grepo Bocholt-Hemden, Borken-Bahnhof

Nürnberg-Fürth

Area:
Reg. Bez. Ober-und Mittelfranken, Niederbayern-Oberpfalz, Mainfranken and Eger
In direct control of:
Reg. Bez. Ober-und Mittelfranken, *Reg. Bez.* Mainfranken
Address:
Ludwigstr. 36
Tel: 25541 and 27741
Chief:
SS-Sturmbannführer Dr. Otto
Under:
B.d.S. Nürnberg
Supervising:
St. Karlsbad
St. Regensberg
Branch office:
AuDSt Würzburg

Posen

Area:
Reichsgau Wartheland
In direct control of:
Reg.Bez. Posen, Kreise Altburgund, Dietfurt, Hohensalza, Gnesen
Address:
Ritterstr. 21a
Tel: 4365, 8261
Chief:
SS-Obersturmbannführer Stossberg
Under:
B.d.S. Posen
Supervising:
St. Litzmannstadt
Branch offices:
AuDSt Posen, Gnesen, Hohensalza.
Jarotschin, Kosten, Lissa, Samter
Arbeitserziehungslager Posen and Hohensalza

Prag

Area:
248   Böhmen

In direct control of:
Böhmen
Address:
Bredauergasse 21
Tel: 30041
Chief:
SS-Obersturmbannführer Dr. Gerke
Under:
B.d.S. Prag
Branch offices:
AuDSt Beneschau, Budweis, Jitchin, Jungbunzlau,
Kladno, Klattau, Kolin, Königgratz, Paradubitz,
Pilsen, Tabor
Grepo Prag (Airport)
Polizeigefängnis Theresienstadt
Arbeitserziehungslager Hradischko, Plan/Leinsitz,
Miroschau/Pilsen-Land

Reichenberg (Süd)
Area:
Reg. Bez. Aussig
In direct control of;
Reg. Bez. Aussig
Address:
Lerchenfeldgasse 3
Tel: 2554, 4665, 4666
Chief:
SS-Sturmbannführer Denk
Under:
B.d.S. Dresden
Branch offices:
AuDSt Aussig, Brüx, Komotau, Leitmeritz,
Teplitz-Schönau, Tratenau, Warnsdorf
Greko Böhmisch Leipa, Gablonz

Stettin
Area:
Provinz Pommern (*Reg. Bez.* Stettin, Köslin,
Schneidemühl)
In direct control of:
Reg. Bez. Stettin, *Reg. Bez.* Köslin
Address:
Auguststr. 47
Tel: 35321
Chief:
SS-Obersturmbannführer Bruno Müller

Under:
B.d.S. Stettin
Branch offices:
AuDSt Bütow, Dramburg, Flatow, Greifswald
Köslin, Kolberg, Neustettin, Schneidemühl,
Stolp,(also *Greko*) Woldenberg/Neumark
Greko Stralsund controlling:
Grepo Stolpmünde
Arbeitserziehungslager Hägerswelle/Stettin-Pölitz

Stuttgart
Area:
Land Württemberg and *Reg. Bez.* Sigmaringen
In direct control of:
Land Württemberg and *Reg. Bez.* Sigmaringen
Address:
Wilhelm-Murr-Str. 10
Tel: 28141, 29741/5
Chief:
SS-Obersturmbannführer Mussgay
Under:
B.d.S. Stuttgart
Branch offices:
AuDSt. Heilbronn/Neckar, Oberndorf/Neckar,
Sigmaringen, Ulm
Greko Friederichshafen
Grepo Stuttgart-Echtendingen (Airport)
Stapo Ellwangen, Tübingen
Arbeitserziehungslager: Oberndorf-Aistaig, Rudersberg/Schorndorf

Wien
Area:
Reichsgaue Wien, Niederdonau, Oberdonau, Steiermark,
Kärnten, Salzburg, Tirol-Vorlarlberg
In direct control of:
Reichsgaue Wien and Niederdonau
Address:
Morzinplatz 4
Tel: A 17580
Chief:
SS-Brigadeführer und Generalmajor der Polizei Huber
Under:
B.d.S. Wien
Supervising:
St. Graz
St. Innsbruck

St. Klangenfurt
St. Linz-Donau
Branch offices:
AuDSt Sankt Pölten, Wiener Neustadt, Znaim
Greko Eisenstadt controlling:
Grepo Bruck/Leitha, Kittsee, Sauerbrunn and *Nebenstelle* Zwettl
Greko Lundenberg controlling:
Grepo Lundenberg-Bahnhof
Greko Wien controlling:
Grepo Aspern (Airport), Engerau, Marchegg, Wien-Reichsbrücke

Entrance to the Criminal Police Office in Berlin, a department of the Security Police.

251

Coming Attractions

The microfilms which make up the body of the Müller files contain over 800,000 pages of historical, political and criminal records gathered by the German Gestapo, SD, Foreign Office and other state and Party agencies prior to and during the course of the Third Reich.

There are dossiers on the royal houses of England, Holland, Denmark, Belgium, Italy, Romania, Bulgaria, Norway and Sweden; dossiers on leading political and military leaders of most major nations in existence at that time; a tremendous volume of paperwork on the Soviet intelligence networks throughout the world, with especially important data on their penetration of the highest social, political and military levels in both Great Britain and the United States. Documents on various dissident Germans, both in Germany and abroad; information on Müller and the Gestapo's difficulties with Jewish emigration in 1938-1939; wartime and postwar commentary on German and refugee Jewish funds hidden in Swiss banks and those who looted the funds in 1948 are crammed into a historical jumble like the antechambers of King Tut's tomb.

Since the files are only copies of the originals, they cannot be considered German official property (only the originals can be so described) and, therefore, belong to anyone who possesses them and may be used as any historian sees fit. Secrets that the Nazis and their enemies sought, and still seek, to keep safely out of sight are there for anyone to see. Hundreds of pages about Stauffenberg's perverse habits nestle cheek by jowl with reports on currency violations, political assassinations, disrespectful authors, and prominent academics informing on their fellow savants. There are lists of Gestapo officials used by the US…and Britain…after the war. There is information on Nazi dominance of the early BND and its control over General Gehlen. Documentation is contained of Müller's new career in the United States as a high-level advisor and his final rank, high-level dealing in stolen art to stuff the coffers of several Western intelligence agencies. There are reports by British agents from the Near East concerning their use of such Nazi escapees as Alois Brunner,

Odlio Globocnik and Christian Wirth, inventor of the gas chamber. All of this information has provided constant amazement and entertainment to the author, as well as those reliable experts with whom he has shared his historical finds.

To publish all of this material would be impossible. To make it available to any researcher for unlimited use is the eventual goal of the author and his associates. The general attitude of libraries, when approached, is one of instant horror and revulsion. While some of the material might suit their needs, most of the material would certainly not. And they have, without exception, balked at a wholesale display. The political, religious and personal views held by the officials who control the library and the employees who run it play an important part in what is displayed—and what is not. Academia tends to be very responsive to government needs. This is called the "Grant Syndrome" and dictates close, warm cooperation with a bureaucracy from which all blessings, and grant money flows. A very conservative administration in the United States would, no doubt, delight in releasing negative material on the reign of Franklin Roosevelt, whereas a very liberal administration would shudder at the profanation of their deity.

Because of a long history of repression and official duplicity, no British or German official agency has ever been, nor ever will be approached. As France came off very well in the Müller files, and as the French are possessed of a considerable Latin clarity of thought, they might well be a suitable candidate for his papers. After all, the early relatives of the former Gestapo Chief's family were French in origin which explains a good deal about Müller's own penetrating intelligence, sarcastic humor and ability.

Volume III will concern itself with communist penetration in England, the discovery of the Globocnik horde, maltreatment and the killing of German civilians and military prisoners of war and other historically fascinating material.

APPENDICES

APPENDIX 1

Lfde. Nr.	Name, Vorname	Degen/Ring	Dienststellung	Partei-Nr.	ʍ-Nr.	Geburts-datum	Führer- bzw.Offz.-Dienstgrad bei der Waffen-ʍ, Wehrmacht, Polizei	Gruppen-führer

ʍ-Gruppenführer:

98	*Rodenbücher Alfred, ⚔ I M. d. R.	⬤	b.ʍ-Pers.Hauptamt	413 447	8 229	29. 9. 00	Korv. Kpt. d. R.	9. 9. 31
99	Frhr. von Holzschuher Wilhelm, ⬤ ⚔ II ⬤ ⬤ ⬤ Reg. Pr. a. D.	⬤	b. Stab Oa. Main	75 001	214 975	2. 9. 93	Lt.-a. D.	9. 9. 34
100	Kaul Curt, ⬤ ⚔ I ⬤ ⬤ ⬤ 🂠 ⚔ II M. d. R.	⬤	ʍ-Pers.Hauptamt, z. Zt. W.ʍ	244 954	3 392	5. 10. 90	Gen. Lt. d. P.	20. 4. 37
101	Hennicke Paul, ⬤ ⚔ I ⬤ 🂠 ⚔ I St. Rat, M. d. R.	⬤	kdrt. ʍ-Hauptamt	36 492	1 332	31. 1. 83	Gen. Lt. d. P.	30. 1. 38
102	Willikens Werner, ⬤ ⚔ I ⬤ ⬤ ⬤ 🂠 ⚔ I St. Sek., St. Rat, M. d. R.	⬤	b. RuS-Hauptamt	3 355	56 180	8. 2. 93	Hptm. z. V.	30. 1. 38
103	Reischle Hermann Dr., ⬤ ⚔ I ⬤ ⬤ ⬤ ✚ II M. d. R.	⬤	b.ʍ-Pers.Hauptamt	474 435	101 350	22. 9. 98	Hptm. d. R.	11. 9. 38
104	Sporrenberg Jakob, ⬤ ⚔ I ⚔ I M. d. R.	⬤	Stab Oa. Nord	25 585	3 809	16. 9. 02	Gen. Lt. d. P.	1. 1. 40
105	von Bomhard Adolf, ✚ I ⬤ ⬤ ⬤ ⚔ I	⬤	Hauptamt O. P., Gen. Insp. Pol.Sch.	3 933 982	292 711	6. 1. 91	Gen. Lt. d. P.	9. 11. 40
106	Riege Paul, ⚔ I ⬤ ⬤ ⬤ ⚔ L	⬤	b. Stab Oa. Südost	2 658 727	323 872	27. 4. 88	Gen.Lt.d.P.a.D.	9. 11. 40
107	Bracht Werner, ✚ I ⬤ ⚔ I	⬤	Stab RF ʍ	2 579 550	310 475	5. 2. 88	Lt.d.R. a.D.	20. 4. 41
108	Turner Harald Dr., ⚔ I ⬤ 🂠 🂠 ⚔ I St. Rat	⬤	Stab RF ʍ	181 533	34 799	8. 10. 91	m. d. U. d. Gen. Lt. W.ʍ	27. 9. 41
109	Streckenbach Bruno, ⬤ ⚔ ⬤ ⚔ I ⚔ I ⬤	⬤	Kdr. 19. W. Gr. Div. ʍ	489 972	14 713	7. 2. 02	Gen.Lt. d. P. u. W.ʍ	9. 11. 41
▶ 110	Müller Heinrich, ⚔ I ⬤ ⬤ ⚔ ⛨ ⚔ I	⬤	RSi-Hauptamt, Chef Amt IV	4 583 199	107 043	28. 4. 00	Gen. Lt. d. P.	9. 11. 41
111	Schreyer Georg	⬤	b. Stab Oa. S-U	766 705	207 410	16. 7. 94	Gen. Lt.d.P.a.D.	9. 11. 41

	⬤ ⚔ I Reg. TI.							
149	Lörner Georg, ⚔ II ⬤ ⬤ ⚔ I	⬤	ʍ-W.-V.Hauptamt, Chef Amtsgr. B	676 772	37 719	17. 2. 99	Gen. Lt. W. ʍ	9. 11. 43
150	Glücks Richard, ✚ I ⬤ ⚔ I	⬤	ʍ-W.-V.Hauptamt, Chef Amtsgr. D	214 805	58 706	22. 4. 89	Gen. Lt. W. ʍ	9. 11. 43
151	Wappenhans Waldemar, ⚔ I ⬤ ⬤ ⬤ ⛨ ⚔ I	⬤	ʍ-Pers. Hauptamt	456 090	22 924	21. 10. 93	Gen. Lt. d. P.	9. 11. 43
▶ 152	Müller Heinrich Dr. Dr., ⬤ ⚔ II ⬤ ⬤ ⬤ ✚ I St.Mi. a. D.	⬤	RSi-Hauptamt	343 344	290 936	7. 6. 96	Lt. d. R. a. D.	9. 11. 43

Illustrated is a page from the November 9, 1944 SS Rank List. Note that both Heinrich Müllers were the same rank and were in the same office. To avoid confusion the #110 Müller was nick-named "Gestapo Müller."

Above right: Müller's full medal bar consisting of: 1914 Iron Cross 2nd Class with 1939 Clasp, War Service Cross in Bronze with Swords, Bavarian WWI War Service Cross with Swords, 1914-1918 Frontline Combatant, Police 18-year Service Cross, Olympic Order 2nd Class, Austrian Anschluss Medal and Sudeten Anschluss Medal with Prague Bar. Below the medal bar is his 1914 Iron Cross 1st Class with Clasp and his WWI Bavarian Retired Pilot's Badge.

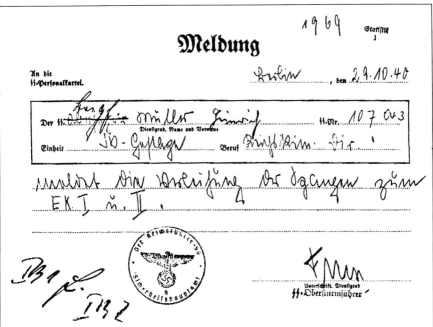

A notification that Müller had been awarded the Clasp (Spange) to the 1st and 2nd Class Iron Cross, dated October 29, 1940.

APPENDIX 2

AGENT REPORT

KTC/ter

1. NAME OF SUBJECT OR TITLE OF INCIDENT	2. DATE SUBMITTED
German Nationalist Underground (Communist Penetration) RE: Activities in the British Zone RE: Project HAPPINESS/11	2 December 1948
	3. CONTROL SYMBOL OR FILE NO.
	IV-3090/11.13

4. REPORT OF FINDINGS

1. Reference is made to paragraph 161, Consolidated Orientation and Guidance Report, Headquarters, 7970th CIC Group, EUCOM, dated 9 July 1948.

2. Allegedly the DAHLKE Group is an armed group in the German underground and all its members possess firearms. The group is also alleged to have connections with the SED. The most prominent personalities of the group are:

1. Walter DAHLKE, HAMBURG (L54/S55), Kielortallee 2
2. Alexander DOLEZALECK, former SS Hauptsturmfuehrer
3. Dr. Herbert BEER, LUETJENBURG (Ostholstein)
4. Dr. Herta SUADICANI, BERLIN-WILMERSDORF

a. Walter DAHLKE, former Captain in a German Armored Division, is now a student of law at the HAMBURG University where he is in contact with communist students. He is described as a very complicated and mistrusting person. He was recently contacted by members of the National Committee Freies Deutschland, who are said to have furnished identification and gave DAHLKE messages from a Captain who resides in the Soviet Zone. DAHLKE told sub source that all illegal transports of arms are brought into the Western Zones at a point between JERXSHEIM and GUNZ-LEBEN near HELMSTEDT. The transports are camouflaged as furniture transports from LEIPZIG.

b. Alexander DOLEZALECK, former SS Hauptsturmfuehrer in the Germanische Leitstelle, participated in the so called "Action Koenigsgraetz" in 1944 (groups within the SS and the German Foreign Office who secretly sided with the Soviet Plan to murder HITLER and replace him with HIMMLER). DOLEZALECK has resided in the Soviet Zone since 1945 and is working actively for the SED, FDJ and the Trade Unions. He has a leading position in SCHWEIN, and under the alias of BOMHOFF, attends to the cultural administration for the SED. He is a member of the Deutscher Volksrat and participated in the meetings of this organization. On 19 March 1948, he held a secret meeting with the DAHLKE Group in HAMBURG. He crossed the border illegally under the name of DORRNICK and was accompanied by a former German professional officer whose name is not known but who is allegedly a leading personality in the FDJ in DRESDEN (N52/F29). At this meeting, DOLEZALECK stated that it is his task to establish contact with illegal national groups in the Western Zones and to find a common basis for common action. Stress was also put on the Bodenreform and Socialization during the meeting but a complete agreement was not reached. It was agreed that close contact should be maintained between DOLEZALECK, DAHLKE and Dr. BEER also went there in May 1948. DOLEZALECK also has the task of bringing former members of the "Amt VI of the RSHS" (Reichssicherheitshauptamt) into the Soviet Zone. When DAHLKE returned from his first visit to the Soviet Zone, he told sub source about the secret training of former German Army personnel in the vicinity of FUERSTENWALDE and DESSAU. DOLEZALECK is expected to return to HAMBURG in the middle

5. TYPED NAME AND ORGANIZATION OF SPECIAL AGENT	311	6. SIGNATURE OF SPECIAL AGENT
ERNEST J. GUNTHER, 7970th CIC Gp, Reg IV		*Ernest J. Gunther*

WD FORM 341 1 JUN 47

The 1948 US CIC report that verifies the Soviet plan to assassinate Adolf Hitler in 1944. The subjects of this paper are identified as Soviet agents and Dolezaleck, one of the identified individuals, has written to the author to admit the existence of, and his participation in, the plot (although denying any role as a Soviet agent). Another of Dolezaleck's associates admits that he was a resident in the Soviet Zone at the period and location covered by this report.

of December 1948 for another meeting.

      c. Dr. Gerbert BEER was a Major and Commanding Officer of an Engineer-
ing Unit in the German Army. In 1946, he started extensive political activity
and built up an organisation of his many friends from both the Western and Eastern Zones of Germany. Allegedly he was imprisoned by the Soviets, NKVD, at the
end of 1945 and entered the Western Zones in 1946. He is also supposed to be
covering his activity by working for British Intelligence, knowing that he is
closely watched by the British, he claims that he has succeeded in fooling his
British liaison about his real activity. Besides his home in LUETJENBURG (M55/
N83), where he runs a translation office, he has another apartment in HAMBURG,
Isestrasse 139/III.

      d. Dr. Herta SUADICANI, BERLIN-WILMERSDORF, was also a member of the
"Germanische Leitstelle" and works with BEER, DOLEZALECK, and travels between
BERLIN (N53/Z75), NUERNBERG and MUNICH. When in MUNICH, she resides at the
apartment of former SS Standartenfuehrer SPAARMANN, MUNICH, Anglerstrasse 18.
She is also very friendly with Gerhard RIEMER, MUNICH, Agnes BERNAUERSTRASSE 86,
the former Ortsgruppenleiter of the NSDAP in POLAND. He is an employee of the
laboratory of the METZELER tire factory in MUNICH and also works for BEER.

      e. Gerda KICHERER, STUTTGART-BAD-CANNSTADT, maintains liaison for
BEER and he stays at her apartment when visiting STUTTGART (L49/802).

      f. Professor Dr. Rudolf SEWIG, BRAUNSCHWEIG (M53/I90), Campestrasse 7,
works with DAHLKE and BEER. SEWIG is a leading employee of the Photo firm
VOIGTAENDER and maintains another apartment in the same house as Dr. BEER in
HAMBURG, Isestrasse 139.

      g. Otto ZANDERER, former Hauptbannfuehrer of the HJ (Hitler Youth)
succeeded Reinhold SCHLOESSER as chief of the Cultural Department of the "Reichs-
jugendfuehrung", is now chief of the Cultural and Political Department of the
"National Zeitung" in BERLIN and also belongs to the DOLEZALECK Group.

      h. Dr. BEER is also well acquainted with Generalarzt Dr. SCHREIBER,
the right hand man of General SEYDLITZ. SCHREIBER recently escaped to the
Western Zones. BEER, who is regarded as SCHREIBER's future son-in-law told
Source that it was untrue that SCHREIBER, as officially reported, used the
first opportunity to escape to the Western Zones when he was brought to the
Soviet Zone. BEER also stated that SCHREIBER has been in BERLIN several times
since 1945 and each time traveled back to MOSCOW on the "Blue Express". DAHLKE
said that SCHREIBER's escape to the Western Zones was a well organized maneuver
on the part of the Soviets.

      i. Dr. BEER is in contact with a former member of the Waffen SS, Fnu
KOELK, LENSAHN (Oldenburg). KOELK brought two members of the RSHA Amt VI, whose
names are not known at present, into the Soviet Zone where they received good

312

IV-2090/11.13 Subj: German Nationalist Underground (Communist Penetration)
Re: Activities in the British Zone Re: Project HAPPINESS/11 dtd 2 December
1948 Continued Page 3

positions with the Soviet Intelligence. This was accomplished with the aid of
a female Russian refugee in LUEBECK, whose name is unknown.

SOURCE: P-3518-IV-G   EVAL: B-3

3.

6USC 552 (b) (1)

APPROVED:

MARIE T. CLAIR
Special Agent, CIC
Case Officer

OPS

313

SECRET

44682

258

APPENDIX 3

<table>
<tr><td colspan="2" align="right">Aktennummer:</td></tr>
</table>

M u e l l e r

Zuname

Heinrich
Vorname

Beruf:

geb. am: 28.4.oo

in: München

Wohnung:

SS-Brigadeführer,
Generalmajor der
Polizei

Amtschef von Amt IV
-Gegner- Erforschung
und Bekämpfung-

Adjudant: SS-U'Stuf.
Duchstein
(RSHA Berlin)

Anmerkung: Dem Amtschef unmittelbar
unterstellt:
IV (N) Nachrichtensammelstelle
IV (P) Verkehr mit ausländischen
Polizeien.
Generalgrenzinspektor: Amtschef IV
SS-Brigadenführer Generalmajor der
Polizei Mueller.
Vertreter: SS-Standartenf. Krichbaum. ◀

Ort: Berlin,   b.w.

11. 60 L L 10 000 B II 776 a

A portion of a file in the German Federal Records at Ludwigsburg that deals with wanted Third Reich personalities. Note the reference to Willi Krichbaum (arrow) who is identified as Heinrich Müller's Deputy in the Gestapo. Both Krichbaum's membership in the SS, his assignment to the Gestapo and his position in that organization has been contested by the CIA official who ran the Gehlen organization to which Krichbaum belonged.

Siehe (Dok.) Geschäftsverteilungs-
plan des RSHA vom 1.3.1941 (Stand
1.1.1941) Seite 12/13.

ohne Az
Müller
Lt. Befehlsblatt der Sipo und SD
Nr, 8/41 zum Generalmajor der
Polizei ernannt. (Amtschef im RSHA)

VI 415 AR 13 1o/63
Ref.IV (Amtschef),Sipo:Vertr.S(PP)
f.Abt.II, S(PP II), S (PP IIB), S
(PP II D), S(PP II-Ber.),Gestapo II
E1,E2,E4, E5,E7,E8,E9,E11,E12,E14,
E15,E16,E17,(E18,E19,E2o,E21) E 22

M. sollte lt.Sterbeurkunde des StA
Berlin-Mitte Nr. 11 7o6/45 verstorbe
sein. Dies ist zweifelhaft. Gegen M.
ist deshalb bei dem GStA b.d.KG Berlin 1 Js 1/68 (RSHA)-ein Ermittlungs
verfahren wegen Mordes anhängig,das
die gesamte Tätigkeit des M.im RSHA
in seiner Eigenschaft als Amtshef
IV in den Jahren 1939-45 umfaßt.Un-
terbrechung der Verjähr. ist erfolg
Fahndung läuft.Das Verf.ist gem. §
2o5 StPO vorläufig eingestellt.
E 18 bis E 21 verbunden zu E 4 am 2
4.66.

259

APPENDIX 4

A Wallenberg Retrospective

In this work, reference has been made to Raoul Wallenberg, a Swedish diplomat in Budapest, Hungary during World War II. A member of the powerful and wealthy Swedish banking and industrial family, Wallenberg vanished at the end of the war and has since been the subject of considerable literary effort, all of which seems to be directed at proving the thesis that Raoul Wallenberg was abducted by the Soviets when they captured the Hungarian capital on January 15, 1945. Various sightings of the missing diplomat have been extensively reported, but no substantive material has ever surfaced other than some of his personal belongings, including his diplomatic passport and 1945 personal notebook, which the Soviets turned over to Swedish representatives in October 1989.

In his interview, Heinrich Müller states, categorically, that he had Wallenberg shot by his chief deputy, Willi Krichbaum, for interfering in the deportation process of Hungarian Jews in 1944. Those who have written books stating that Wallenberg was, or had been in the hands of the Soviets, have argued this statement because it would, if true, invalidate their writings.

The question of Wallenberg's assassination by the Gestapo has been raised in an official publication of the Swedish Ministry for Foreign Affairs of 1988.[1] After giving an overview of Wallenberg and his activities in Budapest in 1944, this work states that "the Swedish Ministry for Foreign Affairs in Stockholm received a message indicating that Hungary's Kossuth radio station had broadcast a message on March 8 (1945) saying that Raoul Wallenberg had disappeared on January 17 and had later probably been murdered by Gestapo agents."

Aside from this unsubstantiated report, there is the statement made by Müller to his CIA interrogator in 1948. The question now arises as to whether or not Müller was being truthful with him. To freely admit to being the moving force behind the murder of a neutral diplomat would only result in antagonizing his future employers. It would not be an event one would fabricate to impress someone.

There was no hint of retribution from the Americans for this act and while the interrogator was obviously shocked, Müller's employment by the US was never in question. The sole purpose of the extensive 800 page interview was to iron out any future difficulties associated with the inclusion of the former Gestapo Chief in the upper echelons of US intelligence. Müller was, by nature, a brutally frank and direct man who, when he could do so safely, had no

---

[1] Raoul Wallenberg, Swedish Ministry for Foreign Affairs, "UD informerar," Uppsala 1988, pp. 5-9.

problem in discussing his actions, and those of others, in the most direct manner.

Another question concerning the allegation that the Soviets seized Wallenberg and kept him incommunicado for years is that there was no valid reason for their doing so. In the postwar years, Stalin and his minions have been blamed, often without justification, for bad weather, aircraft accidents, outbreaks of disease and any nastiness that one can conceive of. In the case of Wallenberg, there was no motive for kidnapping and incarcerating a man with family connections with the Swedish government and business circles. Revenge by the Soviets against a Germany-friendly Swede would indicate that other Swedish diplomats would also suffer the same captivity, but this did not happen although these diplomats fell into Soviet hands in March 1945. All were duly sent back to Sweden with the exception of Wallenberg.

In spite of his ruthlessness in domestic matters, Stalin was a shrewd and capable leader in matters of foreign policy. His country had been economically devastated by the war and he eagerly sought assistance in rebuilding his shattered infrastructure. In October 1946, the Soviet Union and Sweden signed a Credit and Trade Agreement where Stalin's government received a Swedish credit of one billion Swedish crowns to be repaid in ten years with an interest rate of 2.38%. The Soviets eagerly bought important military supplies like ball bearings from the Swedes, something they continued to do during the course of the Cold War. There was no reason for the Soviets to antagonize Sweden at the end of the war or in the immediate postwar years, and no reason to kidnap or murder a minor diplomat with connections to a family whose generosity Stalin actively sought.

The Soviet dictator exercised absolute control over his military and civil establishments and no Soviet general would have dared to arrest Wallenberg without Stalin's orders, or would the Soviet secret police hide such a person in their jails without similar orders. It is not conceivable that Stalin would issue such an order. Wallenberg was of no importance to him and, according to Müller's statements, the young diplomat was pro-Soviet and had been suggested for his position by the Soviet Ambassador in Stockholm.

All complex scenarios which delight writers dealing with conspiracies are easily demolished by the application of the rule that entities must not be multiplied beyond necessity. That is to say, that the simplest explanation to a complex problem is generally the correct one.

If this dictum, known as Ockham's Razor after the 14th century British philosopher who first expressed it, is applied to the disappearance of Raoul Wallenberg, it is evident that an assassination by the Gestapo is far more realistic than abduction and lengthy imprisonment by the Soviets.

Müller worked for US intelligence for a number of years, and one of the terms of his employment was that he turn over his files, or the greater part of them, to his new employers. There is no doubt, whatsover, that much of the information used in this series on the former Chief of the Gestapo is already in the hands of at least one US agency.

Given the unpleasant results which any official acknowledgment of Müller's postwar employment could cause, it appears doubtful if any of his papers, other than a small amount of official correspondence now in the US National Archives, would ever be released, even to the powerful Wallenberg family.

As a parallel case, in the trans-atlantic radio-telephone conversation between Churchill and Roosevelt on November 26, 1941, Churchill clearly indicates a pending Japanese attack on Pearl Harbor on the 8th of December, not the 7th (due to the Japanese use of their own time zone). The German State Archives in Koblenz has shown a suspicious reluctance to discuss the existence of this intercept in their own files.

It was recently discovered that the original intercepts were captured by American forces in Bavaria at the end of the war, and they eventually ended up in the National Archives in Washington. With the West German government as an obedient ally, most of their records held by the US were duly returned. Considering the explosive nature of the 1941 intercept and its negative impact on a number of Amercian political and military institutions, a search of the National Archive holdings would only be fruitful in theory.

Once a government has control over controversial material, it rarely admits to having it, let alone releasing it to the public.

The copies of Müller's files, which contain information from many diverse German intelligence agencies besides his Gestapo, are filled with a legion of answers to many historical questions which vex historians today. As a half-century has passed since copies of these files passed into American control, it would seem reasonable that historians of whatever persuasion might be permitted free access, but reasonable theory is superseded by unreasonable pragmatism as it always has been.

It is ironic that Müller, who was bitterly anti-communist, could have supplied information which would tend to exonerate his arch-enemies of a crime for which they have been persistently blamed for half a century.

Bibliography

Akten zur Deutschen Auswärtigen Politik: 1918-1945, Erster Band, Baden-Baden, 1961

Akten zur Deutschen Auswärtigen Politik: 1918-1945, Dritter Band, Frankfurt, 1963

Allen, Peter, *The Windsor Secret,* Briarcliff Manor, New York, 1984

Bauer, Fritz, *Die Kriegsvebrecher vor Gericht,* Zürich, 1945

Best, S. Payne, *The Venlo Incident,* London, 1950

Best, Werner, *Die deutsche Polizei,* Darmstadt, 1941

Bloch, Michael ed. *Wallis & Edward, Letters 1931-1937,* New York, 1986

Brassey's Naval Annual, *Fuehrer Conferences on Naval Affairs,* 1939-1945, 1948

Corson, William R. *Widows,* New York, 1989

Costello, John, *The Mask of Treachery,* New York, 1988

Cray, Ed, *General of the Army: George C. Marshall, Soldier and Statesman,* New York,1990

Dallin, David, *Soviet Espionage,* New Haven, 1955

Deakin, F.W., *The Brutal Friendship: Mussolini, Hitler and the Fall of Italian Fascism, Part 1.* New York, 1966

Dulles, Allen Welch, *Germany's Underground,* New York, 1947

Goralski, Robert, *World War II Almanac: 1931-1945,* New York, 1981

Harman, Nicholas, *Dunkirk: The Patriotic Myth,* New York, 1980

Hillgruber, Andreas, *Staatsmänner und Diplomaten bei Hitler,* Frankfurt, 1970

Hinsley et al, *British Intelligence in the Second World War,* London, 1980

Hoffmann, Peter, *Die Sicherheits des Dikators,* Munich, 1975

Howell, Edgar M., *The Soviet Partisan Movement: 1941-1944,* Department of the Army,1956

Jacobsen, Hans-Adolf, *Fall Gelb*, Wiesbaden, 1957

von Lang, Jochen, *The Secretary*, New York, 1979

Leasor, James, *Rudolf Hess: The Uninvited Envoy*, London, 1961

Macmillian, Harold, *The Blast of War-1939-1945*, New York, 1967

Navy Department, Bureau of Ordnance, *German Explosive Ordnance*, Vol. 1, 1946

Reitlinger, Gerald, *The SS- Alibi of a Nation*, New York, 1947

Ribbentrop, Joachim von, *Zwischen London und Moskau*, Leoni, 1961

SS-Personalhauptamt, Dienstältersliste der Schutzstaaffel der NSDAP-Stand vom 9.November 1944, Berlin, 1944

Simpson, Christopher, *Blowback*, New York, 1988

Taylor, A.J.P., *The Origins of the Second World War*, New York, 1961

Thomas, W. Hugh, *The Murder of Rudolf Hess*, New York, 1979

U.S. Department of State, *Spanish Government and the Axis*, Washington, DC, 1946

Vaksberg, Arkady, *Stalin Against the Jews*, New York, 1995

Whiting, Charles, *The Hunt for Martin Bormann*, New York, 1973

Woodward, Sir Llewellyn, *British Foreign Policy in the Second World War*, London, 1962

Wulf, Josef, *Die SS*, Bonn, 1954

Microfilm Records of the U.S. National Archives, Washington, D.C.
Roll 229, Frame 2767262 et seq. History of Gestapo, 1934-1939.

Roll 432, Frame 2962655 through 2962689, Gestapo offices and officials, 1945.

Files of Heinrich Müller
File on the Duke and Duchess of Windsor containing Gestapo, SD and Foreign Office. Reports, correspondence between the Duke and Hitler and von Ribbentrop.

File on German scientists working on SS-sponsored atomic research.

File on Soviet penetration of United States official positions and abstracts of U.S. Counterintelligence material.

File containing inventory of fine art in the Müller collection, and a list of art dealers used by Müller and various transactions involving art works.

File on Rudolf Hess.

Files containing microfilms of Adolf Hitler's personal files and papers taken in Berlin in 1945.

File containing two reports on Raoul Wallenberg.

File of correspondence between Müller, his representatives and representatives of the Swiss government.

File containing material on bank accounts, money transfers and stock holdings.

Records of the Office of Strategic Services (OSS)
OSS Archives of the Central Intelligence Agency
Overseas Cable File NN3-226-88-5

Records of the Washington Radio & Cables and Field Photo Branch NN3-226-86-2
COI/OSS Central Files NN3-226-87-1
COI/OSS Central Files NN3-226-94-001.

Records of the New York Secret Intelligence Branch NN3-226-79-1
London Field Station Files NN3-226-79-1
Field Station Files: Bern and Madrid NN3-226-90-1
Field Station Files: Barcelona, Bern, London NN3-226-90-1
Field Station Files: Bern, Stockholm & Caserta NN3-226-86-6.

Records of the Director's Office: Minutes and Correspondence with the Navy, State and War Departments and with Franklin D. Roosevelt and HST NN3-226-86-3.

Index

(Note: Page numbers listed in italics indicate a picture of the subject.)